HANDBOOK OF BIBLICAL CRITICISM

Second Edition
(Revised and Augmented)

by Richard N. Soulen

JOHN KNOX PRESS
ATLANTA

Library of Congress Cataloging in Publication Data

Soulen, Richard N., 1933–
    Handbook of Biblical criticism.

    Bibliography: p.
    1. Bible—Criticism, interpretation, etc.—
Dictionaries. I. Title.
BS511.2.S68   1981   220.6   81–2674
ISBN 0–8042–0045–9 (pbk.)   AACR2

© copyright 1976 and 1981 John Knox Press
Second edition, 1981
10 9 8 7 6 5 4 3
Printed in the United States of America
John Knox Press
Atlanta, Georgia 30365

Acknowledgments

Acknowledgments are due and here gratefully given to the many whose assistance has made this Handbook possible. I should like to mention first of all those whose research is reported in these pages. Unfortunately, the nature of this Handbook has prohibited a wide use of bibliographic data, which for several reasons needed to be limited to essential quotations and to a few suggested readings. (Additional reference works consulted are listed at the end of the volume.) And of course I am especially grateful to those persons who so magnanimously laid aside their own work to correct drafts of articles and to offer suggestions about various portions of the manuscript. I am particularly grateful to Drs. Paul and Elizabeth Achtemeier, respectively Professor of New Testament and Visiting Professor of Homiletics at Union Theological Seminary in Virginia; Dr. William Jerry Boney, Professor of Theology and Philosophy, The School of Theology, Virginia Union University; Professor Alexander A. Di Lella, O.F.M., Holy Name College, Washington, D.C.; Dr. Balmer Kelly, Professor of Biblical Theology, Union Theological Seminary in Virginia; Dr. Douglas M. Parrott, Chairman, Program in Religious Studies, The University of California, Riverside; Dr. Donald T. Rowlingson, Professor Emeritus of New Testament Studies, Boston University School of Theology; Dr. Irving Alan Sparks, Associate Dean, Graduate Division, San Diego State University; Dr. Gene M. Tucker, Professor of Old Testament, Candler School of Theology, Emory University; Dr. Dan O. Via, Jr., Professor of Religious Studies, The University of Virginia; and Dr. Lamar Williamson, Professor of Biblical Studies, The Presbyterian School of Christian Education, Richmond, Virginia. Needless to say, however much I am indebted to these people, I alone am responsible for any errors of fact or judgment in the articles themselves or in their selection.

Of no less fundamental assistance to me has been the staff of The Library, Union Theological Seminary, Richmond, Virginia, which serves as the principal library for the institutions of the Richmond Theological Center. Dr. John B. Trotti, Head Librarian, Mrs. Martha Aycock, Research Librarian, and Mrs. Judy Webster, Mrs. Jean Coats, and Mrs. Sarah Peterson of the staff all receive my heartfelt thanks, not only for their invaluable help but also for their good spirit.

I wish also to express my indebtedness to Dean Paul Nichols of The School of Theology, Virginia Union University, for providing secretarial assistance at the beginning of the project in the persons of Mrs. Gayla Sandel Woody and Mrs. Ella N. Grimes. The project would scarcely have been possible without them. A special word of appreciation goes to Mrs. Gordon B. English for her inimitable skill in preparing the manuscript for publication. Finally, I am grateful to my children, Kendall, Jonathan, and Kathryn, for their helpfulness at many points and to my wife, who provided a constant source of support and encouragement throughout. To her this book is dedicated.

August 1976
Richmond, Virginia

Preface to the Second Edition

In the five brief intervening years since the first publication of the *Handbook,* the field of Biblical criticism has undergone a change so radical as to be described by one noted New Testament scholar as nothing less than a second revolution, analogous to the introduction of the historico-critical method into Biblical studies two centuries ago. This revolution, says J. D. Crossan, has transformed Biblical studies from a single discipline to a field of disciplines, each with its own theoretical assumtions and methods so diverse and complex (even contradictory) that no one practitioner of Biblical criticism can master them all.

This edition of the *Handbook* tries to bring the student up to date with these new developments. It does so by concentrating on fields of study rather than on a plethora of technical terms within these larger areas. Over forty new articles have been added, including Canonical Criticism, Semiology, Structure, Sociological Interpretation, Reception Theory, Rhetorical Analysis, Theological Interpretation, Biblical Theology (Movement), Linguistics, Topos, etc. Another forty have either been revised or expanded. Many readers have asked for suggested readings to augment definitions, and so bibliographical data is now a part of all major articles. This should not only stimulate further research but also serve to call attention to glossaries and lexica dealing with the specialized terms which could not be included in this work. It seemed good also to include, as an appendix, a simplified guide for writing an exegetical paper. It is limited to the Synoptic Gospels for the sake of precision and clarity. Instructors using the handbook will want to adapt it as they see fit, since it is in the main a traditional approach to exegesis, one making more use of structuralist and other perspectives deemed too complex to be included in a handbook of this nature. Those wishing a purely structuralist approach will find help in the bibliography found in the articles on structure and related terms.

These remarks would be incomplete without a word of thanks to the many whose assistance in so many diverse ways has made a revised edition possible. Above all, to Dr. Richard A. Ray, Director of John Knox Press, for his wise counsel and friendship over the years and for his kind support of this project from its inception, I wish to express my deep appreciation. Gratitude is also to be expressed to the Deutscher Akademischer Austauschdienst of the Federal Republic of Germany, to the Association of Theological Schools in the United States and Canada, the Andrew W. Mellon Foundation, and the Arthur Vining Davis Foundation, whose research grants enabled me to spend the academic year, 1977–1978, on sabbatic leave at the University of Heidelberg, where work on this and other projects was carried out. The cordiality of the theological faculty there was beyond all expectation, and I remain indebted to them for their help in academic as well as human concerns. I wish especially to thank Dr. Christoph Burchard, Dr. Hartwig Thyen, Dr. Lothar Steiger, and Dr. Ekkardt Stegemann for their hospitality, as well as members of the Doktoranden-Kolloquim for inclusion into that spirited group. Dr. Wolfgang Stegemann, pastor of the Evangelische Landeskirche in Nussloch, Dr. Paul Phillippi of the theological faculty and his wife, and Frau Elka Kruger, Assistant Librarian in the Theologisches Seminar, through their generous self-giving, made the stay in Germany an exceedingly happy as well as rewarding year.

Suggestions for the revision have come from so many sources that I cannot begin to list names. Hopefully colleagues and students alike will see the fruit of their advice, although regretfully, not every recommendation could be acted upon.

I cannot fail to express appreciation to the Spence Library staff once again, especially Mrs. Martha Aycock, Research Librarian, and her able assistant, Ms. Cecelia Clark. Mrs. Portia Williamson, M.Div. candidate at the School of Theology of Virginia Union University, and Ms. Virginia Glen-Calvert assisted in various stages of research and are also due my thanks, as is David Hagstrom, Th.D. candidate at Union Theological Seminary in Va., who graciously consented to write the article on Canonical Criticism, having just completed a Master's thesis on the subject, and Mrs. Louise English, who turns questionable manuscript into beautiful typescript with amazing dexterity. And of course the initial dedication is now more in order than ever before.

CONTENTS

Introduction   9

Handbook of Technical Terms with Names and Tools   13

Abbreviations in Textual Criticism
  plus common Latin words and phrases   215

Abbreviations of Works
  commonly cited in Biblical studies   221

Major Reference Works Consulted   233

Appendix: A Simplified Guide for Writing an Exegetical Paper   235

To Margaret Ann

Introduction

This book is for the beginning student in the critical study of the Bible. It is not for advanced students in the field—though perhaps it is for the professional religionist whose bailiwick lies elsewhere and for whom the penumbra of forgetfulness in Biblical matters grows increasingly large. It is a *hand*book, a pocket reference for library or lecture hall, to be used whenever a name, a term, or an abbreviation is met for the first time unidentified, unexplained, or without a clarifying illustration; or, when its meaning is simply forgotten.

The novice in Biblical studies constantly finds himself or herself in just such a predicament. The sea of technical terms and names expands yearly and the crosswinds of scholarship keep them in such flux that even the specialist feels swamped once familiar waters are left behind. It is little wonder that scholars in Old Testament and New Testament studies rarely enter each other's domain. The student's plight is far less enviable. Introductory texts, purportedly designed for the beginner, often presuppose knowledge few possess. This is particularly true of translated works originally prepared for European students. Furthermore, classroom lectures are not uncommonly written with the same erroneous assumption about the hearer's fund of knowledge. And it is the characteristic of lecturers, with too much to cover in too little time, not to wait for the student who in his or her confusion thinks a Nestle Text is the label on a can of chocolate mix. It hardly needs to be added that scholarly journals and monographs are the frontiers of research as well as its depository; they represent an even more formidable challenge to the beginner in Bible study.

For this reason, it seems to me, a handbook of technical terms, tools, and names, however limited or incomplete, is a pedagogical necessity. The present volume represents an initial effort to meet that need. It is designed to aid the student in two ways: first, as an abbreviated introduction to the methodologies of Biblical criticism, including the related, initiating bibliographies; and, second, as a book to facilitate the use of established tools of scholarly research as suggested above.

The entries fall into the following general categories:

(1) *Methodologies:* Textual Criticism, Literary Criticism, Historical Criticism, Form Criticism, Tradition Criticism, Redaction Criticism, Her-

meneutic(s), Structuralism, et al. A historical overview of these methodologies is to be found in the article **"Biblical Criticism."** The reader who begins there may then wish to turn to the individual articles for a brief sketch of their beginnings, a partial listing of related technical terms and names which are also discussed in greater detail separately, and for an introductory bibliography. These articles on methodologies provide a backbone to the total work and give it the stamp of a handbook.

(2) *Technical Terms and Phrases* associated with the above methodologies. The selection of terms is of course somewhat arbitrary, and indeed had to be considering the immense number of entries possible. This Handbook focuses on terms deemed of greatest interest and importance to the beginning student. Terms which present no problem to understanding are in the main excluded; when they are included, it is because of their historical interest, their current prominence, or in order to supply illustrative or other detailed information about them.

(3) *Research Tools and Texts,* primarily for study in English but also for beginning students in Hebrew and Greek. The key article in this regard is **"Exegesis";** additional information is found under **"Bibliography."** The former entry lists basic beginner's tools and texts. This Handbook also attempts to note the various types of tools (commentary, concordance, monograph, version, paraphrase, etc.) and to cite those leading "Guides to Biblical Study" which are currently available.

(4) *Names.* Those listed are limited, except in a very few instances, to scholars now deceased whose insights and labor are most frequently cited as constituting lasting contributions to the field of Biblical criticism. For names not listed, the reader is directed to Werner G. Kümmel's, *The New Testament: The History of the Investigation of Its Problems*, trans. S. MacLean Gilmour and Howard C. Kee (Nashville: Abingdon Press, 1972; London: SCM Press, 1973), pp. 466–498, and to the major reference works cited at the end of this volume.

(5) *Theological Terms.* A few terms not strictly within the terminology of Biblical criticism are nevertheless so closely connected with it that their absence would be sorely missed, e. g., apocalyptic, eschatology, epiphany, etc.

(6) *Abbreviations.* Two lists are found at the end of this Handbook:(a) Latin abbreviations (and phrases) basic to textual criticism yet rarely translated as found in critical texts of the Old and New Testament and in such volumes as the *Synopsis Quattuor Evangeliorum.* (b) Abbreviations of periodicals, reference works, Bibles, and Biblical books, etc., often unidentified, as for example in periodical literature. Both lists of abbreviations, however, are of necessity limited.

Finally, a word about the definitions themselves. They are offered as working definitions, not more. The task of Biblical criticism is after all largely one of defining its subject matter, of delineating the nature of the Bible and its content in ever more precise terms. This is the genius of Biblical criticism and its grief. In short, I do not pretend here to solve the specialist's perplexities concerning terminology. This Handbook is not intended to be a contribution to the ongoing debate. Only in a few instances have I made remarks at all prescriptive rather than descriptive (e. g., see: **Late Judaism** and **Lower Criticism**). The intent throughout has been to simplify exceedingly complex issues for the sake of clarity and brevity. This is the pedagogical task.

HANDBOOK OF TECHNICAL TERMS
WITH NAMES AND TOOLS

Acrostic. A series of lines or verses whose initial, final, or other identifiable letters form a word, a phrase, the initial letters of a phrase, or the alphabet. Acrostics in the Hebrew OT include in whole or part Pss. 2; 9–10; 25; 34; 37; 111; 112; 119; 145; Prov. 31:10–31 and Nahum 1:2–10. In some instances the acrostic is formed on every other line, in other instances more than one line opens with the same letter; e. g., Ps. 119 is formed of 176 lines, eight lines for each of the twenty-two letters of the alphabet. Unfortunately, acrostics are inevitably lost in translation.

Agrapha is a Greek term meaning literally "unwritten (sayings)" and was first employed by the German scholar Alfred (not Arnold) Resch in 1889 to designate sayings attributed to Jesus but not found in the canonical Gospels. The A. are also occasionally referred to as the "unknown" or "lost" sayings of Jesus. Since it is known that Jesus' teachings were first passed down orally, it is presumed that certain of these escaped the knowledge of the evangelists and were subsequently lost except as they are alluded to or preserved by early Christian writers, e. g., by Paul in Rom. 14:14. Resch claimed to have recovered a large number of these from Paul's writings (such as 1 Cor. 2:9: " 'What no eye has seen, nor ear heard, nor the heart of man conceived, what God has prepared for those who love him,' " RSV), which purportedly derived from a pre-canonical gospel (but cf. Isa. 64:4).

Current scholarship rejects Resch's loose definition and limits the term A. to sayings (not allusions) explicitly attributed to Jesus. Sayings having some possible claim to authenticity but not in the Gospels can be found in: (a) the NT (Acts 20:35 and 1 Thess. 4:16f.); (b) ancient MSS of the NT (such as the addition to Lk. 10:16 in Codex Koridethi or the substitute reading of Codex Bezae at Lk. 6:5: "Man, if indeed you know what you are doing, you are blessed; but if you do not know, you are cursed and a transgressor of the law"); (c) the Church Fathers (such as Justin Martyr, Clement of Alexandria, Origen, etc., who in the main do not record oral tradition but passages from non-canonical gospels); (d) the Gospel of Thomas, some of whose 114 sayings are also found in Oxyrhynchus Papyrus 654; and (e) Oxyrhynchus Papyrus 1, 655, and 840.

Additional sayings attributed to Jesus can be found in the Talmud ('Abodah Zarah 16b 17a and Shabboth 116 a, b) and in Mohammedan writings and inscriptions, all of which are deemed spurious. (See Joachim Jeremias, *The Unknown Sayings of Jesus* [London: S.P.C.K., 1958].)

Aktionsart (Ger.: type or kind of action) is a German technical term employed by grammarians to characterize an aspect of Greek verbs and participles not present in like manner in English (or German), viz., the kind of action involved in the verb. Greek verbs have two kinds of action: punctiliar and linear (Moulton). Whereas in English the primary task of the verb is to tell the time of an action or event (past, present, or future), in Greek the *kind* of action *(A.)*, whether extended (linear) or momentary (punctiliar) in time, is primary. Although exceptions to this generalization are numerous, in the main the present stem of a Greek verb (from which the imperfect tense is formed) denotes an action or an event continuous in time and can be translated into English only with auxiliary words, e. g., "I am praying" (or "I was praying"). The aorist stem (from which the future, perfect, and pluperfect tenses are also formed) denotes an action or an event momentary (punctiliar) in time, though its effects may still continue (perfect) or have continued for some time in the past (pluperfect), e. g., "I prayed."

Albright, William Foxwell (1891–1971). Born in Coquimbo, Chile, the son of Methodist missionaries, A. received his Ph.D. in Semitic Studies at Johns Hopkins University in 1916. He was first a research associate and then director of the American School of Oriental Research in Jerusalem from 1920–29 and 1933–36, becoming W. W. Spence Professor of Semitic Languages at Johns Hopkins in 1929. An outstanding archaeologist and teacher, A. was the leading OT scholar in the U.S. from 1930–1950 and the recipient of six honorary degrees from foreign universities, and twenty from institutions in the United States.

Alexandrian Text. In NT Textual Criticism, AT is one of the geographical place names given to MSS of the NT bearing the same textual characteristics and thought to come from a common ancestor originating in Alexandria, Egypt. Also called the "Egyptian Text" or, more commonly and preferably perhaps, the "Neutral Text"—so called by F. J. A. Hort (1882) on the theory that it was an essentially pure representative of the NT autographs. The principal witness to the Neutral Text is the 4th cent. MS Codex Vaticanus (B), whence the more recent designation "Beta." According to E. J. Epp *(JBL,* 93 [September 1974], pp. 386–414), the Neutral Text-type is one of only two distinct early text-types (with the Western) and can be traced from (i. e., identified with) P[75], P[23], P[20], P[50], etc. to Codex B and to more recent witnesses, such as Codex L (8th cent.), MSS 33 (9th cent.), 1739 (10th cent.), and 579 (13th cent.). Whether the AT is closer to the original than the Western is still a matter of dispute. See: **Byzantine Text; Western Text.**

Allegory (Greek: "saying something other than one seems to say"). In literary criticism the term A. is used to denote both (1) an allegorical representation and (2) an allegorical interpretation. (1) By the former is meant the presentation of an abstract or spiritual concept in the guise of concrete images and events. John Bunyan's *The Pilgrim's Progress* is an allegory based on the Puritan concept of sin and salvation. Here the series of characterizations and actions are ultimately governed not by the narrative's own inner logic but by the pattern of concepts outside the work, to which the narrative is made to conform. (2) An allegorical interpretation on the other hand is that kind of interpretation which assumes that the text to be interpreted says or intends to say something other than its literal wording suggests, that it contains hidden within it a deeper, mystical sense not derivable from the words themselves (cf. Gunkel, *RGG*[1]). Here, as in (1) above, the images and actions of the text represent meanings originating outside the work itself. (Note: Just as the noun has both these meanings, so the verb "to allegorize" is both transitive ["to make or treat a thing as allegorical"] and intransitive ["to construct or utter allegories"] —Oxford.)

The term A. first appears in the Hellenistic period arising probably within Cynic-Stoic philosophy, where in order to modernize and thus preserve them it refers to attempts to find deeper meanings behind the ancient Greek myths (see Plutarch, "How to Study Poetry," 11, 19e). In this sense, the practice of interpreting ancient texts and myths for their deeper meaning passed over into Hellenistic (esp. Alexandrian) Judaism (e. g., Aristobulus of Alexandria, 2nd cent. B.C.), Philo and Josephus (1st cent. A.D.) and was adopted by Christian writers, esp. Mt. and Paul. (Some scholars however find A. already in the OT, e. g., Isa. 5:1–6; Ps. 80:8–16; Prov. 5:15–23; Eccles. 12:1–6.)

In Paul's letters, the allegorical interpretation of OT themes is found in 1 Cor. 5:6–8 (leaven); 9:8–10 (law); 10:1–11 (Exodus); and Gal. 4:21–31 (Hagar and Sarah; see vs. 24 where the word A. is used).

According to Joachim Jeremias, there are no allegories among the authentic teachings of Jesus. In time, however, Jesus' parables, removed from their setting in life, became obscure (see Mk. 4:10–12) and were subjected to allegorizing tendencies. The attempt to reclaim the parables from obscurity by way of allegorical interpretation is apparent in the Gospel accounts: in some instances allegorical interpretations have been added, e. g., the interpretation of the sower (Mk. 4:12–20 pars.), of the tares (Mt. 13:36–43), and of the seine-net

(Mt. 13:49–50); in other instances allegorical elements themselves have been added, adjusting the parable to the delay of the *parousia* or to historical events subsequent to and including the crucifixion (e. g., Mt. 22:11–13; 24:43–44, 45–51; 25:12–30; Mk. 2:19*b*-20; 13:33–37). Also, Mk. 12:10–11 pars., which may be linked to Isa. 5:1–6.

The early Church Fathers nurtured this predilection for allegory (see the Epistle of Barnabas, Clement of Rome, Irenaeus, Tertullian, etc.); a classic example is Augustine's interpretation of the good Samaritan (*Quaestiones Evangeliorum*, 11, 19; abbreviated English trans., C. H. Dodd, *The Parables of the Kingdom* [London: Nisbet & Co., 1953; New York: Charles Scribner's Sons, 1961], p. 11).

See: **Parable; Typology;** also **Anagogy; Tropology.**

Alt, Albrecht (1883–1956). Professor of OT: *Privatdozent* in Greifswald (1909–12), professor in Basel (1914–20), Halle (1921), and Leipzig (1922–48). From 1921–23, he was the Director of the German Evangelical *Institut für Altertumswissenschaft des Heiligen Landes* in Jerusalem, and from 1925–45, President of the *Deutscher Verein zur Erforschung Palästinas* (Society for Palestinian Research). A's extensive knowledge of the ancient Orient, its geography, history and the documents pertaining to it, caused his writings to exert a profound influence on OT studies in general and particularly on the formulation of a new understanding of the history of Israel. (See: Alt, *Essays on OT History and Religion* [Oxford: Basil Blackwell, 1966].) See: **Law.**

Amanuensis (Latin: by hand). One who is hired to write from dictation, a scribe or secretary. The apostle Paul frequently used an A.; see Rom. 16:22; 1 Cor. 16:21; Gal. 6:11; Col. 4:18; 2 Thess. 3:17.

Amarna Tablets were accidentally discovered in 1887 at Tell el-Amarna situated on the Nile River in Egypt, halfway between Memphis and Thebes. Archaeological excavations (1890–91; 1907–14; 1920–37) unearthed the royal archives, bringing the total number of cuneiform tablets to about 377. Most contain diplomatic correspondence written in Akkadian (also Hittite and Canaanite) by vassal kings and governors in Palestine, Phoenicia, and southern Syria to Amenhotep IV (Akhenaton) and his father, Amenhotep III, during the short period in the early part of the 14th century B.C. when Amarna was the capital of Akhenaton's declining empire. Of considerable interest and controversy is the reference in the texts to the 'Apiru, whom some identify as the biblical Hebrews. For some of the texts in English, see: *ANET.*

'Am Ha'arez (Hebrew: lit., "the people of the land") is a Hebrew term of varied meaning depending on the period of its use. In pre-Exilic Judah, the *AHa* appear to have played a role in the political, social, and economic life of

the nation just below that of the priests (Jer. 1:18; 34:19; 37:2; 44:21, etc.), holding slaves (Jer. 34) and being open to the charge of oppressing the poor (Ezek. 22:29). In post-Exilic Judah, the term (frequently plural, so Ezra 10:2, 11; Neh. 10:30–31) refers to the people(s) of the land(s) who had not been carried into exile (the exiles being called the "people of Judah," Ezra 4:4) and whose blood and religion had become mixed with foreign elements and thus impure. In the rabbinic literature of the Christian period, the term is one of contempt and designates those who are either ignorant of or indifferent to the law (cf. Mk. 7:1–5; Lk. 6:1–5; 11:37–41; Jn. 7:49).

A minore ad majus means "from the lesser to the greater"; it is the Latin equivalent to *Kal wahomer* (Heb.), the first of Hillel's seven principal rules of interpretation; also translated "from the easy to the difficult." Where the rule is used the *protasis* states: "If such be (true) . . ."; and the *apodosis* states: "then how much more (must it be true that). . . ." In the NT see: Mt. 7:11; 10:25 *b;* 12:11f., pars.; also Rom. 11:12, 24; Heb. 9:13f.; etc. (best observed in RSV). See: **Hermeneutics.**

Anacoluthon is a grammatical non sequitur in which the structure of a sentence as initially conceived is not carried out; sometimes A. is due to popular idiom, sometimes to the author's losing his train of thought (e. g., Gal. 2:4–6; 2 Thess. 2:2; 1 Tim. 1:3ff.).

Anagogy, Anagogic (Greek: to lead). One of the fourfold senses of Scripture, along with literal (historical), allegorical (mystical) and tropological, as developed by John Cassian (*ca.* 360–435) though traceable back to Origen, Gregory of Nazianzus, Jerome, et al., and favoritely employed in the hermeneutical theory of the Middle Ages. The A. sense of Scripture refers to its spiritual meaning as it pertains to future and heavenly, i. e., eschatological realities. For example: Jerusalem is interpreted as a type of the heavenly Jerusalem (Gal. 4:26), or Melchizedek (Heb. 6:20; 8:1) and the High Priest (Heb. 9:7, 11, 24) as models of the priesthood of Christ in heaven. See: **Allegory; Hermeneutics;** *Sensus Litteralis;* **Tropology.**

Analogy (Greek: proportion, correspondence; Rom. 12:6). To "draw an analogy" is to make a comparison between the similar features or attributes of two otherwise dissimilar things, so that the unknown, or less well known, is clarified by the known. Strictly speaking, an analogy is predicated on the similarity of relationships which two things (concepts, entities, etc.) have: Paul refers to the soldier as one who does not serve at his own expense as an analogue to the apostle's right to recompense (1 Cor. 9:7); he compares the meaninglessness of speaking in tongues with a war bugle that gives forth only an indistinct sound (1 Cor. 14:6–8); and, in 15:18, he uses sleep as an analogue of death, since in both there is a cessation of activity and an attendant repose. As in the last example, there is no clear line between A. and other types of comparisons (parables, allegories, images, etc.), cf., 1 Thess. 2:7; 5:1–11; Gal. 3:15–18; 3:23–4:7; 4:19, etc. In theological language, A. stands between literalism on the one hand and symbolism on the other.

Analytical [Greek; Hebrew] Lexica are volumes containing all the words and inflected forms of the Hebrew/Aramaic OT and the Greek NT, arranged in alphabetical order, parsed and defined. Useful in identifying the stem of irregular verbs. Such editions are currently published by the Zondervan Publishing House, Grand Rapids, Michigan (Greek, 1967; Hebrew and Chaldee, 1970; 1974²).

Anaphora (also epanaphora; Greek: to bring or relate back to).

(1) In grammar, A. denotes the use of a word as a grammatical substitute for a preceding word or group of words. In Acts the use of the article in "the Spirit" is anaphoric in that it denotes a specific spirit, viz., the Holy Spirit of Pentecost, e. g., Acts 2:4; 8:18; 10:44 (see BDF, para. 257).

(2) In rhetoric, A. denotes the repeated use of the initial word or words of two or more clauses, lines or strophes in a sequence, usually for poetic or rhetorical effect. The repetition of "How long?" in Ps. 13 and "By faith" in Heb. 11 are examples of A.; also, in Paul's letters (though occasionally lost or altered in translation): 1 Cor. 3:9; 10:21, 23; 2 Cor. 7:2, 4; Gal. 3:28; 4:4–5; 5:26; Phil. 2:1; 3:6; 4:12, etc.; in Hellenistic rhetoric: Epictetus I 4, 14; 5, 7; 16, 3; 28, 28–30; III 22, 48, etc.

(3) In ecclesiastical usage, A., here meaning "offering," is the name of the central prayer in the Eucharistic Liturgy.

See: **Epiphora.**

ANET, ANEP. Common abbreviation (acronym) for *Ancient Near Eastern Texts Relating to the Old Testament,* ed. James B. Pritchard (Princeton: Princeton University Press, 1969³), and by the same editor and press, *The Ancient Near East in Pictures Relating to the Old Testament* (1954). Selections from the two are available in a combined, supplemented version in paperback (1971⁵). An indispensable tool for OT study, containing the texts in translation from **Ras Shamra** and **Amarna.**

Angelophany. See: **Epiphany.**

Annotated (Study) Bible is a Bible supplied with clarifying historical, literary, and theological notes in introductory sections or paragraphs and/or footnotes, with maps, charts, concordance, cross references, etc. The notations provided represent the opinion of the editor(s) and may reflect a given theological position: conservative, fundamentalist, Roman Catholic, liberal Protestant, Jewish, etc.

An ecumenical (Jewish, Catholic, Protestant) AB. is: *The New English Bible with the Apocrypha,* Oxford Study Edition; Samuel Sandmel, M. Jack Suggs, and Arnold J. Tkacik, eds. (London: Oxford University Press, 1976).

The RSV "Common" Bible, approved by Protestant, Roman Catholic, and Eastern Orthodox Churches, and including 3 and 4 Maccabees and Psalm 151 (which appear only in the canon of the Eastern Orthodox Churches) is: *The New Oxford Annotated Bible, with the Apocrypha,* Expanded Edition; Herbert G. May and Bruce M. Metzger, eds. (London: Oxford University Press, 1977).

Antiphrasis (Greek: to speak the opposite). The use of a word when its opposite is meant; hence, often ironic or sarcastic, e. g., 2 Cor. 11:19;12:11*b*, 13*b*, etc. See: **Irony; Meiosis.**

Antistrophe. See: **Epiphora.**

Antithetic Parallelism. See: **Parallelism.**

Aphorism (Greek: a short, pithy sentence; a definition) is the name given to a principle or general truth expressed succinctly; syn.: adage or maxim. In the *Aphorisms* of Hippocrates (5th cent. B.C.): "If a woman is pregnant with a male child she is of good complexion; if a female, of a bad complexion" (V, XLII) —now "an old wives' tale." Webster defines A. as a "pithy epigram" requiring "some thought." The Epistle of James is frequently termed "aphoristic" because of its tendency to reduce religious faith to general moral truths. See: *Volksspruch.*

Apocalypse, The; The Little Apocalypse. A. is a common name for The Revelation to John, the last book of the NT, and is also the Greek name and the opening word of the Greek text; the term in Greek means "revelation." "The Little Apocalypse" refers to the 13th chapter of Mk. and, to a lesser extent, its parallels in Mt. and Lk., containing a vision of the destruction of Jerusalem and a prediction of the coming of the Son of Man. See: **Apocalyptic; Eschatology.**

Apocalyptic, Apocalyptic Literature, Apocalypticism (Greek: fr. apocalypse: revelation). Apocalyptic is a collective term, appearing in Biblical criticism at the beginning of the 19th cent. to designate those ancient visionary writings or parts of writings which, like the NT apocalypse from which the name is derived, viz., the book of Revelation, purport to reveal the mystery of the end of the world (age) and of the glories of the world (age) to come.

19

In a broader and looser sense, the term A. may simply refer to the matrix of concepts and theological motifs typical of this type of literature.

A. is a distinctly Jewish and Christian phenomenon that flowered in the three centuries between 200 B.C. and A.D. 100, with roots extending back into the 6th and 5th cent. B.C. Two of the best exemplars of the genre, Daniel and the book of Revelation, stand respectively at the beginning and end of this period. Other passages of the OT and NT, however, are classed by some scholars as A. in outlook and style: Isa. 24–27 (the "Isaiah Apocalypse"); Joel 2; Zech. 9–11; 12–14; Ezek. 38–39; Amos 5:16–20; 9:11–15 (?); Mk. 13; Mt. 24–25; Lk. 21; 1 Thess. 4–5; 2 Thess. 2:1–12; and 1 Cor. 15. Recently, Paul Hanson has called Second Isaiah (Isa. 40–55) "proto-apocalyptic" and Trito-Isaiah (Isa. 56–66) "early A." (See: Hanson, *The Dawn of Apocalyptic* [Philadelphia: Fortress Press, 1975].) Many of the Pseudepigrapha and Apocrypha are called Apocalypses and, though no complete agreement exists, those so designated usually include: A. of Abraham; A. of Baruch (II or Syriac Baruch); A. of Esdras (IV Ezra 3–14); I Enoch; Bk. of Elijah; I Baruch; A. of Moses, or the Life of Adam and Eve; A. of Sedrach; A. of Elijah; II Enoch; Assumption of Moses; the Sibylline Oracles; Bk. of Jubilees; Testament of Abraham; Testament of the Twelve Partriarchs; Ascension of Isaiah, et al. Of these, the first four, plus the canonical apocalypses, are the most notable as a literary type. A. of a "cooled down" variety also characterizes the DSS, with A. features in almost all the documents, but particularly in the War Scroll, the Description of the New Jerusalem, and the Thanksgiving Psalms. Found among the DSS were previously known apocalypses: Daniel, I Enoch, and Jubilees.

The question remains: What is A.? Opinions vary widely. Whether it constitutes an identifiable literary genre is debated; the negative argument is that it simply uses, adapting and transforming, all the older traditional genres. According to Klaus Koch, however, six general literary features are present: (1) discourse cycles (frequently called "visions") between the A. seer and a heavenly being, revealing the secret of man's destiny; (2) formalized phraseology depicting the spiritual turmoil of the seer (catalepsy, trance, etc.) that accompanies the vision; (3) a paraenetic discourse conveying an eschatological ethic, or an introductory legend (e. g., Daniel) illustrating proper behavior; (4) pseudonymity, bearing the name of some ancient worthy—although the book of Revelation is an exception; (5) mythical images rich in symbolism (animals, angels, demons, cosmic phenomena); and, (6) a composite character (70 percent of the book of Revelation is derived from previously written sources).

In terms of general content, A. is characterized by the belief (1) that the radical transformation of this world lies in the immediate future (Dan.12:11–12; Rev. 22:20; II Bar. 85:10; IV Ezra 4:50); (2) that cosmic catastrophe (war, fire, earthquake, famine, pestilence) precedes the end; (3) that the epochs of history leading up to the end are predetermined; (4) that a hierarchy of angels and demons mediate the events in the two worlds (this world and the one to come) and that victory is assured to the divine realm; (5) that a righteous remnant will enjoy the fruits of salvation in a heavenly Jerusalem; (6) that the act inaugurating the kingdom of God and marking the end of the present age is his (or the Son of Man's) ascension to the heavenly throne; (7) that the actual establishment of the New Kingdom is effected through the royal mediator, such as the Messiah or the Son of Man, or simply an angel; and (8) that the bliss to be enjoyed by the righteous can only be described as glory (Rev. 21:1; Dan. 12:3; I Enoch 50:1, etc.; see Klaus Koch, *The Rediscovery of Apocalyptic* [London: SCM Press, 1972]).

The origin of A. is variously ascribed to Hebrew prophecy, Iranian religion, Hellenistic syncretism, and Old Canaanite myths, with the greater number of scholars acknowledging at least the influence of eastern religion, particularly Zoroastrianism. For a total reappraisal of the question of the origins of A. and of the methodology used to answer it, see Paul Hanson, op. cit.

The moot point in contemporary NT scholarship is whether, or to what extent, Jesus was an apocalypticist, and whether A. views world history with unrelieved pessimism, the kingdom of God being discontinuous, not continuous with world time, and whether only a heaven can vindicate both the righteous and God. See: John J. Collins, ed., *Apocalypse: The Morphology of a Genre* (Semeia 14; Missoula: Scholars Press, 1979).

See: **Eschatology.**

Apocalyptic Eschatology. See: Eschatology.

Apocrypha, The (Greek: "hidden things"). The books and portions of books present in the LXX (or its Old Latin translation) and accepted by Hellenistic Judaism and by the early Church as sacred scripture but not found in the Hebrew OT.

In preparing his edition of the Bible in Latin (called the Vulgate), Jerome (*ca.* 400) chose to follow the Hebrew canon rather than the LXX, separating the writings found therein into a distinguishable corpus, which he then termed "apocrypha." These he also described as "ecclesiastical books" in contradistinction to the "canonical books" of the Hebrew OT.

Since Jerome, the theological and physical place of the Apocrypha in the Christian canon has continued to be a matter of dispute, with the Orthodox, the Roman Catholics, and the Protestants accepting differing solutions as indicated below.

The Apocrypha comprise:

(A) Tobit; Judith; The Wisdom of Solomon; and Ecclesiasticus or the

21

Wisdom of Jesus, the Son of Sirach—and of the apocrypha these alone were accepted as canonical by the Eastern Church at the Synod of Jerusalem in 1672.

(B) Baruch; the Letter of Jeremiah (or Baruch, ch. 6; in the LXX these two writings appear as additions to the book of Jeremiah); the Prayer of Azariah and the Song of the Three Young Men (or Holy Children); the History of Susanna; and Bel and the Dragon (in the LXX these last three appear as additions to the book of Daniel; see that book in the Jerusalem Bible, chs. 3:24–90; 13; and 14 respectively); and, 1 and 2 Maccabees—these writings, plus (A) above, were confirmed as canonical by the Council of Trent in 1548, though called "Deuterocanonical" because they do not appear in the Hebrew Bible.

(C) 1 Esdras (called Esdras A [Greek for Ezra] in the LXX, III Esdras in the Vulgate where Ezra and Nehemiah are called I & II Esdras): contains portions of 2 Chron. (Ezra and Nehemiah plus other material); 2 Esdras (called IV Esdras in the Vulgate, also known as "The Ezra Apocalypse" [specif. chs. 3–14]; chs. 15–16, in some MSS called V Esdras, are a composite work, and do not appear in the LXX); and, the Prayer of Manasseh, a brief penitential prayer—these writings were not confirmed as canonical by the Council of Trent and consequently appear in Catholic Bibles in an appendix or not at all (so Jerusalem Bible).

In modern Protestant editions of the Apocrypha (RSV, NEB), all of the above (A–C) are included.

(D) In the LXX and in the Appendix to the Greek canon are Ps. 151 and III & IV Maccabees.

Modern translations of the Apocrypha are found in complete editions of the **JB, NAB, NEB, RSV:** individual books are appearing in the Anchor Bible commentary series.

Apocryphal NT (Greek: adj., hidden; also called "The NT Apocrypha" in contradistinction to the [OT] Apocrypha, that is, Jewish writings of the intertestamental period). Uncanonical writings dating from the second to the sixth centuries, written in the form or carrying the name of gospels, acts (histories), letters, and apocalypses, and purporting to tell of events, teachings, and prophecies (apocalypses) related to Jesus and the early apostles but not recorded in the canonical Scriptures. These writings contain little of historical value in terms of the subjects with which they deal (the birth of Mary, the childhood of Jesus, etc.), but they are of inestimable value in understanding the mind of both orthodox and heterodox Christianity of the early centuries.

For the English texts of the following, see M. R. James, *The Apocryphal New Testament* (Oxford: Clarendon Press, 1924; rep. 1950), or Edgar Hennecke and Wilhelm Schneemelcher, *New Testament Apocrypha* (Philadelphia:

The Westminster Press, 1963; London: SCM Press, 1974); the latter includes writings not listed below.

Gospels: Arabic Gospel of the Infancy; Armenian Gospel of the Infancy; Assumption of the Virgin; Gospel of Bartholomew; the Book of the Resurrection of Christ by Bartholomew; Gospel of Basilides; Gospel of Cerinthus; Gospel of the Ebionites; Gospel According to the Hebrews; Protoevangelium of James; History of Joseph the Carpenter; Gospel of Marcion; Gospel of the Birth of Mary; Gospel of Philip; Gospel of Pseudo-Matthew; Gospel of Thomas.

Acts: Apostolic History of Abdias; Acts of Andrew; fragmentary Story of Andrew; Acts of Andrew and Matthias; Acts of Andrew and Paul; Acts of Barnabas; Ascent of James; Acts of James the Great; Acts of John; Acts of John by Prochorus; Martyrdom of Matthew; Acts of Paul; Passion of Paul; Acts of Peter; Acts of Peter and Andrew; Acts of Peter and Paul; Passion of Peter and Paul; Acts of Philip; Acts of Pilate; Acts of Thaddaeus; Acts of Thomas.

Epistles: Epistles of Christ and Abgarus; Epistle of the Apostles; Third Epistle to the Corinthians; Epistle to the Laodiceans; Epistle of Lentulus; Epistles of Paul and Seneca; Apocryphal Epistle of Titus.

Apocalypses: Apocalypse of James; Apocalypse of Paul; Apocalypse of Peter; Revelation of Stephen; Apocalypse of Thomas; Apocalypse of the Virgin.

Additional writings, known by little more than name, could be added, as well as literature commonly classed in other categories.

See: **Nag Hammadi Codices; Oxyrhynchus Papyri; Agrapha; Pseudepigrapha.**

Apodictic Law. In form-critical studies of the OT, AL refers to unconditional (divine) law, e. g., the Ten Commandments. According to Albrecht Alt, AL was singularly characteristic of Israelite religious law, in contrast to the secular, casuistic law of Canaan (see: *Essays on Old Testament History and Religion* [Oxford: Basil Blackwell, 1966], pp. 81–132). According to Alt, AL may open with (a) the second person, negative: "Thou shalt not . . ."; (b) with a participle (lost in English translation): "Whoever strikes his father or mother shall be put to death" (Ex. 21:15); or (c) a curse: "Cursed be he who removes his neighbor's landmark." (Dt. 27:15–26) In some instances, apodictic forms have been molded with casuistic ones (Ex. 21:23–25), indicating (so Alt) the encounter of two cultural traditions. According to more recent opinion, AL is not limited to Israel, or to her settlement period, or even just to religious law. That it is the primary characteristic of Israel's understanding of her covenantal relationship to God is also disputed (see: Dennis J. McCarthy, *Old Testament Covenant: A Survey of Current Opinions* [Oxford: Basil Blackwell,

1972; Richmond: John Knox Press, 1972]). Its predominantly religious subject matter has caused some (Klaus Koch) to prefer not the word law, but commandment or prohibition. See: **Alt; Form Criticism; Law.**

Apodosis. See: **Protasis.**

Apology (an apologetic; Greek: a defense). In the NT the Greek noun and verbal forms of A. *(apologia)* appear frequently (e. g., Acts 22:1; 24:10; 25:8, 16; 26:1–2; 1 Cor. 9:3; Phil. 1:7, 16, etc.) in the sense of a verbal defense or explanation of one's conduct or opinions. Luke's presentation of the story of Paul and of the early Church in Acts is that of a defense or A. According to H. D. Betz, Paul's defense of his apostleship and gospel in 2 Cor. 10–13 is an ironic parody (esp. 12:2–4, 7–10) of the rhetorical A. as found among Sophists and among Paul's opponents in Corinth, in that here Paul inverts characteristic self-acclaim by pointing to his human weaknesses and failure. See: **Irony.**

Apophthegm (pl.: apophthegmata; also apothegm[s]; Greek: "to utter forth"). "A terse pointed saying, embodying an important truth in a few words" (OED). Note: Although the longer spelling conforms to the Greek, being a transliteration, in English the shorter is both older and easier to pronounce.

In form-critical studies, the classification A. has received no clear definition. According to Dibelius, in ancient usage A. applied both to (a) sayings introduced without a setting, and (b) answers of a specific nature set within concrete situations which are narrated either briefly or at length. (The latter [b] Dibelius viewed as a subcategory of A. called *Chriae.*) So defined, the term fits the material in the *Apophthegmata Patrum* (Migne, *Patrologia graeca,* 65, 71–440).

According to Bultmann, A. are "sayings of Jesus set in a brief context"; so defined they correspond to (b) above, viz., Dibelius' *"Chriae."* However, since for Dibelius the synoptic *Chriae* arose out of the Church's need for sermon illustrations, he chose the term "paradigm" for (b). Thus, the paradigms of Dibelius and the A. of Bultmann are basically the same. According to Bultmann, the A. are not historical reports but idealized constructions designed to illustrate some principle which the early Church has traced back to Jesus. Bultmann categorizes A. according to content: (a) conflict and didactic sayings (e. g., Mk. 3:1–6, 22–30; 7:1–23; 10:7–22, 35–40; 12:13–17) and (b) biographical apophthegms (e. g., Mk. 1:16–20; Lk. 9:57–62; 10:38–42, etc.). Bultmann finds twenty-four in the first category, twenty in the second (which he thinks arose as sermonic paradigms).

See: **Bultmann;** *Chria;* **Form Criticism; Paradigm.**

Apostolic Fathers is the title given by general consent to those Christian authors of the 1st and 2nd cent. whose works, though ultimately deemed non-canonical, were often read and valued by the early Church. The term, first used in the 17th cent., designates no firm corpus, varying from eight to twelve in number, viz.: I Clement (*ca.* 95), II Clement (*ca.* 150), the Epistle of Barnabas (2nd cent.), Epistle of Diognetus (late 2nd or 3rd cent.), the (seven) Epistles of Ignatius (*ca.* 115), the Epistle of Polycarp to the Philippians (*ca.* 150), the Shepherd of Hermas (*ca.* 145), the Didache or the Teaching of the Twelve Apostles (late 1st or early 2nd cent.); the Martyrdom of Ignatius and the Martyrdom of Clement are sometimes included. (See: *The Apostolic Fathers,* ed. R. M. Grant [New York: Thomas Nelson and Sons, 1965].)

Apostolicon (Greek: pertaining to an apostle). This neuter substantive had several meanings among the early Church Fathers. It referred to (a) a quotation from the Gospels; (b) a quotation from Paul; (c) (plural) the epistles as part of the NT; (d) the corpus of epistles collected into a volume, being the name given to Marcion's corpus of Pauline letters; and (e) a lectionary reading from one of the NT epistles, in contradistinction to a reading from the Gospels, called an *evangelistarion.*

Apothegm. See: **Apophthegm.**

Apparatus criticus. See: **Critical Apparatus.**

Aquila (abbrev.: 'A). A proselyte from Christianity to Judaism in the 2nd cent., noted for his literalistic translation of the Hebrew OT into Greek (*ca.* A.D. 140) which was accepted as the official Greek Bible of the Jews until replaced by Arabic translations of the 7th cent. His translation appeared in Origen's *Hexapla* and is extant only in fragments (Psalms and Kings), in marginal readings in certain LXX MSS, and where quoted by the Church Fathers. Aquila's recension of Ecclesiastes, however, appears in the LXX in place of the original Old Greek translation. See: **Symmachus; Theodotion.**

Aramaism. See: **Semitism.**

Aretalogy (fr. Greek: *arete:* virtue) is a t.t. used in contemporary criticism with three closely related but distinguishable meanings: (1) a collection of miracle stories, existing independently of hortatory or didactic material and essentially functioning for propaganda purposes; (2) a celebration of the virtues and/or deeds of a god; e. g., concerning the god Isis in Apuleius' *The Golden Ass* (XI 22, 6); (3) a celebrative biography of a religious hero or semi-divine being *(theios aner);* e. g., Porphyry's *Life of Pythagoras,* Philo's *Life of Moses,* and Philostratus' *Life of Apollonius of Tyana.*

25

An aretalogist is thus a kind of evangelist who, it is suggested, related evidence of the supernatural power of a god or divine man to gain devotion to his person and adherence to his teachings. The vision of the true apostle (or the true prophet: see the Elijah and Elisha cycles in the OT) as a divine man who performed miracles seems to underlie some of Paul's difficulty with the church at Corinth (see 2 Cor. 10–13).

The critical question is whether or to what extent the NT Gospels belong to the "genre" of A., or the above aretalogies to the "genre" of gospel.

The term A. is frequently misspelled as aretology which, now archaic, referred to that part of moral philosophy dealing with virtue.

See: Theodore Weeden, *Mark: Traditions in Conflict* (Philadelphia: Fortress Press, 1971).

Argumentatio. See: *Rhetorical Analysis.*

Arndt-Gingrich. See: **Bauer, Walter; Exegesis:** Tools, Lexicons.

Assimilation is the term in textual criticism for the most common of all errors in textual transmission: the replacement of the original reading of a passage by a reading which comes from another document; in the NT, the assimilated passage usually comes from another Gospel. However, the Lukan account of the institution of the Last Supper (Lk. 22:19–20) as preserved by Codex Sinaiticus and Codex Vaticanus (cf. RSV and KJV) has undoubtedly been assimilated to 1 Cor. 11:23–25; Codex Bezae et al. do not contain vs. 22:19 *b*–20 (so RSV). Cf. also Lk.'s account of the Baptism and of the Lord's Prayer in the above MSS. In linguistics A. refers to the disappearance of consonants when two or more morphemes are joined together, as in the "assimilation" of the n and the reduplication of the l in the word "illogical," formed of "in" = "not" + "logical." The phenomenon is frequent in the Hebrew Bible. See: **Conflation; Gloss; Textual Criticism**

ASV (NASB). Common abbreviation for the American Standard Version of the Bible (1901), being in turn a revision of the Revised Version prepared by British scholars completed in 1885. Both are extreme efforts at literal translation, the ASV incorporating decisions of the American delegation to the RV translation committee. Most notably, the ASV translated the Hebrew name *Yahweh* with "Jehovah" instead of "LORD," as in KJV, RV, and in the New American Standard Bible (NASB), which is a revision (1963) of the ASV in the direction of "more current English idiom" (Preface). It remains the most literal of modern translations. See: **Douay; JB; NAB; KJV; RSV; TEV; Paraphrase; Version.**

Asyndeton (pl.: asyndeta; Greek: not joined together) is a t.t. in rhetoric denoting the absence of particles or conjunctions ordinarily linking coordinate words or sentences. It is characteristic of Aramaic, and its presence in Mk. and Jn. has been used in an attempt to prove an Aramaic origin for these Gospels. The frequency of A. in first century Greek papyri and in the writings of Epictetus shows this assumption to be in error (see: E. C. Colwell, *The Greek of the Fourth Gospel*, Chicago: University of Chicago Press, 1931). In Mt.'s use of Mk., however, A. is frequently eliminated by the insertion of a connective; cf. Mk. 3:35; 5:39*b*; 10:27, 28, passim with Mt. parallels.

Authenticity. See: **Criteria of Authenticity.**

Autobiography. In the OT, A., as the memoirs of an official, first appears in the Persian period, in the books of Ezra and Nehemiah. First person accounts are, however, much older, particularly as preserved in oral accounts of the dreams and visions of Israel's Patriarchs (Gen. 37; 40; 41; Judg. 7:13–14; 1 Kgs. 3:4–15; 22:17–22) and prophets (Amos 7:1–9; 8:1–3; 9:1–4; Jer. 1; Isa. 6; Ezek. 1–2; Zech. 1–8; Dan. 7–12, etc.). In these accounts and others, poetic, prophetic, and allegorical features often override historical reminiscence in the service of religious interpretation.

In the NT, A. appears particularly in the letters of Paul. These passages are classified by Beda Rigaux (*Letters of St. Paul* [Chicago: Franciscan Herald Press, 1968], pp. 122–123) as: (a) simple A.: 1 Cor. 16:5–9; 2 Cor. 7:5; Rom. 1:11–14; Phil. 1:12–26; (b) apostolic A., dealing with Paul's pastoral role: 1 Thess. 2:1–12, 18; 3:1–2, 6; 1 Cor. 1:12–16; 2:1–5; 3:1–4, 9–13; 7:8; 11:23; 2 Cor. 1:6–8, 10; Rom. 15:17–21; Col. 2:1–3; 4:7–9; 2 Thess. 3:7–9; (c) apologetic and polemic A.: 1 Cor. 9:1–27; 15:9; 2 Cor. 10:1–12:21; Gal. 1:11–2:14; (d) mystical A.: 2 Cor. 12:1–10; Eph. 3:1–13; and, (e) a special "I" type of A.: Rom. 7:14–25. Some scholars believe authentic A. is also to be found in the Deutero-Pauline Pastorals, e. g., 2 Tim. 4:10–18.

See also: **We-sections.**

Autograph refers to the original copy of an author's work. In every instance, the A. of the biblical books is lost; extant MSS of the Bible are only later, imperfect copies of the A. Some fragments of NT writings do fall within 100 years of the originals, and certain fragmentary MSS of the Jewish sectarian community of Qumran appear to be closer still to the As of some of the late books such as Daniel.

See: **P; DSS; Textual Criticism.**

Babylonian Talmud. See: **Talmud.**

Barth, Karl (1886–1968). The son of Fritz Barth, prof. of NT at Bern, Switzerland, KB studied theology in Germany, later becoming a pastor in Geneva (1909–11) and Safenwil (Aargau, Switz., 1911–1921). His *Commentary on the Epistle to the Romans* (*Der Römerbrief,* 1919; 2nd ed. 1921; Eng.: London: Oxford University Press, 1933), inaugurated an era of theological thought known as Dialectic Theology, of which the journal *Zwischen den Zeiten* ("Between the Times," 1923–33) was the principal organ. Prior to his expulsion from Germany by the Nazis in 1935, B. taught at Göttingen (1921–25), Münster (1925–30), and Bonn (1930–35), then became professor of theology at Basel where he taught until his retirement in 1962; he himself never held an earned doctorate. He is often called one of the most outstanding Protestant theologians since the Reformation (16th cent.), his own thought being most akin to that of John Calvin (1509–64), hence the appellation "Neo Orthodox theology" commonly attached to his major work, *Church Dogmatics* (1932–67; 4 vols. in 13 parts; 9000 pages). The *CD* marked a break with his theological approach prior to 1932 and with his principal dialogists of that period: Friedrich Gogarten, Emil Brunner, and Rudolf Bultmann.

Bath Qol (also *Bat Kol;* Heb.: lit., "daughter of a voice") is the name given to a heavenly voice which revealed God's will to man. The term first appears in rabbinic tradition where it is asserted that the *BQ* had been heard already in the patriarchal period concerning Tamar, and later Moses, Samuel, Solomon, David, etc. After the cessation of prophecy, the *BQ* remained as the only means in rabbinic theology of God's direct communication with man. In the NT, a *BQ* is heard at Jesus' baptism (Mk. 1:11), Transfiguration (9:7), and crucifixion (Jn. 12:28), at Paul's conversion (Acts 9:4, etc.), and Peter's vision (10:13).

Bauer, Walter (1877–1960). Taught NT studies in Marburg (1903–1913), Breslau (1913–1916), and Göttingen (1916–1945) in Germany; noted principally for his Greek-German lexicon of the NT, translated into English by W. F. Arndt and F. W. Gingrich.

Bauer-Arndt-Gingrich. See: **Bauer, Walter; Exegesis:** Tools, Lexicons.

Baur, Ferdinand Christian (1792–1860). Professor of church history and dogmatics in Tübingen, Germany (1826–60), B. became in effect the founder of historical theology through his development and application of principles of historical criticism to the history and theology of the canon. His critical research led to several lasting (though still debated) insights: (1) the opposition between Peter and Paul and their adherents in the early Church; (2) the secondary and late character of the Pastorals; (3) the historical value of the synoptics over John; and, (4) the ameliorating tendencies of the Acts of the

Apostles regarding the split between Peter and Paul, between Christianity and Rome, and its secondary value as a historical source for the life and thought of Paul. The frequent characterization of B. as an uncritical Hegelian who applied the Hegelian dialectic between thesis and antithesis to every problem in the history of primitive Christianity has, in recent years, been proved a misleading if not false generalization. (See P. C. Hodgson, *The Formation of Historical Theology: A Study of Ferdinand Christian Baur* [New York: Harper and Row, 1966].) What is perhaps Baur's most important work exists in English translation: *The Church History of the First Three Centuries,* vols. I-II (London: Williams and Norgate, 1878–79).

B.C.E.; C.E.   Before the Common Era; the Common Era. Terms employed particularly by non-Christians as non-theological equivalents of B.C. and A.D. (*Anno Domini;* Latin: "In the year of our Lord").

BDF (Blass-Debrunner-Funk). See: **Exegesis:** Reference Grammar.

Beatitudes.   See: Blessings.

Benedictus is the traditional name of Zechariah's hymn of prophecy concerning John the Baptist, recorded in Lk. 1:68–79, from the opening word of the Latin text: *"Benedictus Dominus Deus Israel"* ("Blessed be the Lord God of Israel . . ." RSV). The language of the hymn is styled after the Greek OT and hence offers one of the best examples of "Septuagintism" in the NT. See: *Magnificat; Nunc Dimittis;* **Septuagintism.**

Ben Sira (The Wisdom of Jesus ben Sira, or Sirach; also Ecclesiasticus). See: **Wisdom Literature.**

Biblical Criticism refers to that approach to the study of Scripture which consciously searches for and applies the canons of reason to its investigation of the text; it comprises a large number of distinguishable but interrelated methodologies, the terminology and leading practitioners of which make up this Handbook. Until quite recently, BC was synonymous with **Historical Critical Method** (q. v.) which began to appear less than two centuries ago; today that definition is too narrow.

The antecedents of BC are quite ancient, if by BC we mean simply the use of reason in interpreting sacred traditions concerning God's self-revelation in history. So defined, BC is as old as Scripture itself. 1 and 2 Chronicles contain a critique of the interpretation of history found in 1 Kings–2 Samuel; Job presents a critique of the Deuteronomic view of history; Jesus' concept of the kingdom of God implies a critique of the idea of history in normative Judaism of his day; both Mt. and Lk. offer critiques of Mark's interpretation

29

of the life and person of Jesus, and so on. Each judged one view of history (and God's activity in it) by another view thought to be more accurate, just as the modern critic judges ancient texts on the basis of a present and presumably superior understanding of reality.

The search for the meaning of history and for the appropriate rules to guide the interpretation of texts pertinent to it is in practice the oldest of all types of critical inquiry. Such rules of interpretation arose in Biblical times (see: *A minore ad majus*). Jesus, for example, drew attention for not following the rules established by tradition in his day (Mt. 7:29). Since the 17th cent. the theory of interpretation has been called **Hermeneutics.** Perhaps of equal antiquity is attention to the wording of the text, for the concept of the "Word of God," born in the prophetic oracle, gave birth with the rise of the written word to the concept of sacred Scripture. The search for the original wording of the text, now known as **Textual Criticism,** appeared in antiquity when it was realized that texts become corrupt in the process of being copied (see: **Kethibh**). Translators of the OT were among the first to note this fact. The Greek version of the OT (the **Septuagint** [*siglum:* LXX]), which the early Church favored partly because of its unique readings, contained words and passages, even books, not found in the Hebrew OT. In reaction to the rise of Christianity and to its use of the LXX, Judaism reverted to the Hebrew text and to more literal Greek translations of it (see: **Aquila, Symmachus, Thedotion**). The ongoing conflict between Synagogue and Church led not only to lists of authorized books **(canon)** within each faith, but also to a type of rudimentary textual criticism. In the Christian Church, **Origen** (*ca.* 185–254) was the first to approach this task systematically (see: *Hexapla*). In subsequent centuries, however, as Scripture gave way to tradition and rite, TC remained a dormant science; interest did not rise again until the Protestant Reformation (16th cent.) placed renewed emphasis on Scripture as the Word of God. It is worth noting as well that by this time the printing press had made a fixed authoritative Biblical text possible (which for the NT came to be called the *Textus Receptus,* 1550); it also made translation profitable (see: **Version**).

With the Enlightenment (17th and 18th cent.), and the subsequent rise of historical consciousness, came a flood of philological, historical, and literary questions regarding the text: date, place, authorship, sources, and intention **(Historical Criticism, Literary Criticism:** Source Criticism, *Tendenz* **Criticism).** As science altered the traditional world view, the desire to reconstruct Biblical history in conformity with the current understanding of reality was irrepressible. The Documentary Hypothesis (see: **Graf-Wellhausen Hypothesis**) concerning the origins of the Pentateuch and the **Two Source Hypothesis** concerning the origins of the synoptic Gospels became the ostensible victors of more than a half century of literary criticism. For political and economic reasons, scholarly research in the Middle East became possible. The discovery of ancient Biblical manuscripts placed **Textual Criticism** and Bible translation on a new footing. Archaeologists began to uncover the past and with it texts astonishingly similar in content to that of the Bible. By the close of the 19th cent., Comparative Religions (see: *Religionsgeschichte*), as the study of the Old and New Testament in terms of their social and religious milieux, had contributed significantly to the understanding of the two testaments. **Form Criticism** came on the scene in the first decades of the 20th cent. as the interest of literary critics shifted from the individual creative genius to the spontaneous self-expression of common people. The study of **Oral Tradition,** in the form of **legends, hymns,** songs, proverbs, **parables,** etc., provided access to the time prior to the fixing of tradition in written form. Occasionally, Form Criticism lapsed into the study of form for form's sake, or pure "formalism." This led in the 1930s to the analysis of how linguistic forms are transmuted in the traditioning process (**Tradition Criticism** or *Überlieferungsgeschichte*). In the field of NT studies **Redaction Criticism** was offered in the 1950s as a counter-balance to the inclination of form critics to treat the Gospel writers not as real interpreters of the tradition but as mere compilers of it. In still more recent years, other terms suggesting new approaches to the text have appeared: **Rhetorical Criticism, Structuralism,** computerized statistical analysis, et al. Indeed, the introduction of literary and structuralist perspectives in the late 1970s became so pervasive and radical as to be described as a second revolution in Biblical studies analogous to the introduction of historical-critical methods two hundred years ago. It is a revolution in which BC has been altered from a single, historical discipline to a field of disciplines (see: **Linguistics; Reception Theory; Semiology; Sociological Interpretation; Structure**). It remains uncertain, however, whether newer methodologies and theories, which are largely *synchronic* in nature, are propaedeutic to or alternatives for traditional historical methodologies, which have tended to be *diachronic* (see Appendix: "A Simplified Guide for Writing an Exegetical Paper . . ."). In addition, recent text and manuscript discoveries at 3rd millennium *Ebla* in Syria and at St. Catherine's monastery near Mt. Sinai (see: **Textual Criticism**) are adding to knowledge at both ends of Biblical history.

This sketch of BC in terms of its methods provides little more than a few signposts along a complex path marked by conflict and controversy. Until recent decades, it was a distinctly Protestant enterprise. Not all Protestants have been receptive to the scientific spirit, however. From the beginning camps formed on both left and right. Fundamentalists responded to BC with the doctrine of **Verbal Inspiration** and were accused by liberal Protestantism of **Biblicism** and **Bibliolatry.** The Roman Catholic Church likewise remained officially opposed to BC until Pope Pius XII's encyclical *Divino afflante Spiritu* (1943).

The openness with which both Conservative Protestantism and Roman

Catholicism now view BC is due not only to an internal change within these bodies but also to the recognition within BC itself of the nature and limits of reason and of the relative character of all knowledge, whether in literary criticism, theology, or physics. This awareness on the part of BC did not occur overnight. It developed within the theoretical reflections of **Hermeneutics** and in concert with the total changing world view of the 20th cent. The relativity of historical knowledge has thrown into question the authority of Scripture as the revealed Word of God and with it the concept of **canon.** Protestant Biblical theology has been occupied with these issues since Karl Barth's break with the Liberal tradition in his *Epistle to the Romans* (Ger.: 1919; Eng.: London: Oxford University Press, 1933). In Europe, the subsequent discussion lasting until the mid-1960s largely divided along lines separating John Calvin and Martin Luther in the 16th cent. American Biblical scholarship in the 20th cent. has been less theological, American theology less Biblical than its European counterpart. This characteristic is not less apt to be true of the last quarter of the 20th cent., as Protestant and Catholic critics seek neutral, non-dogmatic ground on the one hand and as BC is shaped by the increasingly dominant milieu of the state university on the other. (See: **Biblical Theology Movement; Canonical Criticism; Theological Interpretation.** For keeping up with biblical studies in the US and Canada, see: **CSR; SBL; CBA.**)

Biblical Theology (Movement) was "the intellectual side of a more general religious reaction" against "liberal theology and its use of the Bible" which flourished in America (in Great Britain and on the Continent in a less pronounced way) between 1945 and 1960. According to J. Barr, the BTM was characterized by the following features:
> (1) An opposition to the influence of philosophy and philosophical theology.
> (2) An opposition to the presumed systematizing tendency of dogmatic theology.
> (3) An emphasis upon Hebrew thought in contradistinction to Greek thought.
> (4) An emphasis upon the unity of the Bible.
> (5) An approach to Biblical language which concentrated on word studies.
> (6) An emphasis upon the distinctiveness of the Bible vis à vis its environment.
> (7) An emphasis on divine revelation in history.
> (8) The interrelationship of Biblical study and theological concern. (See: IDB, Supplemental volume (V), ad hoc.)

The now classic study of the movement, its rise and fall in America is

Brevard S. Childs' study, *Biblical Theology in Crisis* (Philadelphia: Westminster Press, 1970); but see also James D. Smart, *The Past, Present, and Future of Biblical Theology* (Philadelphia: Westminster Press, 1979).
See: **Theological Interpretation.**

Biblicism refers pejoratively to the uncritical, literal interpretation of Scripture, particularly to the quotation of a passage of Scripture out of context to prove a point of interpretation. See: **Bibliolatry; Historical Critical Method.**

Bibliography. There are numerous bibliographical tools for the study of the Bible and related subjects. Although some of these are noted elsewhere in this volume under specific subjects, the total list cannot be enumerated here. Rather, the following are to be consulted for more specific bibliographic information:

Bibliographic Index: A Cumulative Bibliography of Bibliographies. New York: The H. W. Wilson Company. Published semi-annually (April and August), the *BI* is a subject list of bibliographies published separately or appearing as parts of books, pamphlets, and periodicals when such lists contain fifty or more entries.

Elenchus Bibliographicus Biblicus, published by the Pontifical Biblical Institute in Rome, from 1920–68 as a part of the periodical *Biblica* and thereafter separately, is the most exhaustive Biblical bibliography available; it includes listings of books, articles, and reviews dealing with both Testaments, and the intertestamental and patristic periods.

A recent single-volume OT bibliographic guide is Brevard S. Childs, *OT Books for Pastor and Teacher* (Philadelphia: Westminster Press, 1977).

The most recent single-volume NT bibliographic aids are:

Hurd, J. C., Jr. *A Bibliography of New Testament Bibliographies.* Naperville, Ill.: Alec R. Allenson, 1966. A comprehensive listing covering all facets of NT criticism.

Scholer, David M. *A Basic Bibliographic Guide for New Testament Exegesis.* Grand Rapids: William B. Eerdmans Publishing Company, 1973². A handy, inexpensive aid to exegesis, including bibliographic tools, with commentary selections weighted on the evangelical side.

OT bibliographic aids in a single volume comparable to Hurd and Scholer do not exist at this time. Worth noting, however, are:

A Basic Bibliography for the Study of Semitic Languages. Edited by J. H. Hospers. 2 vols. Leiden: E. J. Brill, 1973. For the specialist.

Bible Bibliography 1967–73. Edited by P. R. Ackroyd. Oxford: Basil Blackwell, 1973 (1975). Its predecessors are *Eleven Years of Bible Bibliography* (1946–1956) and *A Decade of Bible Bibliography* (1957–66), edited by H. H.

Rowley and G. W. Anderson, respectively. The Society for Old Testament Study publishes an annotated "Book List" annually, the above volumes being composites of these lists.

Danker, Frederick W. *Multipurpose Tools For Bible Study.* London: Concordia Publishing House, 1960; St. Louis: Concordia, 1970.

Periodical bibliographic aids most helpful are: *Internationale Zeitschriftenschau für Bibelwissenschaft und Grenzgebiete* (from 1951; currently published by Patmos-Verlag, Düsseldorf). Although reviews are mainly in German, this aid to periodical literature can be used to locate articles in English on OT, NT, and related areas.

New Testament Abstracts (from 1956; published by Weston College of the Holy Spirit, Weston, Mass.). Abstracts in English of articles and reviews from over 250 periodicals from around the world.

Old Testament Abstracts (from 1978; published by the Catholic Biblical Association; The Catholic University of America, Washington, DC). The format and content are that of *NTA* above.

See: **Exegesis;** also: **Dead Sea Scrolls; Nag Hammadi Codices.**

Bibliolatry is a pejorative term connoting the idolization of the Bible in such a way as to make it, instead of God, the object of reverence. Coined by G. E. Lessing, German dramatist and theologian, in 1777 in his argument against the "bibliolatry" of J. M. Goeze, a Lutheran pastor in Hamburg. See: **Biblicism; Historical Critical Method; Lessing.**

Bicolon. See: **Colon.**

Bildhälfte (Ger.: lit., "picture half") is a German t.t. sometimes used in the interpretation of the parables of Jesus to refer to the imagery of the parable, in contrast to its subject matter, content, or "reality" part *(Sachhälfte).* The "point of comparison," or *tertium comparationis,* is that point in the parable where, as it is argued, the picture and the meaning come together and are one. Recent interpreters have rejected this analysis of parables, which limits the parable to a single point, as too rationalistic. (For the terms see, Eta Linnemann, *Jesus of the Parables* [New York: Harper and Row, 1966]; published in Britain as *Parables of Jesus* [London: S.P.C.K., 1966].) See: **Metaphor; Parable.**

Blessings. Broadly speaking B. are words uttered to evoke, create, or pronounce well-being, to extol or praise God for his providence, or to consecrate or make (someone or thing) holy. More specifically the term may refer to: (a) the actual words of blessing, (b) the power inherent in the utterance to produce an effect, or (c) the effect engendered or intended (health, prosperity, success, etc.).

The word B. is used to translate two Hebrew nouns, *Berakah* and *Ashere,* the latter more often designating the state of being blessed, i. e., "happy." In the LXX, these terms are translated by *eulogia* and *makarios* (in Latin, respectively *benedictio* and *beati*) which distinction is preserved in more recent English translations by the words "blessing" and "happy," as in the Beatitudes (Mt. 5; see JB, TEV).

Biblical B. have been categorized in a variety of ways; one proposal is according to the subject and object of blessing: (1) God subject—man object: Gen. 1:22 (creation); 1:28; 5:2; 9:1; 12:2–3; 22:17 (Patriarchs); Ex. 20:24; Lev. 26:3–13; Dt. 28:1–14 (the people of Israel); Dt. 7:13; 11:26–30; Judg. 13:24; 2 Sam. 6:11–12 (the faithful); also God blessing through his Elect or Anointed One: Gen. 12:2–3; 39:5; Num. 24:9; Isa. 19:24; in NT, through Jesus Christ or an angel: Acts 3:26; cf. Rev. 14:13; 16:15; 19:9; 20:6; 22:7, 14. (2) Man subject—man object: Gen. 9:26–27; 27:23–29 (heirs); Ex. 39:43; Lev. 9:23; Dt. 33 (leaders bless people); Num. 6:23–27 (priests—though God blesses); 2 Sam. 6:18 (king); 1 Kings 8:66 (people bless king); as in rabbinic literature, children and disciples are blessed (Mk. 10:16; Lk. 24:50); Jesus commands disciples to bless those who curse (Lk. 6:28; cf. Rom. 12:14; 1 Cor. 4:12; 1 Peter 3:9).(3) Man subject—God object: Gen. 14:20; 24:27; Ex. 18:10; 1 Sam. 25:32; Ps. 28:6; 1 Chron. 29:10–13 (here in the sense of praising God for what he has done); Mk. 6:41; 8:7 (also for food); in the Eucharist God is praised for a past act by a petition for his continued blessing (Mt. 26:27; Mk. 14:22; 1 Cor. 11:24—here praise is called a "thanksgiving"). Cf. also Rev. 5:9–10, 13–14.

For B. in Qumran, see 1QSb; 1QS 11:1–4; in the Gospel of Thomas, *Logion* 69.

B. (Benedictions) commonly used since the Late Middle Ages to conclude divine worship: Num. 6:24–26 (Aaronic blessing); Rom. 15:13; 16:25–27; 2 Cor. 13:14; Heb. 13:20–21, 25; 1 Thess. 3:11–13; 5:23; Jude 24–25; Eph. 3:20; 6:23; Philem. 25.

Bousset, Wilhelm (1865–1920). Born in Lübeck, Germany, B. taught NT theology at Göttingen and from 1916 at Giessen. Considered one of the founders of the *Religionsgeschichtliche Schule,* a method which he applied to his study of the relationship of Hellenistic religions to early Christianity and Judaism, B. is particularly noted for *Die Religion des Judentums im späthellenistischen Zeitalter* (1903; 1926³ rev. Hugo Gressmann; 1966⁴); *Hauptprobleme der Gnosis* (1907; 1973); and, *Kyrios Christos* (Ger.: 1913; Eng.: Nashville: Abingdon Press, 1970).

Brown-Driver-Briggs. See: **Exegesis:** Tools, Lexicons.

Bultmann, Rudolf (1884–1976). A student of Wilhelm Bousset, Hermann Gunkel, Wilhelm Herrmann, Adolf von Harnack, Adolf Jülicher, and Johannes Weiss, and later a colleague of Martin Heidegger at Marburg, B. taught NT in Marburg (1912–16), Breslau (1916–20), Giessen (1920), and again in Marburg (1921) until his retirement in 1951.

Few names in 20th cent. NT criticism and theology equal that of RB and none exceeds it. As one of the inaugurating volumes on Form Criticism, his *History of the Synoptic Tradition* (1921) is still an indispensable tool of NT criticism. His debates with Karl Barth during the formative period of Dialectic Theology (1919–1933) helped shape the principal themes of Continental theology for more than a quarter century; his program of "Demythologization," that is, the interpretation of the Biblical world view and its language by way of existentialist (Heideggerian) categories, was the dominant issue in Biblical theology until the 1960s. The most readily accessible introduction to his theology remains his little book, *Jesus Christ and Mythology* (New York: Charles Scribner's Sons, 1958).

See: **Apophthegm; Demythologization; Existentialist; Form Criticism; Hermeneutics; Myth.**

Byzantine Text is the name in Textual Criticism given to that form of the Greek NT current in Constantinople (earlier Byzantium), the capital of the Eastern Empire (A.D. 330 to A.D. 1453). This text-type, which is found among the majority of extant MSS, became the basis of Erasmus' Greek NT (1516) and later of the *Textus Receptus* (q.v.), the primary Greek source consulted in the preparation of the KJV of the NT (1611). The antecedent of the BT may be the work of Lucian of Antioch (d. 321), whose edition of the Biblical text Jerome (*ca.* 403) acknowledged as the *"koiné"* or "common and widespread" text, referring to it also as the "Lucianic" text. Also called Antiochene or Syrian, the BT is characterized by clarifying the harmonizing interpolations, and a general smoothing of diction. Major witnesses are codices Alexandrinus (A), Ephraemi (C), Washingtonianus (W), and the *Koiné* group (E.F.G.H., etc.) and most minuscules. Note: In the OT, Lucian's recension (LXX^L) is based on a revision of Old Greek MSS, called the Proto-Lucianic recension. See: **Alexandrian Text; Codex; Family; Western Text.**

Caesarean Text, The. In Textual Criticism, CT is one of the geographical place names by which MSS of the NT bearing similar textual characteristics are sometimes identified (along with Alexandrian, Western, and Byzantine). The theory of the CT as a distinct text-type was proposed by B. H. Streeter (*The Four Gospels* [London:Macmillan and Co., 1924]); it is based on the knowledge that in the two halves of his commentary on John, Origen quoted from different MSS of the NT, the former available while he was in Alexandria, the latter while in Caesarea. Streeter deduced from this that a distinct Caesarean text-type existed which he identified with Codex Koridethi

(θ) and two families of minuscules (Families 1 and 13; see: **Family**). Recent text critical studies seem to indicate, however, that the witnesses purportedly within the CT type do not represent a text-type sufficiently distinct from the two major strains, the Alexandrian (Neutral) and the Western, to warrant a separate designation. (See E. C. Colwell, *Studies in Methodology in Textual Criticism of the New Testament* [Leiden: E. J. Brill, 1969].)

Canon (adj.: canonical) is a transliteration of the Greek word *kanon* meaning rule. In its general sense, C. denotes a collection or list of books accepted as an authoritative rule of faith and practice. The Christian C. varies according to Protestant, Roman Catholic, or Eastern Orthodox traditions. The beginning of the idea of a sacred C. is discernible in Scripture itself; see the "canonical" formulas in Deut. 4:2; 12:32; Jer. 26:2; Prov. 30:6; Eccles. 3:14; 2 Peter 3: 15–16; Rev. 22:6–8, 18–19. See: **Apocrypha;** *Sui ipsius interpres.*

Canonical Criticism is a relatively new term still used rather ambiguously to refer to a variety of interpretive approaches which share a common concern with regard to the nature, function, and authority of canon.

James A. Sanders coined the term canonical criticism (*Torah and Canon* [Philadelphia: Fortress Press, 1972]) to denote a method of biblical criticism which operates subsequent to form and redaction criticism and seeks to determine the function of Biblical texts in their historical contexts and investigate the nature of their authority. The essence of canonical criticism, as practiced by Sanders, lies in discerning the hermeneutics by which the ancient traditions were adapted for use in new contexts. (See also "Adaptable for Life: The Nature and Function of Canon," pp. 531–60 in Cross, Lemke, and Miller, eds., *Magnalia Dei: The Mighty Acts of God* [Garden City: Doubleday, 1976], pp. 531–60; and "Biblical Criticism and the Bible as Canon," *Union Seminary Quarterly Review* 32, [1977], pp. 157–65.)

The term canonical criticism is also frequently applied to the approach to interpretation advocated by Brevard Childs (*Introduction to the Old Testament as Scripture* [Philadelphia: Fortress Press, 1979]; or, in briefer scope, cf. "The Exegetical Significance of Canon for the Study of the Old Testament," *SVT* 29 ([1978], pp. 66–80). With Sanders, Childs shares a broad definition of canon, a concern for the theological significance of the Biblical texts, and a concern for the function of the Biblical texts within the community of faith which preserved and treasured them. However, Childs himself disavows the term canonical criticism as applied to his approach; he does not consider the canonical approach to be another Biblical critical method such as form criticism or rhetorical criticism, or the like. "Rather, the issue at stake in relation to the canon turns on establishing a stance from which the Bible can be read as sacred scripture" (*Introduction,* p. 82).

Contrary to Sanders, Childs does not seek to determine the hermeneutics employed in the canonical process. Rather, the stance developed by Childs focuses on the shape and function of the final canonical text. Childs carefully describes and analyzes the final received form of the OT books. His primary concern is not with any particular editorial layer, but rather with the final resultant product. According to Childs this final shape is of special significance because: (1) it alone displays the full history of revelation witnessed to by Scripture; (2) in it the community has exercised its critical judgment on the received traditions and modified them accordingly; and (3) by showing how the texts were actualized by generations removed from the original event and composition of the writings, the canonical shape may provide a hermeneutical key as to how we may actualize the text in our day.

Sanders and Childs both operate with a definition of canon considerably more broad than that in common parlance. They argue that the notion of canon should be understood as including not only the final literary stage in the Bible's development, but also that development process itself. Moreover, they suggest that such a broadening is not a novel suggestion but results from a critical reevaluation of Semler's narrowing of the concept—upon which the 19th century critical consensus was based.

Along with Childs and Sanders a number of other scholars have shown an interest in a new understanding of canon. Among the other studies which might be comprehended by the term canonical criticism, the following are of special note: Joseph Blenkinsopp, *Prophecy and Canon* (Notre Dame, Indiana: University of Notre Dame Press, 1977); Ronald Clements, "Covenant and Canon in the Old Testament," pp. 1–12 in McKinney, ed., *Creation, Christ, and Culture* (Edinburgh: T. & T. Clark, 1976); and the volume of essays edited by George Coats and Burke Long (*Canon and Authority* [Philadelphia: Fortress Press, 1977]).

Case, Shirley Jackson (1872–1947). Born in New Brunswick, Canada, he studied at Acadia Univ. (A.B., 1893; M.A., 1896), Yale Divinity School (B.D., 1904; Ph.D., 1906), and the U. of Marburg (1910). He taught NT and early Church history at the University of Chicago Divinity School (1908–38), serving as dean from 1933 until his retirement (1938), thereafter becoming dean of the School of Religion, Lakeland, Florida. He was managing editor of the *American Journal of Theology* (1912–20), editor of the *Journal of Religion* (1927–39), and *Religion in the Making* (1940–43). A student of Christian mysticism and millennialism, a supporter of the social gospel movement, he is best known in Biblical Criticism for his book, *Jesus: A New Biography* (Chicago: University of Chicago Press, 1927).

Casuistic Law. In OT Form Criticism, the term casuistic is used to denote a class of case law, in contrast to apodictic or absolute prohibitions. The CL is characterized by an opening conditional clause *(protasis)* in which the case is described, beginning "If . . . ," followed by a statement of the penalty in the *apodosis* or main clause, "then . . ." or "he (or she) shall . . ."; e. g., Deut. 22:23–29. According to Albrecht Alt (see: **Apodictic Law**), CL was the typical formulation of law in the ancient Near East generally. See: **Apodictic Law;** *Sätze heiligen Rechtes.*

Catalog of Vices: See: *Lästerkataloge.*

Catalog of Virtues: See: *Lästerkataloge.*

Catechesis, catechetic, catechetical (fr. Greek: oral instruction). Oral instruction in matters of faith; or a book or collection of materials so used. According to Form Criticism, catechetical needs were formative influences in shaping Biblical material; this is particularly evident in Deuteronomy and the Deuteronomistic redactions of the OT and, more perspicuously still, in the structural patterns of the Gospel according to Mt. in the NT. Materials from a Eucharistic C. for example may possibly be found, it is suggested, not only in the pericope of the Last Supper (Mt. 26:14–30) but also in the miracles of feeding (Mt. 14:15–21; 15:32–38). See: **Credo.**

Catena (pl.: *catenae*) is a technical term borrowed from Latin (meaning "chain") and connoting a connected series, whether of sayings, quotations, liturgical formulae, miracle stories, or all. In Textual Criticism, as in Roman Catholic tradition, a *C.* is a series of quotations extracted from the writings of the Church Fathers *(catena Patrum)* and used as a commentary on a passage of Scripture (see, e. g., Codex 747 in J. H. Greenlee, *Introduction to NT Textual Criticism* [Grand Rapids: William B. Eerdmans, 1964], plate 6).

Catholic Epistles consist of James, 1 & 2 Peter, 1, 2 & 3 John, and Jude; also called the "General Epistles," i. e., letters treated as being addressed to the whole church. Sometimes referred to in German as "church epistles" *(Kirchenbriefe);* however, 1 Peter, 2 and 3 John identify their intended recipients and cannot in the strict sense be considered "catholic," i. e., addressed to all Christians. The names of the epistles are derived from the (putative) authors, rather than from the recipients as in the case of the Pauline letters. See: **Pastoral Epistles.**

Catholicizing Tendency refers to the movement already evident in the 1st cent. toward the institutionalization of Christian belief and practice, particularly with the waning of the expectation of the imminent return of Christ. In the NT, see Mt. 16:19; 18:18; Eph. 4; 1 Tim. 3, etc., and the whole of Acts.

CBA (CBQ). The Catholic Biblical Association of America, founded in 1938, publishes the *Catholic Biblical Quarterly* (CBQ); *Old Testament Abstracts,* and the *CBQ Monograph Series;* Active and Associate Membership is open "to those who qualify as specialists in biblical studies." Address: The Catholic Biblical Association of America, The Catholic University, Washington, DC 20064. See: **CSR; SBL.**

C.E. is an equivalent of A.D. and means "Common Era"; see: B.C.E.

Cento (Latin: patched cloth; plural: *centos*). In Biblical criticism, a *C.* is a patchwork of Scriptural quotations (e. g., Rom. 3:10*b*–18; 11:34–35; 1 Peter 2:6–8; Heb. 1:5–13).

Chenoboskion is the name of the site of the first Christian monastery, founded by Pachomius *ca.* A.D. 320 and located on the Nile river in Egypt, approximately forty miles northwest of Luxor near the modern town of Nag Hammadi. For reasons of historical interest primarily, the name *C.* was attached to the Coptic Gnostic MSS discovered near there in 1945–46; these MSS are now commonly referred to as the Nag Hammadi Codices. See: **Nag Hammadi Codices.**

Chiasmus (chiasm; also called chiastic or inverted parallelism). A Latinized word based on the Greek letter X *(Chi)* to symbolize the inverted sequence or cross-over of parallel words or ideas in a bicolon (distich), sentence, or larger literary unit. *C.* appears for example in Mk. 2:27: "The sabbath [a] was made for man [b], and not man [b'] for the sabbath [a']," taking the simple form: a b b' a'. A *C.* which appears in the Greek or Hebrew is often lost in translation, appearing only as simple synonymous parallelism. Its preservation can also be confusing, as in Matt. 7:6, which parallels in chiastic form "dogs" with "attack" and "swine" with "trample": "Do not give dogs what is holy; and do not throw your pearls before swine, lest they trample them under foot and turn to attack you." (RSV) In prophetic literature, Isa. 6:10 is a chiasm of two tricola (tristichs):

    A Make the heart of this people fat,
    B and their ears heavy
    C and shut their eyes;
    C lest they see with their eyes,
    B and hear with their ears,
    A And understand with their hearts,
       And turn and be healed. (RSV)

Chiasm in prose literature is more difficult to identify, its role in interpretation somewhat less significant. Jn. 6:36–40; Rom. 2:7–10; 11:30–31; Mt. 9:17; 1 Cor. 7:3; 9:19–22; 11:8–12; Col. 3:3–4, etc., are cited as examples, perhaps indicating an underlying Semitic influence on the writers. Nigel Turner (in *A Grammar of New Testament Greek*, vol. III: *Syntax* [Edinburgh: T.&T. Clark, 1963]) suggests that 1 Cor. 5:2–6 is *chiasmus* within *chiasmus:*

A	B		C		B		A
puffed up	misconduct	A	Lord Jesus	A	Satan	A	boasting
	presence	B	you	B	distortion	B	
	presence	B	me	B	flesh	C	
	misconduct	A	Lord Jesus	A	spirit	C	
					salvation	B	
					day of word	A	

For an overzealous but helpful analysis of *C.,* see Nils W. Lund, *Chiasmus in the NT* (Chapel Hill: University of North Carolina Press, 1942).
See: **Parallelism; Colon.**

Chria (pl.: *Chriae;* also Greek: *Chreia;* pl.: *-ai*) is a Greek technical term used in ancient rhetoric to denote a literary form containing an epigram or "a sharp pointed saying of general significance, originating in a definite person and arising out of a definite situation" (Dibelius). In Hellenistic culture, *C.* were told about and in honor of a famous man or simply as a means of preserving a humorous saying or incident concerning him. Dibelius distinguishes the *C.* from (a) the larger grouping of "Apophthegmata" by noting the former's connection with a particular situation, and from (b) the Gnome by its connection with a person (*From Tradition to Gospel* [London: Ivor Nicholson and Watson, Ltd., 1934; repr. James Clarke, 1971; New York: Charles Scribner's Sons, 1935], pp. 152f.). Examples of *C.* are to be found in Xenophon's *Memorabilia,* e. g., "On a man who was angry because his greeting was not returned: 'Ridiculous!' he [Socrates] exclaimed, 'You would not have been angry if you had met a man in worse health; and yet you are annoyed because you have come across someone with ruder manners!' " (III. xiii.)

According to Dibelius, literary tendencies within the early Church, particularly seen in Luke's Gospel, caused sayings of Jesus to be adapted to the *C.* form, e. g., Lk. 3:21–22; 8:21; 9:61–62; 11:27–28; 19:39–40, 45–46, etc.

Christ (Greek: lit., "anointed one"). In Greek the word *Christos* approximates the Hebrew *māshi ᵃḥ* (Messiah) also meaning, the "Anointed One" (of

God). However, in Greek culture, the term C. in no way bore the connotations associated by the Jews with its Hebrew equivalent, viz., one invested by God with a unique power and mission. Hence, C. soon became a proper name (Gal. 1:6; Heb. 9:11), with "Son of God" becoming the honorific designation (cf. Mk. 1:1).

Christophany, meaning "an appearance, or manifestation, of Christ," was first used by D. F. Strauss (1836; II, 621) of the appearances of the risen Jesus to the disciples and women (e. g., Mt. 28:9–10, 16–17; Mk. 16:9–10, 12, 14—the long ending; Lk. 24:13ff., etc.). Other passages are variously described as C., such as the Transfiguration (Mk. 9:2ff. pars.) and Paul's confrontation on the road to Damascus (Acts 9:3–16, etc.). According to some conservative theologians, even OT theophanies are to be understood as C. See: **Epiphany.**

Codex (pl.: codices). An ancient manuscript in book form, made of papyrus or vellum. When the C. as an alternative to the scroll originated is uncertain. But its existence in the 2nd cent. A.D. is certain. The C. found particular favor among Christians, perhaps because it facilitated locating Scriptural passages of interest and placing works in canonical order. (See: Frederic G. Kenyon, *The Text of the Greek Bible,* 3rd rev. and aug. ed. by A. W. Adams [London: Duckworth Press, 1975]; also Eric G. Turner, *The Typology of the Early Codex* [no location cited: The University of Pennsylvania Press, 1977].)

Codex Alexandrinus (*siglum:* A) is a 5th cent. MS of the Greek Bible, presently housed in the British Museum, earlier a gift from the Patriarch of Constantinople to James I (1603–25). The text-type in the NT is both Byzantine (Gospels) and Alexandrian (Acts and Epistles). Of the NT, most of Mt. is missing, as are Jn. 6:50–8:52 and 2 Cor. 4:13–12:6. The MS includes I and II Clement and contains, with P[47], one of the best texts of the book of Revelation. In the OT, the text is eclectic.

Codex Bezae Cantabrigiensis is a 5th cent. Graeco-Latin MS of the Gospels and Acts (*sigla:* D or D[ea] [Greek] and d [Latin]). It receives its name from Theodore Bezae and the University of Cambridge to which he presented it in 1581, having obtained the MS from St. Irenaeus' monastery in Lyon, France. Its origin is unknown but is probably Western Mediterranean. D is the principal representative of the Western text, which orders the Gospels: Mt., Jn., Lk., Mk. Though filled with innumerable orthographic and grammatical errors, the text, which is arranged colometrically, is of interest because of its omissions (called "Western non-interpolations" by Westcott and Hort) in Luke and its additions in the book of Acts, which is 1/10th longer than the "Neutral" text (S, B, etc.). These apparent additions to the text of Acts are dominantly anti-Jewish in nature (see E. J. Epp, *The Theological Tendency of*

Codex Bezae Cantabrigiensis in Acts [Cambridge: The University Press, 1966]). The most famous addition to Luke follows 6:4: "On the same day he saw a man working on the Sabbath and he said to him, 'Man, if you know what you are doing, blessed are you; but if you do not know, you are accursed and a transgressor of the law.' "

Codex Ephraemi Rescriptus (*siglum:* C). A palimpsest codex of parts of the Old and NTs dating from the 5th cent. The text, now in Paris, contains Alexandrian and Western readings, but also later readings of a Byzantine type, hence not of great significance for Textual Criticism. See: **Palimpsest.**

Codex Sinaiticus (*siglum:* ℵ or S) is a 4th cent. vellum MS of portions of the OT and the whole NT, discovered in 1859 by Constantin Tischendorf in the Orthodox monastery of St. Catherine at the foot of Mt. Sinai. Like Codex Vaticanus, the text is Alexandrian. Absent from the text is the longer ending of Mk. (16:9–19) and the *pericope de adultera* (Jn. 7:53–8:11). In order, the Pauline epistles follow the Gospels (canonical order), then Heb., the Pastoral Epistles, Acts, the Catholic Epistles, and Revelation, followed by the Epistle of Barnabas and the Shepherd of Hermas.

Codex Vaticanus (*siglum:* B) is a 4th cent. vellum MS of the Bible, housed in the Vatican library since at least 1481. The text is Alexandrian (or Neutral) and, because of its antiquity, state of preservation, and text-type, is extremely valuable as a textual source. The MS ends at Heb. 9:14. The books missing in addition to Heb. 9:15–13:25, are Philemon, the Pastorals, and Revelation. Also absent are the longer ending of Mk. (16:9–19) and the *pericope de adultera* (Jn. 7:53–8:11). The Catholic Epistles precede the letters of Paul and follow the Acts of the Apostles.

Collate (fr. a Latin verb meaning to compare). In Textual Criticism, collation refers to the critical comparison of ancient handwritten exemplars of a given writing in order to ascertain textual differences with the aim of reconstructing the original text. Usually, MSS are collated against an accepted form of the text, such as the *Textus Receptus* of the Greek NT or a modern critical text. See: **Critical Text; Textual Criticism;** *Textus Receptus.*

Colometric. See: **Colon.**

Colon (pl.: cola). A single verse unit of poetry. As t.ts. for the analysis of Hebrew poetry, the OT scholar W. F. Albright proposed the terms colon, bicolon, and tricolon for the more customary terms: stich (or hemistich), distich (or stich), and tristich, because of the varied usage of the alternative terminology as indicated below. Many have followed Albright's suggestion, but it has yet to win the day. Example:

Judges 15:16
1. "With the jawbone of a donkey:		a. hemistich,	b. stich,	or c. colon
2. Have I mightily raged:	1 + 2:	a. stich,	b. distich,	or c. bicolon
3. With the jawbone of a donkey:		a. hemistich,	b. stich,	or c. colon
4. Have I slain a thousand men":	3 + 4:	a. stich,	b. distich,	or c. bicolon;

Ps. 24:7
"Lift up your heads, O gates:	stich or colon ⎫	tricolon
And be lifted up, O ancient doors!:	stich or colon ⎬	or
That the King of glory may come in.":	stich or colon ⎭	tristich.

(Note: According to Sigmund Mowinckel, Pss. 93; 138; 45:1–16; 24:7–10; 60:8–10; 108:8–10; 79:1–2, etc., are further examples of tricola. Using the alternate terms, he finds tristichs in Pss. 1; 2; 6; 22; 31, et al.; tetrastichs in Pss. 18; 46; 49; 65, et al.; pentastichs in Pss. 20; 99; 104, et al.; heptastichs in Pss. 21; 33; 85; and an octastich in Ps. 119—but here the term "stich" means "bicolon" above.)

In Textual Criticism, the term C. means a line containing a single clause, normally of at least nine syllables but not more than sixteen. Some ancient MSS of the NT are written colometrically, of which Codex Bezae is the most famous; in them, each printed line is composed of one colon or clause. (See: Sigmund Mowinckel, *Real and Apparent Tricola in Hebrew Psalm Poetry* [Oslo: I kommisjon hos Aschehoug, 1957].)

Colophon (Greek: finishing touch) is the name given to an inscription at the end of a book; it may include in whole or in part: the title or subject matter, the author, printer, date and place of publication; or it may contain simply a comment or warning by the author. In the OT a C. can be found at the close of the Holiness Code (Lev. 26:46) and the second book of the Psalms of David (Ps. 72:20); also cf. Job 31:40; in the NT, Rev. 22:18–19 may be so considered. According to B. H. Streeter, a common C. on 11th and 12th cent. minuscule MSS reads, "Copied and corrected from ancient exemplars from Jerusalem preserved on the Holy Mountain." See: *ANET,* 424, 438.

Comedy. Although, as customarily understood, C. appears nowhere in the Old or New Testaments as a literary genre, a medieval definition of comedy (and tragedy) has recently been revived in the employ of parable interpretation. In the Middle Ages C. was defined as a movement from bad to good fortune, whereas tragedy embodied a reversal of fortune from good to bad. It is in this sense that Dante's *The Divine Comedy* is to be understood. For its application to the interpretation of parables see Dan O. Via's *The Parables* (Philadelphia: Fortress Press, 1967) and his *Kerygma and Comedy in the New Testament* (Fortress, 1975).

Commentary. Although varied in form, content, and style, a C. is a book which discusses the Biblical text chapter by chapter and verse by verse, lifting up noteworthy phrases and words for clarification. Critical commentaries, in contrast to homiletical or devotional ones, deal with the text in terms of its linguistic, literary, historical, and religio-cultural setting. Introductory articles often precede the C. proper. Commentaries may appear as single volumes or in series. Among the best of the former are Karl Barth's *The Epistle to the Romans* (London: Oxford University Press, 1933) and Vincent Taylor's *The Gospel According to St. Mark* (London: Macmillan and Co., 1952), although the former is primarily theological, as are the classical commentaries by John Calvin and Martin Luther.

The following are standard English commentaries of the Bible or of the NT alone. Fortunately, a number of the more important German commentaries are becoming available through the *Old* and *NT Library* series (Westminster) and through *Hermeneia* (Fortress).

Anchor Bible, The (Garden City, N.Y.: Doubleday and Co., 1964–   ).
  Not strictly a commentary. Translation with extensive introduction and critical notes.

The Broadman Bible Commentary (Nashville: Broadman Press, 1970–1973).
  Evangelical.

Cambridge Bible Commentary: New English Bible (Cambridge: The University Press, 1963–   ).
  For lay readers by leading British and American scholars (paper).

Cambridge Greek Testament Commentary (Cambridge: The University Press, 1957).
  Prepared for British schools and colleges.

Clarendon Bible, The (Oxford: The Clarendon Press, 1922–1947 [incomplete]).
  Based on RV. Non-technical.

The Expositor's Bible Commentary with The New International Version of the Holy Bible (Grand Rapids: Zondervan, 1979–   ).
  Evangelical.

Harper's New Testament Commentaries (New York: Harper and Brothers, 1957–   ; same as Black's NTC).
  Requires some knowledge of Greek.

Hermeneia (Philadelphia: Fortress Press, 1971–   ).
  Based on Hebrew and Greek texts; for serious students.

International Critical Commentary on the Holy Scriptures (New York: Charles Scribner's Sons, 1896–1937).
  Technical commentary; partly out of date.

The Interpreter's Bible (Nashville: Abingdon Press, 1951–1957).
  Contains exegetical and expository sections.

Layman's Bible Commentary (Richmond: John Knox Press, 1959).
  Non-technical.

Moffatt New Testament Commentary (London: Hodder and Stoughton, 1926–50).
  Non-technical commentary by British scholars.

New International Commentary on the Old Testament (Grand Rapids, Mich.: Wm. B. Eerdmans, 1955–   ) and *NIC on the New Testament* (Eerdmans, 1954). (Same as *The New London OT and NTC*.)
Conservative. Some knowledge of languages helpful.

Old Testament Library, The (Philadelphia: The Westminster Press, 1961–   ).
Contains commentaries and monographs. Scholarly. Languages not required.

Pelican Gospel Commentaries, The (Baltimore: Penguin Books, 1963–   ).
Non-technical (paper).

Tyndale New Testament Commentary (Eerdmans, 1956–   ); *Old Testament Commentary* (1964–   ).
Based on KJV: non-technical, theologically conservative.

The Wesleyan Bible Commentary (Grand Rapids: W. B. Eerdmans, 1964–69). Evangelical.

Westminster New Testament (London: Methuen and Co., 1908–12).
Theologically conservative; less technical than *ICC;* based on Revised Version of 1881.

Recent one-volume Commentaries include:

Interpreter's One-Volume Commentary (Nashville: Abingdon Press, 1971; London: William Collins Sons, 1972).

Jerome Biblical Commentary (Englewood Cliffs, N.J.: Prentice-Hall, Inc., 1969; London: Geoffrey Chapman, 1969).

A New Catholic Commentary on Holy Scripture (Camden, N.J.: Nelson, 1953; rev. 1969).

The New Layman's Bible Commentary (Grand Rapids: Zondervan, 1979).
Evangelical.

Peake's Commentary on the Bible (New York: Thomas Nelson and Sons, 1962).

The Wycliff Bible Commentary (Chicago: Moody Press, 1962).
Conservative evangelical.

Conclusio.   See: *Rhetorical Analysis.*

Concordance.   A C. is an alphabetical listing of all the principal words of a book, including a reference indicating the place where it occurs and usually some portion of the accompanying phrase. Cs of Scripture are numerous, varying in form, language, and comprehensiveness. Cs of Scripture in the original languages are commonly known by the editor's (s') name, such as Davidson, or Mandelkern (Hebrew and Chaldee), Moulton and Geden (Greek NT) Hatch and Redpath (Septuagint), and Schmoller *(Handkonkordanz zum NT)*. A new multivolumed series of Cs of the Scriptures, called *The Computer Bible,* and of ancient texts pertinent to the study of Scripture (called *The International Concordance Library*) is being published by Biblical Research Associates (Wooster, Ohio). The *CB* will include individual Cs devoted to a wide range of analytic data, including morphology, syntax, style, linguistic phenomena, etc.; the *ICL* will include Cs of the Apostolic Fathers, Philo of Alexandria, the Apocryphal NT, the Dead Sea Scrolls, et al.An exhaustive C. to the Greek NT with word statistical studies is being published by K. Aland: *Vollständige Konkordanz zum griechischen Neuen Testament* (Berlin/New York: Walter de Gruyter, 1975–).

English language Cs exist for the major English translations of the Bible. Standard Cs include Creden's (KJV, 1873); Strong's (KJV, reprint 1958); Young's (KJV, 1936); and Nelson's (RSV, 1957); less exhaustive Cs exist for NEB, JB, Moffatt's, etc. A valuable C. to the NT is the *Modern Concordance to the New Testament,* Michael Darton, ed. (Garden City: Doubleday, 1977) which is designed for use with the JB, KJV, RSV, NAB, NEB, and LB(P). Also: Clinton Morrison, *An Analytical Concordance to the Revised Standard Version of the New Testament* (Philadelphia: Westminster Press, 1979).

A C. to the Dead Sea Scrolls has been edited by Karl Georg Kuhn, *Konkordanz zu den Qumrantexten* (Göttingen: Vandenhoeck and Ruprecht, 1960).

Conditio Jacobea (Latin: "the condition of James"), viz., "If the Lord wills." The term applies to Jas. 4:15, but is a misnomer if it be inferred that it originated here (see also Acts 18:21; Rom. 1:10; 1 Cor. 4:19; 16:7; Heb. 6:3; also cf. Phil. 2:19, 24). This apotropaic formula is not found in OT or rabbinic writings although it abounded in the popular piety of the Graeco-Roman culture and still survives in many languages: *deo volente* (Ital.), *Inshallah* (Arabic), etc. Its function is evident by its setting in the so-called travelogue sections of Paul's letters. An amusing and satirical parallel can be found in the *Alphabet of ben Sira,* an 11th cent. Jewish writing; see: Strack und Billerbeck, ad hoc.

Conflation, Conflate Reading. In textual criticism, C. is the term used to denote a scribal error or editorial change in which two variant readings of a text are combined forming a new reading not precisely identical with either of the two source readings. See: **Assimilation; Gloss; Haplography; Homoioteleuton.**

Congregational Rules, Church Rules. See: *Gemeindeordnungen.*

Consistent Eschatology. See: **Eschatology.**

Constructive Parallelism. See: Synthetic Parallelism under **Parallelism.**

Corpus Hermeticum. See: **Hermetic Literature.**

Covenant Form. See: **Treaty Form.**

Covenant Lawsuit. See: *Rîb* **Pattern.**

Covenant Renewal Psalms. See: **Psalms.**

Credo (Latin: I believe). A creed or confession of faith. The C. has its setting in the worship (cultic) life of the believing community. Examples in the OT are Dt. 26:1–11; 6:20–24; 26:5–9; Josh. 24:2*b*–13 (14–25); etc. Creedal themes may appear in prayers, cult lyrics, or narratives, e. g., 1 Sam. 12:8; Pss. 78; 105; 135; 136. Here the major themes revolve around the Exodus, the conquest of the Promised Land, and the Sinai Covenant. In the NT, Christological formulas and hymns constitute parallels to the OT C. See: **Hymn.**

Criteria of Authenticity. What in terms of subject matter has been called the "Quest of the Historical Jesus" can in terms of methodology be called the quest of C. of A., that is, the quest for the conceptual means by which the (synoptic) sayings tradition can be judged to go back either to the Jesus of history or to the early Church. The criteria adduced to determine authentic sayings of Jesus are known as C. of A.; they have been developed over several decades of scholarly debate and recently articulated by Norman Perrin and Reginald Fuller:

(1) The criterion of dissimilarity (so Perrin; Fuller: "distinctiveness"): To be certain or reasonably certain of authenticity, a saying must be dissimilar to both Judaism and the teachings of the Church. Although it is obviously possible and probable that Jesus incorporated Jewish thought into his own theology (e. g., Isa. 61:1–2) or that the early Church transformed authentic sayings into its own (e. g., Mk. 8:34ff.), it is only where the tradition is dissimilar to both Judaism and the Church that (relative) certainty can be assured. A logion that meets this criterion is embedded in the Beelzebul controversy (Lk. 11:14–23); "But if it is by the finger of God that I cast out demons, then the kingdom of God has come upon you" (vs. 20; Mt. 12:28). It should be noted, therefore, that it is an admittedly minimalist criterion. Many scholars question whether any adequate understanding of a highly influential historical figure can be based on a standard requiring absolute historical discontinuity with past and future. Furthermore, the criterion excludes from Jesus the perhaps major and proven characteristic of the early Church, viz., apocalyptic.

(2) The criterion of multiple attestation (Perrin; Fuller: the "cross-section method"): Material whose theme is essentially duplicated elsewhere in the tradition in the same or additional forms, e. g., concern for the common people

of the land, for the least, the lost and the last, is multiple attested in a variety of forms (logia, parables, makarisms [blessings], etc.).

(3) The criterion of coherence (Perrin; Fuller: "consistency"): To be considered authentic, any given saying must cohere with other established material in form and content. Allegory does not cohere with the form of Jesus' parables and must be excluded or held in doubt from the "authentic sayings" (e. g., the allegory of the sower, Mk. 4:1–9, pars., or at least its interpretation, Mk. 4:13–20, pars.). Similarly, the spiritualization of Jesus' sayings, such as Mt.'s version of the Beatitudes (5:3–6), are probably redactional elements. C. of A. can be applied as well to the deeds of Jesus; that he associated with tax collectors and sinners, aroused the antagonism of scribes and pharisees, practiced exorcism, etc., is little to be doubted. (See: Norman Perrin, Rediscovering the Teachings of Jesus [New York: Harper and Row, 1967; London: SCM, 1967] and Reginald Fuller, *A Critical Introduction to the New Testament* [London: Duckworth, 1966, 1974³].)

See: **Apocalyptic; Eschatology; Historical Critical Method; Redaction Criticism.**

Critical Apparatus refers to the text critical footnotes supplied primarily in Hebrew and Greek editions of the OT and NT which cite the MS sources and readings that either support or vary from the printed text; CAs are also found in certain study Bibles such as the **Gospel Parallels** (q. v.). A CA will include the following: papyrus MSS dating from the 2nd-6th cent. (P¹, P², etc.); uncial MSS from the 4th-10th cent. (S, B, C, D, etc.); minuscule MSS from the 9th-15th cent. (1, 13, 181, etc.); versions (Old Latin, Old Syriac, Coptic, etc.); Church Fathers (Clement, Justin, Origen, etc.); and lectionaries. There are approximately 81 papyrus MSS, 266 uncials, 2754 minuscules, and 2135 lectionaries bearing witness to the NT text. See: **Critical Text; Papyrus; Uncial; Minuscule; Version; Lectionary.**

Critical Text. A CT is a conjectural reconstruction of a document of which only divergent recensions are extant; it is therefore a hypothetical text usually based on the one or two best MSS available. A CT is normally accompanied by a Critical Apparatus with alternate readings. The most widely used CTs are Tischendorf (1869); Westcott and Hort (1881); Nestle-Aland (*Novum Testamentum Graece* [New York: American Bible Society, 1898; 1963]); and, *The Greek NT*, edited by Aland, Black, Metzger, Wikgren, and Martini (New York: American Bible Society, 1966, 1968²). Others are R. F. Weymouth (1886); Bernhard Weiss (1894–1900); British and Foreign Bible Society (1904, based on Nestle's 4th ed.; 1958² ed. by G. D. Kilpatrick); Alexander Souter (1910, rev. 1947); H. J. Vogels (1920, 1950⁴); A. Merk (1933, 1965⁹); J. M. Bover (1943, 1968⁵).

Tischendorf's *Editio Octava Critica Maior* (3 vols.; 1869) is historic in the discipline for its scope of method and is still considered the essential Critical Apparatus. Souter's edition reproduced the Greek Text which lies behind the Revised Version (British) of 1881; originally prepared by E. Palmer, it is the closest to the *Textus Receptus* of any widely used Greek NT. The Greek NT of R. V. G. Tasker (1964) represents the text behind the New English Bible (1961)—called an "anachronism" by Kurt Aland for its disregard of modern TC methods.

Cryptogram (Greek: hidden writing). A C. may be either a writing or a drawing which has a hidden or secret meaning. Cs are particularly characteristic of apocalyptic writings, and of oppressed peoples generally, among whom late Judaism and early Christianity must be numbered. The epigraph of Daniel 5 ("Mene, Mene, Tekel, and Parsin") and the mark of the beast (666) in Rev. 13:16–18 are cryptograms. The identifying cryptogram for the early Christian was a simple line drawing of a fish, which name in Greek *(Ichthus)* is an acrostic for Jesus Christ, Son of God, Savior (see, e. g., the *colophon* in the Gospel of the Egyptians, Nag Hammadi Codex III 69, 14–15).

CSR. The Council on the Study of Religion "is a federation of learned societies in religion interested in developing greater coordination of the field as a whole. It seeks to initiate, coordinate and implement projects designed to strengthen and advance scholarship and teaching." The constituent members of the CSR are: American Academy of Religion; American Society of Christian Ethics; American Society of Missiology; American Theological Library Association; Catholic Biblical Association; Catholic Theological Society of America; College Theology Society; Religious Education Association; Society of Biblical Literature; and, Society for the Scientific Study of Religion. It publishes quarterly the *Bulletin* (announcing activities of member societies), *Religious Studies Review,* and TOIL (Teaching Opportunities Information Listing). CSR Executive Office address: Wilfrid Laurier University, Waterloo, Ontario, Canada N2L 3C5.

Cult-Historical Method. See: *Kultgeschichtliche Schule.*

Cultural Translation. See: *LB(P), LNT(P).*

Cursive. See: **Minuscule.**

D: Deuteronomic Code is the name of the nucleus of laws (chs. 12–26) in the book of Deuteronomy; some scholars identify it with the book found in the Temple in 621 B.C. during the reign of Josiah (see: 2 Kings 22–23). See: **De Wette; Law.**

Damascus Document, The. See: **Dead Sea Scrolls.**

Daughter Translation. A translation of the LXX into another language, such as Latin, Ethiopic, Coptic, or Syriac, hence, a translation of a translation of the Hebrew Scriptures. See: **Version.**

Dead Sea Scrolls (abbrev.: DSS). The name given to mainly parchment and papyrus scrolls written in Hebrew, Aramaic, or Greek, and discovered in eleven caves along the northwestern coast of the Dead Sea between 1947 and 1956, generally dating from 250 B.C. to A.D. 68 and assigned to an Essene community located at the archaeological site known as Khirbet Qumran. The term is also used more broadly for texts found during the same and more recent years at Masada, Naḥal Ḥever, Wadi Murabba'ât, Naḥel Ṣe'elim, Khirbet Mird, Naḥal Mishmar, and, occasionally, includes texts from the Cairo Genizah. These MSS are of inestimable value in understanding sectarian Judaism and Christianity of the 1st cent. In addition to the books of the OT (excepting Esther) and portions of the Apocrypha and Pseudepigrapha, the principal scrolls discovered (here listed with their present *sigla* followed by the older abbreviations) were the Manual of Discipline (1QS = DSD), the Rule of the Congregation (1QSa), and the Manual of Benedictions (1QSb) (together constituting one scroll); The War of the Sons of Light Against the Sons of Darkness (1QM = DSW); Commentaries *(pesherim)* on portions of Habakkuk (1QpH = DSH), Nahum (4QpNah), Micah (1QpMi), also on small sections of Isaiah (4QpIsa^a-d), Psalm 37 (4QpPs37), Hosea (4QpHos) and Zephaniah (4QpZeph); The Vision of the New Jerusalem (also called The Temple Scroll, since it describes the ideal temple; 1–5QJN); The Damascus Document (closely related to 1QS, it was previously known from fragments found in a Cairo synagogue in 1896 and called the Zadokite Document; CD = CDC); The Copper Scroll (3QTreasure or 3Q15—thought to be unrelated to Qumran); The Thanksgiving Psalms (also known by the modern Hebrew term *Hodayot,* meaning thanksgiving; hence the *siglum* 1QH = DST); and, The Genesis Apocryphon (written in Aramaic; 1QapGen = DSL); and the *Florilegia,* consisting of The Eschatological Midrashim (4QEschMidr), The Patriarchal Blessings (4QPBless), and The Testimonia (4QTestim). Early translations of the major, non-canonical scrolls are available in paperback: Theodore H. Gaster, *The Dead Sea Scriptures* (Garden City, N.Y.: Doubleday & Co., 1956; revised and enlarged 1964, 1976²); Géza Vermès, *The Dead Sea Scrolls in English* (Baltimore: Penguin Books, 1962; rev. ed., 1975; London: Penguin, 1975). Countless additional fragments remain to be assembled and published, e. g., about 95 percent of the texts from Cave #4 at Qumran alone are presently unpublished.

Note: Each *siglum* above contains the number of the cave in which the scroll was found (1–11), the location of the cave (Qumran), and an initial(s) for the name of the document (p meaning *pesher* or commentary); superscribed letters indicate the copy of the work at a given site (e. g., 4QpIsa^{a-d}). In some listings the *siglum* has prefixed to it an abbreviation of the material from which the text is made (papyrus [p, pap], copper [cu], ostracon [o, os, ostr], wood [lign], parchment [perg], or skin [no abb.]); and an appended abbreviation indicating the language in which the text is written (Hebrew, Aramaic, Arabic, Christian Palestinian Aramaic, Greek, Latin, or Nabatean). For advanced study see: Joseph A. Fitzmyer, S. J., *The Dead Sea Scrolls: Major Publications and Tools for Study* (Missoula, Montana: The Scholar's Press, 1975).

Decalogue (Greek: lit., "Ten Words") is the Greek (LXX) name for the "Ten Commandments" given according to tradition by God to Moses on Mt. Sinai; the term appears in Ex. 34:28; Dt. 4:13; and 10:4; the commandments themselves in Ex. 20 and Dt. 5. A ritual decalogue (expanded to thirteen) appears in Ex. 34:11ff., the fragment of another in 23:14–19. A similar catalog of laws governing sexual relations (Lev. 20:11–21; cf. 18:7–18) and social prohibitions in the form of curses (Dt. 27:15–26) probably also numbered ten originally. See: **Law.**

De-eschatologize. See: **Eschatologize.**

Deissmann, (Gustav) Adolf (1866–1937). Born in Langenscheid (Nassau), Germany, D. taught NT in Marburg (1895–97), Heidelberg (1897–1908), and Berlin (1908–34). D's primary contribution to NT criticism derives from his study of newly discovered (1897–1904) Greek papyri, by which he proved the identity of Biblical Greek with that commonly spoken *(Koiné)* in the 1st cent. His major works in English translation are *Light From the Ancient East* (New York: George H. Doran Co., 1910; rev., 1927) and *Paul* (Doran, 1926). See: **Oxyrhynchus Papyri.**

Deep Structure. See: **Structure.**

Delay of the Parousia. See: **Parousia.**

Demythologization (fr. German: *Entmythologisierung*). As a technical term in the Biblical hermeneutics of Rudolf Bultmann (1884–1976), D. refers to the interpretation of Biblical myths in terms of the understanding of existence which comes to expression in the imagery of the myths themselves. It does not refer to the elimination of myth, but to its reinterpretation in existentialist terms. In this context, the term myth denotes imagery that speaks of the other world in terms of this world, the divine in terms of the human. To speak

52

of God's transcendence in spatial terms as the One who dwells in heaven, or of man's universal sin and finitude in terms of Adam's Fall, are examples. Myths, says Bultmann, are true anthropologically, or existentially, not cosmologically; they are the objectification of man's self-understanding, not a scientific representation of external reality. The essay ("New Testament and Mythology," 1941) which sparked almost two decades of debate is found in *Kerygma and Myth,* ed. H. W. Bartsch (trans. R. H. Fuller; London: S.P.C.K., 1954). See: **Hermeneutics; Bultmann; Existentialist.**

Deuterocanon (-ical) is a Greek term meaning literally, "second canon." As used by Roman Catholics since the Council of Trent (1545–63), D. designates books or parts of books not in the Hebrew Bible (the "proto" canon) but present in the Greek OT (LXX) and accepted as inspired both by early Church Fathers and the Council.

Used broadly, the term is applied to passages whose secondary character has been revealed by textual criticism, such as Mk. 16:9–20; Jn. 7:53–8:11; and I Jn. 5:7 (KJV), all of which are absent from the oldest extant MSS of the NT.

See: **Apocrypha; Codex Sinaiticus; Codex Vaticanus.**

Deuterograph (Greek: second or secondary writing) is a term characterizing the relationship of certain OT writings to each other; e. g., 1 & 2 Chronicles are Ds of 1 Sam.–2 Kings. In a sense Deuteronomy is a D. of sections of Ex.–Num.; it often rewrites older laws in oratorical style, reinterpreting them in the process; e. g., cf. Deut. 15:12–15 and Ex. 21:2; Deut. 19:1–13 and Ex. 21:12–14; Deut. 22:25–29 and Ex. 22:16–17. Cf. also Deut. 5 and Ex. 20 (the Ten Commandments); Ps. 14 and Ps. 53; Ps. 40:13–17 and Ps. 70; Ps. 57:7–11 plus 60:5–12 and Ps. 108; Ps. 18:2–50 and 2 Sam. 22:2–51, etc.

The word may be used to call attention to the repetitive nature of the subject matter of Scripture; it may also be used in a non-critical way to hide the differences in perspective from which the common subject matter is viewed.

Deutero-Isaiah (lit., Second Isaiah). The name commonly given to the author of Isa. 40–55, written most likely during the period when the Jews were exiled in Babylon (586–538 B.C.); some scholars include chs. 56–66, but they are now more often dated later and called Trito-Isaiah.

Deuteronomist (ic History) is the name given to the author/compiler of the OT book of Deuteronomy and/or certain other portions of the OT which reflect the literary and theological characteristics of Deuteronomy, whether found in Gen-Joshua, or Deut-2 Kings, the latter called the "Deuteronomistic History" by the OT scholar, Martin Noth (q.v.).

Noth, in 1943, proposed that Deut-2 Kings was a single work by a single author, written in Palestine during the Exile from earlier oral and written traditions, and expanded through secondary additions by later redactors belonging to the Deuteronomistic School (see his *The Deuteronomistic History* [Sheffield: JSOT Press, 1980]). Noth's proposal of a D. History countered an older view which saw the Hexateuch (Genesis-Judges 1) as a work augmented and redacted by the Deuteronomist. Noth denied any authorial relationship between Genesis-Numbers and the DH, even in those passages of the DH which Noth himself took to be secondary additions.

Noth's hypothesis has been both rejected and vigorously defended (though rarely without qualification). The chief objections to his hypothesis are that it makes an artificial break between Gen-Num and Deut-2 Kings, and that it oversimplifies the literary complexity of the latter.

Deutero-Pauline

Deutero-Pauline is a term applied to those writings in the NT which are explicitly attributed to Paul but which are secondarily (deutero-) Pauline in content and were probably not written by him. Although no uniform agreement exists among scholars as to their number, those most often listed as D-P are 2 Thess.; Col.; Eph.; 1 & 2 Tim.; and Titus. Also called sub-, post-, or pseudo-Pauline.

De Wette, Wilhelm Martin Leberecht

De Wette, Wilhelm Martin Leberecht (1780–1849) was born in Weimar (Germany) and studied under J. J. Griesbach in Jena; in 1810, he joined Friedrich Schleiermacher at the newly founded theological faculty in Berlin, but was later removed at the urging of Pietists for his liberal theological and political views. In 1822, he became Professor of Ethics and Practical Theology at Basel; after F. C. Baur, he was perhaps the leading historical theologian of his time. His earlier writings dealt primarily with Old and NT study; he was the first (1817) to argue persuasively that the Deuteronomic Code was the book found in the Temple in 621 B.C.

Diachronic; Synchronic

Diachronic; Synchronic (Greek: "through time"; "with time"). These two terms of increasing parlance in Biblical criticism are basic concepts in the linguistic theory of Ferdinand De Saussure and his adherents: everything that relates to the static side of a language is S.; everything that relates to the evolution of a language is D. Correspondingly, synchrony designates a language state; diachrony an evolutionary phase. For example: that the accent of a Greek word never falls behind the third syllable from the end (called the antepenult) relates to S.; that over the centuries the final occlusives of Greek words gradually disappeared (*gunaik* becoming *gunai*) relates to D. (See F. De S., *Course in General Linguistics,* trans. Wade Baskin [New York: Philosophical Library, 1959; first pub. 1916; London: William Collins Sons, 1974].) Similarly, whereas a study of the changing interpretation given to the death and resurrection of Jesus by the NT writers relates to D., a study of the structural relationship between the death-resurrection motif in, say, Paul's letters and other Christian and/or Hellenistic literature, irrespective of chronology, relates to S. (See Dan O. Via, Jr., *Kerygma and Comedy in the New Testament* [Philadelphia: Fortress Press, 1975].)

Diatessaron (Greek: through four). See: **Tatian.**

Diatribe (Greek: discourse; short ethical treatise). In contemporary parlance a D. is a harangue, an abusively argumentative speech. In antiquity, as used by Zeno, Cleanthes, et al., it denoted a brief lecture on various ethical issues related to the public good; poverty, old age, banishment, apathy, freedom from affectation, etc. In this sense the D. appears about the 3rd cent. B.C., perhaps a kind of oral propaganda by which philosophical instruction of a popular character was propagated following the extension of Greek hegemony under Alexander the Great (see *RAC*).

According to H. I. Marrou, the D., in literary-critical sense, is an imaginary or fictitious dialogue of moral paraenesis (e. g., Rom. 12–15; Gal. 5–6; Eph. 4–6), characterized by (1) stereotyped address (e. g., Rom. 2:1; 1 Cor. 15:36); (2) rhetorical objections (e. g., Rom. 9:19; 11:19; 2 Cor. 10:10); (3) questions and answers in catechetical style (e. g., Rom. 6:1, 15; James 2:18–22; 5:13); and (4) personified abstractions (e. g., Rom. 10:6–8; 1 Cor. 12:15–20). In terms of its formal structure, the D. is characterized by (1) simple, paratactic style (e. g., Rom. 2:21–22; 13:7); (2) parallelism and antithesis (e. g., Rom. 12:4–15; 1 Cor. 9:19–22; 2 Cor. 4:8–11); (3) rich vocabulary, as in lists of vices and virtues (e. g., Rom. 1:29–31; 1 Cor. 6:9–10; 2 Cor. 11:26–27); (4) imperatives or warnings (e. g., Rom. 12:14–15; 1 Cor. 11:6; Gal. 5:12); (5) conversational tone, play on words, irony (e. g., Jas. 2:2ff.; 1 Cor. 4:8; Gal. 5:12; Phil. 3:19); (6) comparisons out of nature or life (e. g., 1 Cor. 9:24–27; 2 Tim. 2:4–6; Jas. 3:3–6); (7) quotations from famous poets (e. g., 1 Cor. 15:33—Menander; Tit. 1:12—Epimenides; Acts 17:28—Aratus); (8) anecdotes, *bons mots,* historical examples (e.g., I Clem. 55). (See: *RAC* VI, 990–1009.)

Unfortunately, D. is sometimes used to translate the German term *Scheltrede,* but *S.* corresponds to the first definition above and not to its literary and technical meaning.

Dibelius, Martin (1883–1947). Born in Dresden, the son of a leading German pastor and church leader, D. taught NT studies in Berlin (1910–1915), and at Heidelberg (1915–1947). Although best known for his pioneering work in Form Criticism (1919), D. wrote several commentaries on NT epistles, plus studies on the history of the early Church and on NT theology and ethics. He contributed significantly to the theological foundation of the ecumenical movement. See: Martin Dibelius, *From Tradition to Gospel* (London: Ivor

Nicholson and Watson, Ltd., 1934; repr. James Clarke, 1971; New York: Charles Scribner's Sons, 1935).

Also See: **Form Criticism;** *Chria;* **Paradigm.**

Didache; The Didache (Greek: teaching; cf. English: didactic). A common t.t. for the instructional material of the early Church in contrast to *kerygma* or preaching; for example, cf. 1 Cor. 7:1–40 (esp. vs. 10 containing a teaching of Jesus) with the kerygmatic passage in Acts 2:22–24.

The D., or Teaching of the Twelve Apostles is usually described as an early 2nd cent. manual of church instruction, although its first section (chs. 1–6), known as "The Two Ways" (one of life and the other of death), may go back to a 1st cent. Jewish document. These chapters, however, appear to be related in some way to the Epistle of Barnabas, a 2nd cent. Christian writing, the direction of dependence being disputed. The second section (chs. 7–15) contains a series of instructions and admonitions on baptism, worship, the Eucharist, the treatment of apostles and prophets, etc. The only extant Greek copy, dating from A.D. 1056, was discovered in 1875 by P. Bryennios in the library of the Jerusalem Monastery of the Holy Sepulchre in Constantinople. See: Robert M. Grant, ed., *The Apostolic Fathers: A New Translation and Commentary,* Vol. 3: *Barabas and the Didache* by Robert A. Kraft (New York/London: Thomas Nelson and Sons, 1965).

Dilthey, Wilhelm (1833–1911). Born in Biebrich on the Rhein, the son of the court chaplain to the Duke of Nassau (Germany), D. first studied theology and then philosophy and history with Leopold von Ranke in Berlin. He subsequently held professorships at Basel (1866), Kiel (1868), Breslau (1871), and Berlin (1882). Although few of his major works were ever completed (in Berlin, according to F. Rodi, he was known as "the man of Vol. I"), his influence on 20th cent. thought was considerable. Called "the virtual creator of the philosophy of history in its present form" *(ODCC)* and the founder of German *Lebensphilosophie* (life philosophy), he stressed the intuitive non-rational aspects of human life and culture which he termed the true subject matter of philosophy, rather than logical abstractions such as cosmology, transcendence, etc. He is of interest to Biblical criticism and interpretation primarily for his studies in hermeneutics based on Schleiermacher. See: **Hermeneutics.**

Discourse. In NT criticism particularly the term D. is used to characterize in a formal way the distinction between the teachings of Jesus as found in the synoptic Gospels and those in the Gospel of John. Whereas the former are short and pithy sayings (e. g., Mt. 5–7), the latter are extended elaborations (discourses) on major (Johannine) themes: light, life, truth, way, etc., all of which explain the nature of Jesus and his relationship to God and to the true believer (e. g., 3:1–21, 31–36; 4:4–42; 5:16–47; 6:25–71; 7:14–36; and 13: 31–17:26).

Discourse Analysis. See: **Semiology**

Dispositio. See: **Rhetorical Analysis.**

Dittography (Greek: written twice). In Textual Criticism, D. is the technical name for the scribal error in manuscript copying in which a letter, word, or line is mistakenly repeated; the opposite of haplography. In this context, a dittograph is an example of erroneous repetition. See: **Textual Criticism.**

DJD. Abbreviation for *Discoveries in the Judean Desert of Jordan.* Being essentially a facsimile edition of the Dead Sea Scrolls published in Oxford at the Clarendon Press; Vol. I: *Qumran Cave I* (1956: D. Barthélemy and J. T. Milik; text in French, introductory notes in French and English); II, 1 and 2: *Les Grottes de Murabba'ât* (1961: P. Benoît; J. T. Milik; R. de Vaux); III, 1 and 2: *Les 'Petites Grottes' de Qumran* [Caves 2–7 and 10] (1962: M. Baillet; J. T. Milik; R. de Vaux); IV: *The Psalms Scroll of Qumrân Cave 11* (1965: J. A. Sanders, text in English); V: *Qumrân Cave 4* (1968: John M. Allegro; text in English); VI: Qumrân Grotte 4, II: 1. Archéologie, II. Tefillin, Mezuzot et Targums (1977: R. de Vaux and J. T. Milik et al.; text mainly in French). See: **Dead Sea Scrolls.**

Documentary Hypothesis. See: **Graf-Wellhausen Hypothesis.**

Dodd, Charles Harold (1884–1973). Professor of NT and later of Biblical Criticism and Exegesis at Oxford (1915–30), Manchester (1930–35), and Cambridge (1935–49), England. Philosophically a Platonist, Dodd is noted with equal merit for his studies in the Gospel and letters of John, Paul's letter to the Romans, and for *The Parables of the Kingdom* (London: Nisbet and Co., 1935); and *The Apostolic Preaching and Its Development* (Nisbet, 1936); additional research in the area of NT backgrounds, in the study of Scripture and in Biblical theology made him unquestionably the leading British NT scholar of this century, a fact often noted by his peers who chose him to direct the translation of the New English Bible. See: **Eschatology; Parable.**

Dominical Saying (fr. *Dominus:* Latin: Lord). A saying of Jesus.

Douay Bible is a common name for the first English Catholic version of the Bible, with the NT published at Rheims (1582), the OT at Douay (1609–10). Based on the Latin Vulgate, it was revised by Bishop Richard Challones of

London in 1750–63, and by an American, Archbishop Kenrich, 1849–60; and again by the Confraternity of Christian Doctrine (NT), 1941. See: **JB; NAB; KJV; RSV; TEV; Paraphrase; Version.**

Doublet. As a t.t. in literary criticism, D. refers to a parallel narrative, parable, saying, etc., which by oral tradition grew out of or alongside of an original narrative, parable, etc. For example, Mt. 16:19*b* is undoubtedly a doublet of Mt. 18:18; similarly, the two miracles of loaves and fishes (Mk. 6:35–44 and 8:1–9) are probably two accounts of a single event or narrative. In the OT, doublets (or three- and fourfold parallels) are evidence of multiple tradition; e. g., cf. Gen. 12:10–13 and 20:1–18 with 26:6–11 (Sarah and Rebekah); Ex. 20:1–17 with 34:10–28 (Decalogue); Ex. 16 and 17:1–7 with Num. 11:4–35 and 20:1–13 (wilderness miracles).

Double Tradition is a term employed to denote passages in the synoptic tradition common to Mt. and Lk.; it is used to avoid prejudging or implying the nature of its source or the order of dependence.

DSS (abbrev.). See: **Dead Sea Scrolls.**

E: Elohist (fr. Heb.: Elohim: God) is the accepted designation for one of the sources employed in the composition of the Pentateuch, derived from the source's preferred Hebrew name for the Deity, viz., Elohim, commonly translated "God." The provenance, date, and extent of the E document (or oral tradition), whose existence was first proposed by Jean Astruc in 1753, are much disputed. Of all the sources (traditionally: J, E, D, and P), its location in the Pentateuch is the most difficult to ascertain, which leads many scholars to view it as a redactor's supplement to the older J source.

According to Otto Eissfeldt, E views God as more remote and awesome than does J; its interpretation of the covenant is less materialistic and less nationalistic (see e. g., Ex. 19:5–6 and Num. 23:9, 21); and, most obviously, its terminology is different; God is called Elohim, not Yahweh; the sacred mountain is called Mt. Horeb, not Sinai (Ex. 3:12); Amorites, not Canaanites inhabit the promised land (Gen. 48:22; Ex. 23:23; cf. Gen. 12:6; 50:11), etc.

The opinion is generally held that E arose in the 9th OR 8th cent. B.C. in northern Palestine (Ephraim) from traditions that were much older. According to Martin Noth (1902–1968), the following passages (with minor refinements omitted) stem from the E tradition: Gen. 15:1*b*, 3*a*, 5, 13–16 (16:9–10 redactional); 20:1*b*–18; 21:6, 8–34; 22:1–19; 28:11–12, 17–18, 20–22; 30:1–3, 6, 17–19, 22–23; 31:2, 4–16, 19*b*, 24–25*a*, 26, 28–29, 30*b*, 32–35, 36*b*–37, 41–45, 50, 53*b*–55; 32:1–2 (32:13*b*–21); 33:4–5, 8–11, 19–20; 35:1–5, 7–8, 14, 16–20; 37:3*b*, 22–24, 29–36; 40:2–23; 41:1–33, 34*b*, 35*a*, 36–40, 47–48, 50–54;

42:1*a*, 2–3, 6–7, 11*b*, 13–26, 28*b*–37; 45:2–3, 5*b*–15; 46:1–5*a*; 47:5*b*, 6*a*, 7–12; 48:1–2, 7–22; 50:10*b*–11, 15–26.

Ex. 1:15–21; 3:4*b*, 6, 9–15; 4:17, 18, 20*b*; (chs. 7–10 in part); 13:17–19; 14:5*a*, 7, 11–12, 19*a*, 25*a*; 17:3; 18:1–27; 19:3*a* (3*b*–6*, 10–11*a**, 14–15*), 16–17, 19; 20:1–22 (23:1–33* [special source]); 24:1–2, 3–8*, 9–11; 32:1*b*–4*a*, 21–24.

Num. 20:14–18, 21; 21:21–35; 22:1*a* (redactional), 2–3*a*, 9–12, 20, 38, 41–23:27, 29–30.

See: *Grundlage;* **P: Priestly Code.**

Early Church, The is an ambiguous term which may be used to denote the Church at its inception or through its development in the first five centuries. Less broad are the terms "primitive church" or "primitive Christianity," which are translations of the German terms *Urkirche* or *Urgemeinde,* and *Urchristentum* (*Ur-* meaning original, primitive, ancient). These terms, also ambiguous, are used by some to denote Christianity prior to the rise of the institutionalized Catholic Church, whose incipient formation is found in the NT (Ger.: *Frühkatholizismus:* early or incipient Catholicism). This definition is based on the hypothesis that the earliest Christians anticipated the imminent return of Christ and that the institutionalization of Christianity was a product of the "Delay of the Parousia" (i. e., since the Risen Lord had not returned, the Church must act in his stead; see Mt. 16:18–19).

Ebla (Tablets/Texts). Ancient name of the archaeological site known as Tell Mardikh, located between Hama and Aleppo in North Syria. In 1974/75, Italian archaeologists discovered the royal archives of E., comprising several thousand cuneiform texts written in Sumerian (80%) and a previously unknown language called Paleo-canaanite or Eblaite (20%), the latter revealing many striking affinities with Hebrew. The tablets date from Ebla's empire years, ca. 2400–2250 B.C. (Early Bronze IV) and contain: (1) economic-administrative texts, (2) lexical texts (onamastica), (3) historical and juridical texts, (4) literary texts, and (5) syllabaries (the oldest in history). The texts are providing startling new chapters to our knowledge of the history and literature of the ancient Near East of the 3rd Millennium B.C. See *Biblical Archaeologist* 39 (May and Sept.), 1976; 41 (Dec.) 1978; also Chaim Bermant and Michael Weitzman, *Ebla: A Revelation in Archaeology* (New York: Times Books, 1979); Paolo Matthiae, *Ebla: An Empire Rediscovered* (Garden City, N.Y.:

---

*marks points where, according to Bernhard Anderson, many scholars deviate from Noth's analysis; passages in parenthesis are omitted by Noth. For bibliographic information, see: **J** (**Yahwist**).

Doubleday, 1981); and John F. Healey, "Keeping Up with Recent Studies: VII. Ebla: Ancient City of Syria," *ET* 91(1980), pp. 324–28.

Ecclesia (ecclesiastical; ecclesiology) is the English transliteration of the Greek word meaning "assembly," "meeting," or "gathering," which, to Christians later, came to mean "a body (or the whole body) of believers in Christ," i. e., "a (or the) church." The latter term ("church") is thought to come from the Greek adjective *kuriakos,* meaning "belonging to the Lord." In time it took the place of E., which still appears in "ecclesiastical" (pertaining to the church), "ecclesiology" (the doctrine of the church), etc. For the use of E. in the NT see, Kittel's *Bible Key Words,* vol. I; trans. J. R. Coates (New York: Harper and Brothers, Publishers, 1951), or *TDNT,* q. v.

Eichhorn, Albert (1856–1926). Born near Lüneburg (Germany), E. was Assoc. Prof. of Church History in Halle (1886–1900) and Kiel (1901–13). Sometimes considered "the founder of the history-of-religions school" in Germany (H. J. Kraus) or at least one of its co-founders along with Hermann Gunkel, William Wrede, and Hugo Gressmann, E. did not publish any single work of note primarily because of chronic poor health, but his influence was felt in articles and in discussions with the above named and others. See: *Religionsgeschichte.*

Eichhorn, Johann Gottfried (1752–1827), Professor of Oriental languages in Jena (E. Germany) and professor of Philosophy at Göttingen (1788–1827); introduced the concept of Myth as used in classical philology to Biblical studies, often called "the father of OT criticism" for establishing criteria for the discernment of divergent source materials in the OT, such as repetitions, duplicate stories, differences in style, characteristic phraseology and vocabulary, etc.

Eisegesis (Greek: to lead, bring, or introduce into). In the interpretation of Scripture, E. refers to the practice of reading into a text the meaning which one wants to get out of it. As such, the term is the opposite of exegesis and is almost always used pejoratively. See: **Exegesis.**

Eissfeldt, Otto (1887–1973). Born in Northeim, Germany, E. studied OT with J. Wellhausen, R. Smend, and H. Gunkel; he taught OT in Berlin (1913–22) and in Halle (1922–57), becoming one of the most famous students of the Wellhausen-Gunkel school of OT criticism. His rejection of tradition history *(Traditionsgeschichte)* and his avoidance of any theological interpretation of the OT (such as von Rad's), plus his concentration on issues in comparative religions *(Religionsgeschichte),* led to the conservative appearance of his scholarship. A prolific writer, he edited the commentary series *Handbuch zum*

Alten Testament (Tübingen: J.C.B. Mohr [Paul Siebeck], 1937–77) and Joseph Aistleitner's *Wörterbuch der ugaritischen Sprache* (Berlin: Akademie Verlag, 1963). Called "the best of its kind" is his monumental *The Old Testament: An Introduction Including the Apocrypha and Pseudepigrapha* (Oxford: Basil Blackwell and New York: Harper and Row, 1965; German: 1934, 1964³). For a complete bibliography, see: O. Eissfeldt, *Kleine Schriften,* Vols. 5–6 (Tübingen: J.C.B. Mohr [Paul Siebeck], 1973, 1979).

Elohist. See: **E: Elohist.**

Endzeit (German: end-time). The eschaton or the end of the world and its attendant events. E. is the temporal opposite of *Urzeit,* the time of the beginning and the primeval events accompanying it. See: **Eschatology.**

Enthronement Psalms. See: **Psalms.**

Entmythologisierung (Ger.). See: **Demythologization.**

Epanaphora. See: **Anaphora.**

Epigram (adj.: —matic). As made popular by 17th and 18th cent. epigrammatists, the E. is a short poem (frequently an epitaph) stating concisely and often satirically or wittily a single thought or moral; today it may refer to any brief, pithy saying. Prophetic speech, Wisdom, and the sayings of Jesus are in this broader sense epigrammatic: e. g., Amos 3:8 "The lion has roared; who will not fear? The Lord GOD has spoken; who can but prophesy?" (RSV)

Epigraphy (fr. Greek: inscription). That field of study concerned with the classification and interpretation of inscriptions. For biblical studies, the best collection of these texts is found in **ANET(P).** For a popular history, see: Maurice Pope, *The Story of Decipherment: From Egyptian Hieroglyphic to Linear B* (London: Thames and Hudson, 1975).

Epinicion (pl.: epinicia; lit., "upon victory") is a Greek term denoting a song or ode composed to celebrate a victory in war or in athletic competition. Judges 5 is an E. celebrating Deborah's victory over the Egyptian general Sisera in the plain of Jezreel *ca.* 1125 B.C.; see also Judges 15:16; 1 Sam. 18:7*b,* etc.

Epiphany (Greek: manifestation; appearing). In its original sense, E. refers to a sudden and transient manifestation of Divine will and power, in forms more or less perceptible (by hearing, seeing, touching), and either natural or mysterious in character. So defined, E. is a central concept in all religions, the manifestations of the divine in the world of human experience. It may occur through natural objects (stones, trees, animals) or natural events (thunder and lightning, the conjunction of planets), or unnatural events (possession, miraculous healing), or the fate of nations and persons (the Exodus, Fall of Jerusalem, calling of a prophet).

E. is therefore the genus of which NT species are: Theophany (Mk. 1:9ff.: Jesus' baptism; Mk. 9:22ff.: the Transfiguration), Christophany (Mk. 6:45ff. and Jn. 6:16–21: walking on the sea; the Resurrection appearances; Acts 9:4–16: Paul's conversion), Pneumatophany (Acts 2: the Spirit of Pentecost), and Angelophany (e. g., Lk. 1:11, 26; 2:9, etc.).

In the OT, E. as a manifestation of God (or, "the glory of God"; Hebrew: *Kabod*), apart from Gen. 1–3, occurs at decisive points in the history of Israel: the promises to the Patriarchs (Gen. 17; 18; 28; 1 Kgs. 19), the call of Moses (Ex. 3), the Exodus-Sinai tradition (Ex. 13; 16; 19; 24; 40), the accession to the promised land (Josh. 5), and the call of prophets (Isa. 6; Ezek. 1). These theophanies are in the main auditory, revelatory of God's will through his Word. In some instances they are related to holy places (Gen. 12:6–7; Ex. 32:7; Num. 11:24; 1 Chron. 21:26; Isa. 6). Tied to history, they are all irrepeatable. They are celebratively re-enacted (Pss. 1; 18; 50; 77; 97) in the cult (Deut. 5:5, 22–23). The eschatological E. appears in prophetic literature as the ultimate and final manifestation of God's will, viz., the day of Yahweh (Amos 5:18; Isa. 60:1ff.). In the NT, the manifestation of God's will in Christ (Jn. 1; Phil. 2:5–10; Col. 1:15–20, etc.), the continuing presence of his Spirit in the Church and in the Eucharist (see the epiphanic meal in Lk. 24:30–31; Jn. 21:12) stand in tension with the eschatological E. (the Parousia) and the prior E. of the Anti-Christ (2 Thess. 2:7; Rev.) and of Satan (Rev. 6; 12:3 [9]; 13:1).

See: **Christophany.**

Epiphora (also: epistrophe or antistrophe; Greek: repetition) denotes the repetition of a word or words at the end of two or more sequential verse lines, sentences, or strophes. Though often lost in translation, E. may be seen for example in the use of "Egypt" in Ezek. 20:7–9, and in the use of "us" (the Hebrew pronominal suffix *nu*) in the chiastic structure of Ps. 67, which is also an example of symploce (the conjoining of anaphora and epiphora). In Paul's letters, E. is found at 1 Cor. 7:12–13; 9:19–22; 12:4–6; 2 Cor. 11:22, 27, etc. For examples in Hellenistic rhetoric, see Epictetus I 29, 10; II 19, 24; III 22, 105; IV 1, 102; 9, 9. See: **Anaphora;** *Chiasmus.*

Epistle. See: **Letter.**

Epithalamion (pl.: epithalamia) is Greek for nuptial and denotes a poem or song written to honor a bride or groom. In the OT, see Song of Songs 3:6–11 and 6:13–7:5; less certain are the royal psalms, Pss. 2 and 45. It has been suggested that Ps. 2 is an E. acrostic (in Hebrew): "To Alexander Janneus and his wife" (R. H. Pfeiffer). Sigmund Mowinckel, however, designates this an Enthronement Psalm (*The Psalms in Israel's Worship* [New York: Abingdon Press, 1962; Oxford: Basil Blackwell, 1963], II, 61).

Erasmus, Desiderius, von Rotterdam (1466/69–1536). Called "the most renowned scholar of his age" *(ODCC)*, E. is noted in Biblical criticism for his pioneering edition of the Greek NT (1516), which later became the basis of the *Textus Receptus.* His fame as a humanist scholar rests principally on his attacks against evils in the church and state of his day (*The Praise of Folly,* 1509; *Familiar Colloquies,* 1518). His humanist convictions, esp. his abhorrence of violence, led him to reject the Lutheran Reformation, perhaps never fully to understand it. They also led to his repudiation by the Roman Church and by Martin Luther, but likewise to the offer of patronage from the leading princes of his day (Henry VIII, Francis I, Archduke Ferdinand of Vienna), all of which he refused in favor of personal and intellectual freedom. This he found in Basel where he spent the last fifteen years of his life actively engaged in debate with Luther, publishing texts of the Church Fathers, and writing religious tracts. See: **Textual Criticism;** *Textus Receptus.*

Eschatologize, Eschatologizing Tendency (fr. Greek: *eschaton:* last). Transitive verb: "To give an eschatological character to" (Oxford); correspondingly, to "de-eschatologize" means "to remove eschatological character from" (a saying, parable, etc.). In NT criticism what constitutes an ET or a De-ET depends on whether the message of Jesus and/or that of the early Church was itself eschatological, that is, whether it spoke of an imminent and radical transformation of the world by God. If the message of Jesus was non-eschatological, as the 19th cent. thought, then the primitive Church "eschatologized" his message to conform to its expectation of his return. If, however, Jesus was an eschatologist (see, e. g., Mk. 9:1; 13:26; 14:62 and passim) as 20th cent. scholarship tends to believe, then at numerous points and because of the delay of the coming of the kingdom and/or the delay of Jesus' return (parousia; q. v.), many of the original sayings and teachings of Jesus were gradually "de-eschatologized." E. g., Luke de-eschatologizes the teachings of John the Baptist (cf. 3:10–14 with 3:7–9 [Q]). Similarly, the purpose of 2 Thess. seems to be to de-eschatologize the message of 1 Thess., which fact is proffered as argument against its authenticity. See also 2 Peter 3:3–13 for its de-esch. tendency.

Eschatology (fr. Greek: *eschaton:* last). The term E. was first coined in the 19th cent. as the name for that part of dogmatic theology which treated "the doctrine of last things," viz., death, judgment, heaven, hell, and all attendant matters (the nature of resurrection, of the intermediate state of the dead, of Jesus' second coming, etc.). So defined, E. pertains essentially to the world beyond this world, to a time beyond history.

In OT criticism, E. refers to the future course of history, to a radical turn or transformation of this world, not in the domain of nature but of history. The promises of God to Israel (Gen. 49:8–12; Dt. 33:13–17; Num. 23:21, etc.) are in this sense E. The prophetic "day of the Lord" (Amos 5:18; Isa. 2:12), warnings of divine judgment (Isa. 7:3; 37:31; Zeph. 3:12; Jer. 31:7; Ezek.), the concepts of God's kingship, of the Messiah and the messianic era (Isa.) and of a perfected future (esp. Isa. 40–66) are all eschatological in nature. The question is whether or to what extent OT prophetic E. sees the future in continuity or in discontinuity with the present, and whether salvation extends to a transcendent realm beyond this world.

In NT criticism, the definition and role of E. in the teachings of Jesus have been of central importance since the turn of the century. Albert Schweitzer (*The Quest of the Historical Jesus,* 1906) interpreted the E. of Jesus as radically discontinuous with the present: in a future but imminent act, God would bring the present evil age to a close and replace it with his own divine rule. Schweitzer's opinion that Jesus could be understood only from a "consistently eschatological" point of view was countered by C. H. Dodd's concept of "realized E." (*The Parables of the Kingdom,* 1935) in which the rule of God is seen as efficaciously present in Jesus himself. The eternal is present in the now. The consensus position today, which C. H. Dodd himself accepted, is a synthesis of these two, viz., that God's rule is inaugurated in the words and deeds of Jesus though its ultimate fulfillment is still to be realized: hence the catch words: "E. in the process of being realized" or "inaugurating E." (from the German, *sich realisierende Eschatologie*). Nevertheless, the nature of E., the relationship of E. to apocalypticism, the role of E. and apocalyptic in the teachings of Jesus and in the life of the early Church are all very much in debate.

In contemporary NT theology, particularly in Existentialist Interpretation, the Theology of Hope, and in various theologies of the future, E. has played a central, even if radically reinterpreted, role.

Some scholars draw a distinction between Prophetic E. and Apocalyptic E. to differentiate between (a) expectations concerning the future found in the prophetic warnings/promises in the OT and (b) expectations concerning the future in the Intertestamental and NT period (200 B.C.-A.D. 200). The prophets, who had no expectation of a life after death, warned of the loss (or gain) of one's "world" (status, relationships, prosperity, etc.), whereas the apocalypticists warned of the destruction of *the* world. Prophetic E. saw *the* world as the arena of God's activity; Apocalyptic E. saw the world as Satan's, therefore temporary and penultimate.

See: **Apocalyptic; Dodd; Eschatologize; Existentialist; Schweitzer.**

Etiological Legends. See: **Legend.**

Etymology. The nature and scope of E. in the interpretation of Scripture and in the study of language generally is widely debated, a fact hindering its precise definition. According to James Barr, it is necessary to distinguish between scholarly E. and popular E. In general terms, scholarly E. contains three elements: (1) a historical perspective, that is, the tracing of the chronology of linguistic changes; (2) a classification of languages, showing cognate relationships, historical influences, etc.; and (3) an analysis of phonological correspondence between different languages or between different stages of the same language. In practice, however, the term E. has been used, appropriately, to designate one or more of the following linguistic operations: (a) the reconstruction of linguistic form and sense in a prehistoric (i. e., undocumented) proto-language (e. g., proto-Semitic), (b) the tracing of forms and meanings within an observable historical development, (c) the identification and tracing of loan-words from other languages, and (d) the analysis of words into component morphemes (as frequently in this Handbook). Popular E. as found in the OT and NT, but particularly in the Talmud, is not E. in the scholarly sense at all, but simply a play on word similarity, serving a poetic, humorous, or haggadic function, e. g., see in re Moses (Ex. 2:10), Samuel (1 Sam. 1:20), and cf. Peter (Mt. 16:18). (See *Language and Meaning: Studies in Hebrew Language and Biblical Exegesis,* ed. James Barr et al. [*Oudtestamentlische Studien* 19; Leiden: E. J. Brill, 1947].)

Eucharist (Greek: thanksgiving) is the traditional name for the Lord's Supper (Didache 9:1), probably based on Christ's having "given thanks" at its institution (1 Cor. 11:24; Mt. 26:26–28; Mk. 14:22–24; Lk. 22:17–20). The early significance of the eucharistic meal is indicated in Acts 2:42, 46; 20:7; its epiphanic character is suggested by its tie with the Christophany of the Emmaus road (Lk. 24:30–35). It is suggested that the miracles of feeding (particularly in Mt., see chs. 14–15) are part of an early eucharistic catechesis. See: **Apostolic Fathers; Christophany.**

Evangelist. In the broad sense of the term, an E. is anyone who is authorized to proclaim the gospel of Jesus Christ; in its narrower usage within Biblical criticism, it refers to one or the other of the Gospel writers.

Evangelistarion. See: *Apostolicon.*

Example Story. See: **Parable.**

Exegesis, Exegetical Method, Exegetical Tools (Greek: explanation; interpretation; cf. [Greek] NT Lk. 24:35; Jn. 1:18; Acts 10:8; 15:12, 14, etc.).

Broadly speaking, E. is the process by which a text, as a concrete expression of a "sender" to a "receiver," is systematically explained. In Biblical E. only the text itself (and related texts) can provide access to this triad: sender → text → receiver in which the text functioned as the medium of a message between a (human) sender and receiver now gone. In Protestant theology, particularly, E. is based on the presupposition that the Bible is the Word of God and that humanity today is the recipient of its message but that this is not true in such a way that the triad can literally be written: God → text → modern humanity. The exegete is at best a secondary recipient of the text and if the text has been altered in oral or scribal transmission, the exegete is even further removed from the situation of its original recipients. This is *the hermeneutical problem* (q. v., under **Hermeneutics**) which the exegete attempts to overcome, however imperfectly, through E., the systematic ordering of questions to the text. The role of Structuralism in exegesis, its relationship to traditional methodologies, its dependence or lack of dependence upon knowledge of the cultural contexts of texts are all widely debated. (See: **Semiology; Structure.**)

The E. Method does not exist; it varies with each interpreter. The history of E. Method is the history of **Biblical Criticism** (q. v.); its procedures none other than the methodologies sketched in this Handbook. This is to say there are competing and conflicting methods. And although it is *generally* held that all the critical methods should function in concert, few are the exegetes who do not stress one over the other. Concerning the triad above: historical critical methods tend to center on the sender-as-author, editor, or literary artist (so Classical Literary- , Historical- , Redaction- , and "Rhetorical" Criticism), or on the sender-as-social-matrix (e. g., cult, kingship, legal institution—so Form and Tradition Criticism), or on the sender-as-theologian (so certain Redaction and Tradition Critics). The "receiver" is also, in varying degree, a factor in the analysis, particularly of the epistolary texts of the NT and the prophetic texts of the OT. In some instances, God is the intended receiver (as in the Psalter); such texts reflect back upon the situation and faith of the sender(s). Existentialist analysis and the New Hermeneutic have centered on both the sender-text and the text-receiver dimensions of the triad: for example, the parables are said to reveal the "sender" Jesus' self-understanding *and* a new understanding of existence which the receivers (both the original hearer and modern ones) are invited to appropriate as their own. Here it is less the literal images of the text and more the understanding of existence they contain that is "exegeted" (see: **Demythologization**). **Structuralism** (q. v.) focuses on the *text as text,* with no knowledge needed of its historical setting, of its sender or its receiver, or of its composite character as a text. For the structuralist exegete, the "sender" is neither human nor divine in any formerly accepted sense; the sender is at the most the pregiven structure of reality itself, at the least the structure of the human brain. Ultimately, then, it is not the written text, but the structure behind it that is the object of structuralist exegesis—though this is a moot point among structuralists themselves.

Theological E. stands apart from the above. It is that approach to the Biblical text which proceeds in the belief that God himself is in some sense the "sender" of the text whose message, to be illuminated by E., is also in some way intended for people today. (See: **Theological Interpretation.**)

The steps of English E. are interrelated and not necessarily sequential; in highly abbreviated form they are: (1) Delimit the passage for study, noting opening and closing formulae; (2) Determine its context and function within the larger literary unit; (3) Outline the passage, noting interrelationships of elements; (4) Check words of historical and theological import in dictionaries; seek cross-references with other passages by way of a concordance. (5) Compare translations, note significant differences (see: **Paraphrase; Version**). (6) Ask: What is unique about the text? What is typical (such as rhetorical or stylistic devices [parallelism, *chiasmus,* anaphora, epiphora, paronomasia, diatribe, irony, etc.], typical sets of ideas, typical form or "structure," typical concerns, etc.)? How do the typical elements relate to those which are unique? What is their function? (7) What is the setting of the text (see: *Sitz-im-Leben*)? Ask: what is the usual setting of the typical elements discovered? What does this say about the setting of the text at hand? (If the text is composite [as is usually the case in the Pentateuch and the Gospels and frequently elsewhere], several settings may be involved.) (8) What is the function of the passage as now composed? Is it didactic, kerygmatic, emotive, etc.? How is the hearer expected to respond? What does this say about its content? (9) Give tentative answers to: who, where, when, what, how, to whom, why? (10) List questions and problem areas. (11) Consult reference tools. Check commentaries and periodical literature for insights into your own questions. (12) State succinctly the results of your investigation: the text's meaning in its original setting(s). (13) Theological exegesis will ask: What is its meaning for today?

For a simplified guide for writing an exegetical paper following traditional historical-critical methodologies, see appendix.

Selected tools of E. include:
1. Method.
a. Traditional Historical-Criticism.
   Kaiser, Otto, and Kümmel, Werner G. *Exegetical Method: A Student's Handbook.* Trans. E. V. N. Goetchius. New York: The Seabury Press, 1963.

Stuart, Douglas. *OT Exegesis: A Primer for Students and Pastors*. Philadelphia: Westminster Press, 1980.

b. Literary/Structuralist Studies.

Robertson, David *The Old Testament and the Literary Critic*. Philadelphia: Fortress Press, 1977.

Peterson, Norman. *Literary Criticism for New Testament Critics*. Philadelphia: Fortress Press, 1978.

Antoine Gérald, et al. *Exegesis: Problems of Method and Exercises in Reading (Genesis 22 and Luke 15)*. Tr. Donald G. Miller. Pittsburgh: Pickwick Press, 1978.

2. Texts (see also: **Critcal Text**).

Elliger, K. and Rudolf, W., eds. *Biblia Hebraica Stuttgartensia*. Stuttgart: Deutsche Bibelstiftung, 1977 (based on Kittel's *Biblia Hebraica*).

Rahlfs, Alfred, ed. *Septuaginta*. New York: American Bible Society, 1965 reprint of 1935 ed. 2 vols.

Nestle, E. & Aland, K. eds. *Novum Testamentum Graece*. 26th ed. London: United Bible Societies, 1979.

3. Lexicons (see also the entry: **Lexicon**).

Brown, Francis, Driver, S. R., and Briggs, Charles. *A Hebrew and English Lexicon of the Old Testament*. Based on the Lexicon of William Gesenius as trans. by Edward Robinson. Oxford: Clarendon Press, 1959.

Bauer-Arndt-Gingrich. *A Greek-English Lexicon of the New Testament, and Other Early Christian Literature: A translation and adaptation of Walter Bauer's Griechisch-Deutsches Wörterbuch zu den Schriften des Neuen Testaments und der übrigen urchristlichen Literatur*. 4th rev. and aug. ed., 1952, by William F. Arndt and F. Wilbur Gingrich. Chicago: University of Chicago Press, 1957.

Revised and Augmented 2nd ed. by F. W. Gingrich and F. W. Danker, 1979.

4. Grammars.

Weingreen, Jacob. *A Practical Grammar for Classical Hebrew*. 2nd ed. Oxford: Clarendon Press, 1959.

Goetchius, E. V. N. *The Language of the New Testament*. New York: Charles Scribner's Sons, 1966.

Funk, Robert W. *A Beginning-Intermediate Grammar of Hellenistic Greek*. 3 vols. Missoula: Scholars Press, 1973^2; Workbook, 1977.

5. Reference Grammars.

Gesenius, Heinrich F. W. *Hebrew Grammar,* as ed. and enl. by E. Kautzsch. 2nd Eng. ed., rev. in accordance with the 28th Ger. ed. (1909) by A. E. Cowley. Oxford: Clarendon Press, 1910.

Blass-Debrunner-Funk. *A Greek Grammar of the New Testament and Other Early Christian Literature* by F. Blass and A. Debrunner. A trans. and rev. of the 9th–10th Ger. ed., incorp. suppl. notes of A. Debrunner, by Robert W. Funk. Chicago: University of Chicago Press, 1961.

6. Concordances (see the entry: **Concordance**).

7. Dictionaries.

See: *IDB,* HDB, HDCG, and *TDNT, NIDNTT, TDNT,* and *TDOT* (under Abbreviations of Works, pp. 221–231)

McKenzie, John Lawrence. *Dictionary of the Bible.* Milwaukee: Bruce Publishing Company, 1965; London: Geoffrey Chapman, 1966.

Richardson, Alan. *A Theological Word Book of the Bible.* New York: The Macmillan Co., 1950; London: SCM Press, 1972.

8. Commentaries (See the entry: **Commentary**).

9. Background. (See: **Sociological Interpretation**)

a. Old Testament.

Bright, John. *A History of Israel.* 2nd rev. ed. Philadelphia: The Westminster Press, 1972; London: SCM Press, 1972.

Childs, Brevard S. *Introduction to the Old Testament as Scripture.* Philadelphia: Fortress Press, 1979.

Eissfeldt, Otto. *The Old Testament: An Introduction.* Trans. Peter R. Ackroyd. New York: Harper and Row, 1965; Oxford: Basil Blackwell, 1965.

Noth, Martin. *The Old Testament World.* Trans. V. I. Gruhn. Philadelphia: Fortress Press, 1966; London: A. & C. Black, 1966.

b. New Testament.

Barrett, Charles Kingsley, ed. *The New Testament Background: Selected Documents.* New York: Harper & Row, 1956; London: S.P.C.K., 1974.

Kümmel, Werner Georg. *Introduction to the New Testament.* 17th rev. ed. (1973). Trans. Howard Clark Kee. Nashville: Abingdon Press, 1975.

c. Related Texts.

See: *ANET;* **Dead Sea Scrolls; Nag Hammadi Codices;** and Barrett (above).

10. Translations and Versions.

See: **ASV; Douay; Interlinear Greek NT; JB; KJV;** *LB(P);* **NAB; NAS; NEB; Paraphrase; RSV; TEV; Version.**

For Gospel study, see: **Synopsis.**

On the theory of translation: Nida, E. A., and Taber, Charles R. *The Theory and Practice of Translation.* Leiden: E. J. Brill, 1969.

11. Journals.

See: Abbreviations of Works, pp. 221–231.

12. Bibliographic aids.

Wagner, Günter, ed. *An Exegetical Bibliography* (nos. 1–14). Rüschlikon-Zürich: Baptist Theological Seminary, 1973–1979. Deals with books of the NT.

See: **Bibliography.**

Existentialist, Existential (adjectives) are the English spellings of two

terms central to the Biblical hermeneutic of Rudolf Bultmann (1884–1976); in German they appear as *existential* and *existentiel* respectively, and are essentially parallel to Martin Heidegger's terms *existenzial* and *existenziel.* The former, as employed in the term Existentialist Interpretation, refers to an analysis of the structures of human existence and essentially corresponds to the term ontological in philosophy. The two all-inclusive structures of existence (called existentials) in Heideggerian philosophy are authenticity and inauthenticity, which correspond in Bultmann's thought to faith and unfaith (or sin). The latter term, existential, denotes a concrete act of existing and corresponds to the term ontic in philosophy. The two terms are thus related, as reflection is to the subject of reflection, but they are fundamentally distinct. (See: Walter Schmithals, *An Introduction to the Theology of Rudolf Bultmann*, trans. John Bowden [Minneapolis: Augsburg Publishing House, 1968].) See: **Bultmann; Demythologization; Eschatology; Hermeneutics.**

Exordium. See: **Rhetorical Analysis.**

Exposition (fr. Latin: *exponere:* to explain, to put forth). In Biblical interpretation, E. is sometimes distinguished from exegesis, usually for the sake of the latter which commonly denotes a special methodological approach to Scripture. When so used, E. is understood to follow after exegesis, building upon it and so elaborating the meaning of a text as to show its contemporary relevance without falsifying its original sense as revealed by exegesis. The standard illustration of the distinction between exegesis and E. is to be found in *The Interpreter's Bible.* There is strong objection to this distinction on two grounds: (1) that E. is etymologically synonyegesis (the latter being of Greek derivation) and (2) that an understanding of the overall meaning of a text cannot be separated from an understanding of its component parts, as the *IB* implies. See: **Exegesis; Hermeneutics; *IB*.**

External Parallelism. See: **Parallelism.**

Extra-canonical means "outside the canon," i. e., outside the Bible. (Since, in Orthodox, Protestant, and Roman Catholic traditions, the canon is not identical, differing with respect to the Apocrypha, some disagreement naturally arises concerning the employment of this term.) See: **Apocrypha; Canon.**

Family is a t.t. in Textual Criticism used to describe the lineal relatioship which invariably exists between extant manuscripts of the Bible. Since every MS is a copy of a previously existing MS and, as the term suggests, is therefore related both to its predecessors and to all other MSS subsequently copied from it, determination of a F. grouping is as important in fixing the value of a particular MS as is ascertaining its age. A MS from an early but inferior F. is less important than a later MS from a good F. in establishing the original reading of the text. Two of the better known F. groupings of minuscule MSS are "The Lake Group" (F. 1; *siglum:* λ) and "The Ferrar Group" (F. 13; *siglum:* φ). Note: The term F. denotes a smaller and more closely related group of MSS than the more general term "text-type."

Festschrift. A writing (Ger.: *Schrift*) occasioned by the celebration (Ger.: *Fest*) of a special event in the life of a famous scholar, often a birthday or retirement; usually a collection of essays by colleagues, students, and admirers.

Figura etymologica. See: **Paronomasia.**

Five Scrolls, The. See: *Megillah.*

Floating Logion. See: **Logion.**

Florilegium (pl.: *-ia;* Latin: a gathering of flowers) is a learned name for an anthology, being also the literal translation of the Greek word into Latin; from *antho* (flower) and *legein* (to gather). (Cf. *The Little Flowers [Fioretti] of St. Francis,* which is a collection of brief anecdotes about Francis.) Certain documents of the **Dead Sea Scrolls** (q. v.) are referred to as *Florilegia,* consisting of The Eschatological Midrashim (4QEschMidr), the Patriarchal Blessings (4QPBless), and The Testimonia (4QTestim).

Formal Parallelism. See: Synthetic Parallelism under **Parallelism.**

Form Criticism (Ger.: *Formgeschichte, Gattungsgeschichte*) may be loosely defined as the analysis of the typical forms by which human existence is expressed linguistically; traditionally this referred particularly to their oral, pre-literary state, such as legends, hymns, curses, laments, etc.

The term FC is a translation of the German word *Formgeschichte* which literally means the "history of form." It first appeared in the title of Martin Dibelius' work, *Die Formgeschichte des Evangeliums* (1919; Eng.: *From [Oral] Tradition to Gospel* [London: Ivor Nicholson and Watson, Ltd., 1934; repr. James Clarke, 1971; New York: Charles Scribner's Sons, 1935]). But the approach in Biblical studies goes back to the OT scholar Hermann Gunkel (1862–1932), whose description of its principles and method (which he called *Gattungsgeschichte,* a history of [literary] types or "genres") is still basic though limited. (See: "Fundamental Problems of Hebrew Literary History" in *What Remains of the Old Testament* [London: George Allen & Unwin, 1928].)

The task of FC at the turn of the century was to go beyond **Literary Criticism** (q. v.) as then defined. LC had recognized the composite character of both OT and NT documents (see: **Graf-Wellhausen Hypothesis; Two Source Hypothesis**), and it had proposed dates and places of authorship for the documents and their underlying sources. But LC treated Scripture, particularly the Pentateuch and the synoptic Gospels, as the literary product of individual personalities and not as the repository of the living traditions of common people, traditions of shared experience and belief as varied as life itself. What was needed to correct LC was an analysis of literary forms in order to rediscover the history of their development.

Gunkel himself noted two broad literary classifications, prose and poetry, the former including myths, folk-tales, sagas, romances, legends, and historical narrative; the latter, wisdom and prophetic oracles, secular lyric poetry, hymns, thanksgivings, eschatological psalms, etc. Gunkel also noted that types are often recognizable by their introductory formulas ("Sing unto the Lord," "How long, O Lord?" etc. see entry: **Formula**); that each type emerges from a specific setting in the life of a people; and further that, because of this, a genre gives insight into the life-situation (**Sitz-im-Leben,** q. v.) in which it arises and the setting in turn illumines the content and intention of the genre itself.

As Gunkel put it: "To understand the literary type we must in each case have the whole situation clearly before us and ask ourselves, Who is speaking? Who are the listeners? What is the *mise en scène* [French: the setting on the stage] at the time? What effect is aimed at?" (ibid., p. 62). Finally, Gunkel suggested that literary types evolve, that they arise, flourish and die or are transmuted, and can therefore be placed in a chronological relationship as well as a formal relationship to each other. Forms provide the data for a literary history of Israel. He described the end of that history: "The spirit loses power. The types are exhausted. Imitations begin to abound. Redactions takethe place of original creations. Hebrew ceases to be the living language of the people. By this time the collections [psalms, laws, legends, proverbs, etc.] are grouped together into larger collections. The Canon has come into being"(ibid., p. 66).

Gunkel applied the form-critical method to Genesis (*The Legends of Genesis* [New York: Schocken Books, 1966[2]; orig. 1901]) and to the Psalms with lasting results. But his hope for a literary history of Israel faded as FC became absorbed in pure formalism. **Tradition Criticism** (q. v.) arose in the 1930s in a renewed effort to analyze the history of the transmission of traditions, their varied settings and their transmutations.

In more recent years, the methodological assumptions of FC have been challenged by **Rhetorical Criticism** (q. v.), structural linguistics (see: **Structuralism**), et al. Under re-examination is the relation of genre to setting, of oral to written traditions, of form to content, of the conventional or typical to the unique within a text, etc. Form critics now suggest that the notions of genre, setting, and function are far more complex than traditional FC allowed, and that the typicality (or typicalities) which govern a text may include one or more factors other than pure morphology, such as setting, function, intention, structure, etc.

The four more or less traditional steps of form-critical method have been outlined by Gene M. Tucker: (1) Structure: An analysis of the outline, pattern, or schema of a given genre; its opening and closing *(inclusio),* conventional patterns (parallelism, chiasm, etc.), etc. (2) Genre: A definition and description of the unit according to its type (however that typicality is defined). (3) Setting: A determination of the social situation (or other factors, e. g., the "style of an epoch") or language (*langue,* in the Structuralist sense) which gave rise to the genre, to other typicalities of the text, or to the individual text at hand. (4) Intention: A statement of the purpose and function, the mood and content, of the genre in general and specifically of the example under study. (See Tucker, *Form Criticism of the Old Testament* [Philadelphia: Fortress Press, 1971]. For a sketch of the history of FC see *Old Testament Form Criticism,* ed. John H. Hayes [San Antonio: Trinity University Press, 1974].)

The literary forms of the OT, and the oral traditions behind them, present the critic with a vastly different problem from those of the New. The OT, in many instances, has hundreds of years of oral tradition behind it; the synoptic Gospels, with which NT FC began, have 30–60 years at most, the letters of Paul even less. Furthermore, OT forms are numerous; NT forms relatively few. For this reason, and others, the two disciplines developed along lines independent of each other.

FC in NT study began with the writings of K. L. Schmidt, Martin Dibelius (op. cit.), and Rudolf Bultmann (*History of the Synoptic Tradition* [Ger. 1921; Eng.: New York: Harper and Row, 1963; Oxford: Basil Blackwell, 1963], still an indispensable tool of Gospel criticism). In England, Vincent Taylor (*The Formation of the Gospel Tradition* [London: Macmillan and Co., 1933]) became a cautious proponent of the method. Since these beginnings the method has been applied to a wide variety of NT material.

As in OT studies, the purpose of NT FC as traditionally defined was to rediscover the origin and history of the individual units and thereby to shed some light on the history of the tradition before it took literary form, that is, to determine whether the various units are traceable to Jesus, to the early Church, or to the redactional (editorial) activity of the Gospel writers. Dibelius began with the assumption that the *setting in the life of the Church* which gave rise to and formed much of the synoptic material was the sermon (kerygma) and Christian teaching (didache). Bultmann also attributed many of the forms to the Church and to redactional activity; he concluded that nothing could be attributed to Jesus with absolute certainty (see: **Criteria of Authenticity**).

An impediment to FC after its initial thrust was the lack of terminological clarity. While some unanimity existed in identifying certain forms (narratives, sayings, miracle stories, etc.) little agreement existed concerning the subdivision of these classifications or the terminology appropriate to them (see, e. g.: **Apophthegm; Pronouncement Story;** *Chria;* **Paradigm**). What has endured are certain of FC's methodological assumptions, viz., that different linguistic forms arise from and elucidate different aspects of life; that differences in the synoptic material are due in part to oral transmission; that form, content, and function are related in varied ways, etc. As mentioned above, however, these assumptions and others are being rethought. It can be said that on the one hand the initial thrust of FC further weakened the Gospels as historical sources for a biography of Jesus, on the other it elevated the importance of the **parables** (q. v.) as that speech form most illuminative of the life and mind of Jesus. Finally, FC's fragmentary approach to the Gospels ignored the thought and setting of the Gospel writers themselves. This oversight was corrected by Redaction Criticism. Structural linguistics challenges the basic assumption that written material can provide any access at all to the period of oral tradition. Others point out that "form" and "structure" are not objective realities but are related to an observer, and that, in any case FC cannot be executed in isolation but involves judgments and knowledge across the spectrum of human existence, from laws of social organization to laments of personal grief. (See: Edgar V. McKnight, *What Is Form Criticism?* [Philadelphia: Fortress Press, 1969]; also *Interpretation,* 27 [Oct. 1973].)

See in addition to terms noted: **Biblical Criticism; Exegesis; Quest of the Historical Jesus.**

Formgeschichte (Ger.: lit., "form history"). See: **Form Criticism.**

Formula (pl.: -ae or -s); formulary. In Form Criticism, a F. is a short literary form, usually not more than a brief phrase or sentence, established principally through use and employed to designate an action (as e. g., a baptismal formulary) or otherwise introduce a longer literary type. The types of formulae are as varied as life: e. g., formulae of asseveration, "Truly, I say to you" (Mt. 18:3, 13, 18, 19, etc.); formulae of accusation (Gen. 3:13; 29:25; Num. 23:11, etc.); prophetic formulae, "Thus says the LORD of hosts" (Jer. 19:11, 15; 20:4, etc.); quotation formulae (1 Kings 11:41; 14:19, etc.); liturgical formulae (Mt. 28:18; 1 Cor. 11:23–26) and so on. It is by way of such formulae that corporate life is formalized and thereby made possible. Though often loosely used in the sense above, the term formulary more precisely refers to a collection or system of formulas.

In the analysis of Biblical poetry, the term F. has been defined as "a repeated group of words the length of which corresponds to one of the divisions in the poetic structure" (usually a half-line or line). Robert Culley has identified approximately 175 formulas or formulaic systems in the poetic material of the Biblical Psalms, e.g., "Incline thy ear (to me; to my cry; O Lord)": Pss. 31:2; 71:2; 102:2; 88:2; 116:2; 86:1. See: R. Culley, *Oral Formulaic Language in the Biblical Psalms* (Toronto: University of Toronto Press, 1967).

Four Document (or Source) Hypothesis of the Synoptic Gospels

as proposed by B. H. Streeter (*The Four Gospels* [London: Macmillan and Co., 1924]):

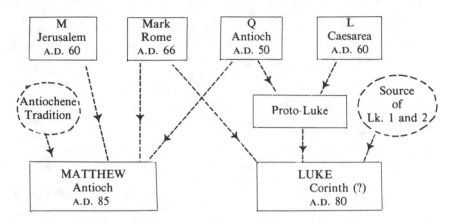

The goal of the FDH was to establish documentary sources essentially equal in antiquity and presumably therefore in authenticity to Mark and Q and thereby to widen the scope of the search for the historical Jesus; it was more widely accepted among English than German scholars. The issue of the sources used by the writers of the synoptic Gospels is still debated in contemporary scholarship.

See: **Proto-Luke; Q; Streeter; Synoptic Problem; Two Source Hypothesis;** *Urmarkus.*

Frühkatholizismus. See: **Early Church, The.**

G. See: *Grundlage.*

Gattung; Gattungsforschung; Gattungsgeschichte (Ger.: *Gattung:* form, type, genre. *Forschung:* research. *Geschichte:* history). In German, the term *G.* denotes a group of things or beings which have important or distinguishing (i. e., "typical") characteristics in common (Duden). In German Biblical criticism usage is disputed. *Gattung* is sometimes used to designate larger literary entities, such as Gospel, epistle, apocalypse, historical writing, etc., in which case *Gs. forschung* designates the study of these literary genres and *Gs. geschichte* the analysis of their historical origin, development and death or transmutation into another literary genre or mixed genre *(Mischgat-*

tung). Here, *G.* is distinct from the German *Form* (*Formen,* pl.) which is used to denote smaller literary units that primarily, but not exclusively, arise in oral tradition. Where *Form* ends and *G.* begins is obviously arbitrary, causing some scholars to reject the distinction altogether so that *Form* and *G.* are essentially identical. In recent Structuralist theory, particularly applied to OT criticism, the term *Form* is used in reference to individual texts; the term *G.* either to a structural model or scheme *(Strukturmuster)* involving at least two exemplars, or to text-type, i. e., the typicality by which a text is governed, whether that typicality be determined by a text's structure, setting, concern, or a specific motif. (See: Rolf Knierim, "Old Testament Form Criticism Reconsidered," *Interpretation* 27 [Oct. 1973], esp. p. 463.)

In English, *G.* is now most frequently translated "genre." *G.* criticism becomes especially problematic when applied to the literature of the early Church because its most important documents, especially the Gospels, represent a new kind of literature, their closest parallels being the so-called aretalogy.

From the perspective of communication theory a genre, according to M. Buss, "is best viewed as an open or virtual class which describes a possibility, rather than as a class of actual objects which meet a certain description." Such a view attempts to understand a given genre, such as a lament psalm, in terms of its actual function in human life, that is, as an expectation of the speaker or hearer, rather than simply as a theoretical and closed construct constituted by the collective elements of all psalms of this type. See: Martin Buss, ed., *Encounter with the Text* (Semeia Supplement; Missoula: Scholars Press, 1979).

See: **Aretalogy; Form Criticism.**

Gemara.   See: **Talmud.**

Gemeindeordnungen, Gemeinderegeln (German: *Gemeinde:* congregation/community. *Ordnungen/Regeln:* rules) are German words meaning "rules for the congregation" and connote a counsel of discipline designed for and originating within the earliest Christian communities, although the ethos which the rules embody may go back to Jesus. Mt. 18 (particularly vss. 15–18) is widely accepted as an example of *G.* placed back, for authority, on the lips of Jesus. *G.* are found throughout the writings of Paul (esp. 1 and 2 Cor.), the Pastoral Epistles, and The Didache (e. g., 1 Tim. 2:1–15; 5:1–21; 6:1–2; 2 Pet. 2:13–3:7; Did. 4:9–11). It should be noted that numbered among the Dead Sea Scrolls are writings known as "The Rule of the Congregation" and "The Manual of Discipline." See: **Dead Sea Scrolls; Household Rules.**

General Epistles.   See: **Catholic Epistles.**

Genre (French: kind, sort, style). See: *Gattung.*

Gloss (fr. Latin: a difficult word requiring explanation). In the narrower sense, a G. is a brief explanation or definition of a difficult word or a translation of a foreign word; more broadly, it is a comment or interpretation. In Textual Criticism it refers to a synonym or brief definition written above a word or in the margin of a text; if continued throughout, the original text is given an interlinear translation, e. g., a Greek MS "glossed" with Latin (so Codex Sangallensis, 9th cent.; see Bruce Metzger, *The Text of the New Testament* [London and New York: Oxford University Press, 1964], plate XIII). In copying MSS, scribes sometimes mistakenly incorporated glosses into the body of the text, thereby corrupting it. See: **Assimilation; Conflation; Interlinear Greek NT.**

Glossolalia (fr. Greek: "speaking in tongues"). An ecstatic state in which unintelligible utterances are purportedly the manifestation and vehicle of prophetic inspiration. G. was undoubtedly common within the early Church; its problematic features, its role in worship, and its status as a gift of the Spirit are discussed by Paul in 1 Cor. 12–14.

Gnosis, **Gnostic, Gnosticism** (Greek: knowledge). The nature and origin of *Gnosis* and the terms by which it is discussed is a matter of scholarly debate. The central issue has been whether Gnosticism is a heretical outgrowth of 2nd cent. Christianity (which is the traditional view apparently held by the early Church Fathers and by scholars up to the turn of this century) or a recrudescence and resurgence of an ancient religion whose origins lay in the East and whose appeal came to rival that of Christianity.

What is indisputable is that there appeared in the 2nd cent. a heresy among Christians which the early Church termed false *"gnosis"* (or "knowledge"; 1 Tim. 6:20) and which today, primarily in English language scholarship, is commonly referred to as Gnosticism. The nature of this heresy has been fairly well known through the quotations of those who argued against it: Irenaeus, Hippolytus, Origen. However, with the 1945–46 discovery near Nag Hammadi, Egypt, of some fifty Gnostic texts, the prospect of detailing the nature of "Gnosticism" more precisely is now immeasurably enhanced. Current research may show that certain of these texts, perhaps in an earlier form, antedate Christianity or reveal a non-Christian origin. Some scholars use the term *Gnosis* broadly as a fairly widespread and highly diverse but generalizable pre-Christian religious phenomenon. When *Gnosis* is thus defined, the term "Gnosticism" is reserved as designating *Christianized Gnosis.* This judgment may however be premature in light of work yet to be done on the Nag Hammadi Codices. Some believe Gnosticism to have originated within sectarian Judaism.

At this stage of understanding, then, how should *Gnosis* be defined? No

77

single term, such as philosophy, theology, or mysticism, suffices. It has been described as "a constellation of religious phenomena" (R. M. Grant) which consists of the following main points:

1. The true God, transcendent and unknowable, is utterly different from and not responsible for the visible creation, which is the work of the demiurge. (Some gnostic systems identify the demiurge with the God of the OT.)

2. Each person's true "self," the "I" of the Gnostic, is a "spark of the divine"; it is therefore unalterably immortal, but "fallen" and imprisoned in corporeality by the powers of this world and, like gold in mud, unable on its own to attain freedom.

3. Only a divine "call" can arouse a person from material stupor, giving him or her "knowledge" *(gnosis)* of the true self, of the self's home in the transcendent realm, and of the true God.

4. This return of the self occurs at the end of the individual life, when the soul travels through the spheres, or at the end of the world, simultaneous with the relapse of materiality to its original chaos or impassivity; the return is therefore resisted by the evil spirits and powers of this world.

Apart from these common elements, there is no single Gnostic system; just as there seems to be no single founder or text from which all the systems flow. There are many systems, each understanding itself to be an extension of the Call which, in Christianized *Gnosis,* proceeds from a Redeemer who has descended from the divine world, imparted *gnosis* and returned to the world above. Gnostic systems are often known by their founder or major teacher, such as Marcion, Basilides, and Valentinus; but the Church Fathers refer to others whose origins are unknown such as the Ophites, Cainites, Naassenes, Peratae, Sethians, etc. (See Werner Foerster, *Gnosis: A Selection of Gnostic Texts,* Vol. I: *Patristic Evidence;* II: *Coptic and Mandean Sources,* trans. R. McL. Wilson [London and New York: Oxford University Press, 1972]; for additional bibliography, see: **Nag Hammadi Codices.**)

The question Biblical interpreters face concerns the nature and role of *Gnosis* in the NT and in the religious milieu to which these writings were addressed. Certainly *Gnosis* in the broadest sense was present, even if incipient and partial, in the 1st cent. in Judaism, in the Dead Sea Scrolls, and in Philo. Christian writings such as the Gospel of John and 1 John show a great affinity for concepts integral to 2nd cent. Gnosticism: the descent and ascent of the Redeemer from and to the heavenly realm (Jn. 1:18; 3:13; 6:33; 12:23, etc.); the revelation of truth about the unknown God (Jn. 1:18; 3:31–36; 14:8–11, etc.); the division of humankind into those who accept and those who reject the truth (Jn. 1:12–13; 8:23, 44; 17:16); the dualism of flesh and spirit (Jn. 3:6; 6:63), of above and below, and so forth. It has been argued that Paul struggles against *Gnosis* in Corinth, having to defend the futurity of resurrection and its "bodily" form (1 Cor. 15), and at Colossae, where he asserts the subjection of all earthly spirit powers by Christ, who is the mediator of creation (Col. 2). By the time of the deutero-Pauline Pastoral Epistles, *G.* has become a rival (1 Tim. 6:20) which Christians are admonished to avoid (1 Tim. 4:1–16; 6:3–5; 2 Tim. 2:14ff.; 4:1–5; Titus 3:9).

See: **Chenoboskion; Nag Hammadi Codices.**

Good News for Modern Man. See: **TEV.**

Gospel (Anglo-Saxon: fr. *Godspell:* good news) is the A-S translation of the Greek word *"euangelion,"* which is used by the NT writers only in the sense of God's good news to men (Mk. 1:15; 10:29; Rom. 1:1–3, 16; 1 Cor. 4:15; 9:18, passim). The term later came to mean a book telling of the life and teachings of Jesus (Didache 8:2; 11:3; 15:3; Justin, *Apol.* 1, 66), perhaps following Mk. 1:1. Some ancient writings, however, though called "gospels," in fact tell nothing of Jesus' life, e. g., the "Gospel of Thomas." Whether or to what extent the four NT Gospels (Mt., Mk., Lk., Jn.) constitute a distinct literary genre is a live question in contemporary criticism. See: **Aretalogy; Genre.**

Gospel Parallel. See: **Synopsis.**

Graf, Karl Heinrich (1815–1869). Born in Mülhausen in Elsass, G. was a private tutor in Paris (1839–43) before becoming a teacher of Hebrew and French in Giessen (1847–68). His suggestion (1866) that the "Foundation Writing" (P) was the latest stratum of the Pentateuch became the basis of Wellhausen's elaborated theory of 1872. See: **Graf-Wellhausen Hypothesis; P: Priestly Document.**

Graf-Wellhausen Hypothesis. A theory concerning the origins of the Pentateuch which, though having numerous antecedents, was most persuasively argued by K. H. Graf (1866) and Julius Wellhausen (1876–1884); it added to the existing hypothesis the argument that written documents, combined and revised over several centuries from varying historical and theological points of view, could be (fairly) precisely dated and placed in an evolutionary sequence. A J (Yahwist) document (*ca.* 850 B.C.) and an E (Elohist) document (*ca.* 750 B.C.) were, according to this hypothesis, combined by a redactor (R^{JE}) around 650 B.C.; the Deuteronomic Code (621 B.C., called D) was added by a redactor (R^D) around 550 B.C.; the Priestly Code (*ca.* 450 B.C.) constituted the final document added by a redactor (R^P) around 400 B.C. Numerous revisions of this hypothesis, which dominated OT criticism until the rise of Form Criticism, have been proposed. See: **D: Deuteronomic Code; E;** *Grundlage;* **J; P: Priestly Document.**

Griesbach, Johann Jakob (1745–1812). Professor of NT at the Universities of Halle (1771) and Jena (1775) in what is now East Germany. He is noted in both Textual and Literary Criticism: he was the first to break with the *Textus Receptus* by developing a Critical Text of his own supplemented with a Critical Apparatus; he was the first to reject the traditional (Augustinian) explanation of the relationship of the first three Gospels (Griesbach Hypothesis); and, denying the possibility of writing a **Harmony,** he created the first Synopsis of the Gospels (Mt., Mk., and Lk.) and the name "synoptic writer" (Ger.: *Synoptiker*).

Griesbach Hypothesis, The seeks to explain the literary relationship of the first three Gospels of the NT by assuming that Mt. is the earliest Gospel, that it was used by Luke, and that Mk. as the latest composition is a radical conflation of both Mt. and Lk. This proposal, made by J. J. Griesbach in Germany in 1783, had been suggested earlier by the Englishman Henry Owen (*Observations on the Four Gospels* [London: T. Payne, 1764]) with little effect. The GH is a modification of Augustine's conjecture that each of the Gospel writers was dependent on the previous author(s), following the canonical order: Mt., Mk., Lk., Jn. In recent years the GH has been revived and revised, most notably by W. R. Farmer (*The Synoptic Problem* [New York: The Macmillan Co., 1964]). See: **Four Document Hypothesis; Synoptic Problem; Two Source Hypothesis; Q;** *Urmarkus.*

Grundlage (Ger.: basis; *siglum:* G). A hypothetical common basis behind the Pentateuchal traditions known as J and E, first proposed by Martin Noth in 1948 to explain the large number of common elements in the two traditions. Noth designated this common basis *(Grundlage)* G. (See: Noth, *A History of Pentateuchal Traditions,* trans. Bernhard W. Anderson [Englewood Cliffs, N. J.: Prentice-Hall, Inc., 1971], p. 38–41.)

Gunkel, Hermann (1862–1932) was born in Springe, Germany, taught NT at Göttingen (1888) before turning to OT studies at Halle (1889–93); he became Assoc. Prof. of OT in Berlin (1894–1907), a full professor in Giessen (1907–20), and ended his career in Halle (1920–27). Although G. was overshadowed by the influence of Julius Wellhausen during most of his own lifetime, G's methodological insights and conclusions have withstood 20th cent. criticism better than Wellhausen's. He has been called "the founder of form-critical and history-of-religions research in the OT" (Kümmel). He was the first to use the terms *"Gattungsforschung"* and *"Sitz-im-Leben"* (setting-in-life), terms which were to redirect the development of literary criticism in NT studies as well. (See: John H. Hayes, *An Introduction to OT Study* [Nashville: Abingdon Press, 1979], pp. 121–49.) With Wilhelm Bousset, G. founded the series *Forschungen zur Religion und Literatur des Alten und Neuen Testaments (FRLANT).* (See his *The Legends of Genesis: The Biblical Saga and*

History, trans. W. H. Carruth [1901] with an Introduction by William F. Albright [New York: Schocken Books, 1964, 1966²].) See: **Form Criticism;** *Sitz-im-Leben.*

Haggadah (or *Haggada*). See: *Halakah.*

Hagiographa means in Greek "the holy (or sacred) writings" and is the name commonly given to the third Jewish division of the OT, also called in Hebrew *Ketubim,* or "The Writings." The H. comprises, in varying order, the Psalms, Proverbs, Job, Song of Solomon, Ruth, Lamentations, Ecclesiastes, Esther, Daniel, Ezra, Nehemiah, and 1 and 2 Chronicles.

Halakah (or *Halacha;* fr. Hebrew: *Halak:* to go, to walk). In rabbinic tradition, *H.* is a t.t. which may refer either to (a) that part of rabbinic literature which contains rules for the daily conduct of the individual's and the community's life, or to (b) the rules and decisions themselves as handed down by the rabbis to be the authoritative interpretation of the written and/or oral Torah. The plural form, *Halakoth* (meaning "rules" or "decisions"), is used as a name for the various collections of these decisions. *H.* is preserved in two forms: as Midrash or as Mishna. As a descriptive term referring to the *legal* content of rabbinic literature *H.* stands in contrast to *haggadah* (plural: *haggadoth;* Aramaic: *aggadah,* meaning "narrative"). *Haggadah* is rabbinic material which seeks to illustrate the Torah, thereby enhancing its narratives with the general aim of winning adherence to its regulations. *Haggadah* varies widely in form (stories, anecdotes, parables, legends, etc.) and in subject matter, with subjects ranging from astrology to mysticism. See: **Midrash; Mishna.**

Hapaxlegomenon (pl.: -a) in Greek means "something said (only) once"; it usually refers to a word that appears but once in either the OT or NT as a whole; it may also be used in a more limited way to the writings of one man, e. g., the letters of Paul.

Haplography is the name of an error in manuscript copying in which a syllable, word, or line is omitted by accidental oversight because of the identity or similarity of adjacent material; the opposite of dittography. See: **Assimilation; Conflation; Dittography; Homoioteleuton; Textual Criticism.**

Harmony (of the Gospels). In current usage, an HG is a work which attempts so to interrelate the materials of the four Gospels that they tell a single and continuous story. The first and most famous was by Tatian (2nd cent.), called the *Diatessaron.* The word H. is at times used as synonymous with "Synopsis," or "Gospel Parallel," but it should be reserved for the former meaning. See: *Diatessaron;* **Synopsis; Tatian.**

Hatch and Redpath is the common call name of the Hatch-Redpath *Concordance to the Septuagint and Other Greek Versions of the OT* (including the Apocrypha) by Edwin Hatch and Henry A. Redpath, 2 vols. (Oxford: Clarendon Press, 1897).

An Expanded Index of the Hatch-Redpath Concordance to the Septuagint (Jerusalem, Israel: Dugith Publishers, 1974) places the Greek words used in the LXX opposite their Hebrew equivalents.

Haustafeln (Ger.: rules of the house). See: **Household Rules.**

Hebraism. See: **Semitism.**

Heilsgeschichte. This compound German term has several English equivalents: redemptive history, salvation history, sacred history; or the history of redemption/salvation, or the history of God's saving acts. The term achieved wide currency in OT and NT theology during the 1950s and '60s, particularly through the influence of Gerhard von Rad's studies in Deuteronomy and the Hexateuch. In contrast to other *"-geschichte"* terms, *H.* does not denote a methodology of Biblical criticism (such as *Formgeschichte* [Form Criticism], *Redaktionsgeschichte* [Redaction Criticism], etc.), but rather a theological principle which interprets Scripture as the ongoing story of God's redemptive activity in history *(Geschichte);* or, it may be used simply as a descriptive term referring to the theology of history found in both Testaments, esp. Deuteronomy and Luke-Acts.

Hendiadys (Greek: "one through two [words]") is the name for a form of parataxis in Greek in which two or more terms are coordinated by the use of "and" *(kai),* rather than by subordinating one term, as e. g., adjective to noun; see Mk. 6:26; cf. Mt. 14:9 (BDF).

Hermeneutics; (The New) Hermeneutic; Hermeneutic Problem; Hermeneutic Circle; Hermeneutic Principle (Greek: *hermēneuein:* to express, to explain, to translate, to interpret).

Hermeneutics is variously defined, from a theory of interpretation to a phenomenology (description) of understanding.

Traditionally, Hs. sought to establish the principles, methods, and rules needed in the interpretation of written texts, particularly sacred texts whose literal meaning was in doubt or had become unbelievable because of shifting world views or deepening moral sensitivity, and thus required reinterpretation in order to be preserved as sacred literature. Hs. in practice thus goes back to antiquity. The OT reveals a continuing effort to reinterpret the nature and will of God, the nature of humanity, the Covenant, etc. The NT depicts Jesus' employing contemporary rabbinic rules of interpretation (see: *a minore ad majus*), just as Paul used rabbinic methods for the interpretation of the significance of Jesus (see: **Typology**). From the Church Fathers through the Middle Ages, four levels of meaning were attributed to the Biblical text: the literal, the allegorical, the anagogic, and the tropological (see: *Sensus Litteralis;* **Allegory; Anagogy; Tropology**). The Reformation inaugurated a new period in Scriptural interpretation; it attempted, unsuccessfully, to limit the meaning of Scripture to its literal sense and offered the principle that the Bible is its own best interpreter (see: *sui ipsius interpres*). With the rise of humanistic letters prior to the Enlightenment came the development of two sets of hermeneutical rules, one for the sacred books of the Bible *(hermeneutica sacra)* and another for all other writings *(hermeneutica profana)*. It was at this time, in the 17th cent., that the term Hs., as the name of a field of inquiry, originated. Friedrich Schleiermacher (1768–1834), following the canons of universal reason attempted to overcome the division between sacred and secular hermeneutics by outlining a General Hs. and a Special Hs., the former devoted to general principles applicable to the interpretation of all languages and writing, the latter to particular books and classes of writings (prophecy, allegory, parable, etc.). This distinction permitted the interpretation of Scripture in the same manner as all other literature, and yet left open the question of its historical and religious uniqueness. Following prior practice, Schleiermacher placed Hs. between grammatico-historical criticism on the one hand and exegesis on the other. In time, however, this division of labor became increasingly suspect and inapplicable in practice, the reason being that the resolution of historical issues regarding a text is dependent upon and not prerequisite to some understanding of the text's meaning. Nevertheless, in conservative circles, traditional Hs. survived (the classic American study is by Milton S. Terry, *Biblical Hermeneutics: A Treatise on the Interpretation of the Old and New Testaments* [1883; reprinted by Zondervan Publishing House, 1952]). Non-evangelical Biblical criticism, from the late 19th cent. on, captivated by the newly discovered tools of historical and literary criticism, evolved in the main without a general theory of interpretation at all. It practiced what in substance was special Hs. The task of general hermeneutical theory was left to European philosophers outside Biblical studies and theology *per se,* most notably Wilhelm Dilthey (1839–1911) and Martin Heidegger (1889–1976). The formulations of these men creatively entered Biblical hermeneutics in the person of Rudolf Bultmann (1884–1976) whose existentialist interpretation (see: **Existentialist**) of the Biblical language and imagery (known popularly as **Demythologization** [q. v.]) dominated Biblical theology for more than two decades.

Hermeneutic (without the *s*) is the name ascribed by American scholars to a school of thought beginning principally with the so-called Later-Heidegger but whose roots go back to Dilthey and Schleiermacher; it differs sufficiently from traditional Hs. to suggest a new designation, hence the altered spelling (a practice not imitated in Germany, where H. is sometimes called "ontological hermeneutics"). H. differs from traditional Hs. in that it is no longer a methodology (as the theory of exegetical method), but a description of what constitutes the phenomenon of understanding as such. It rejects the opinion that a text has meaning autonomous of the interpreter, that the ascertainment of what a text meant in its original setting is a cognitive function separable from the determination of its meaning today. The principal theorist of H. so defined is H.-G. Gadamer (1900–   ); his views are succinctly sketched in Richard Palmer's *Hermeneutics* (Evanston, Ill.: Northwestern University Press, 1969). A defense of objectivity in interpretation is found in E. D. Hirsch, Jr., *Validity in Interpretation* (New Haven: Yale University Press, 1967).

The New Hermeneutic is a designation generally confined to the Biblical hermeneutic of Ernst Fuchs (1903–   ) and Gerhard Ebeling (1912–   ), whose thought rests on or at least shows the influence of the philosophical formulations of Heidegger and Gadamer. It grew out of and in response to Dialectic Theology of the 1920s, which, following the thought of the Protestant Reformers, stated that God has spoken through *(dia)* his Word *(logos)* which is contained in Scripture and made present in the word of proclamation. The NH accepted these theological assertions and inquired into their philosophical basis by analyzing the relationship of language to understanding and to reality. Out of this analysis came the terms **Language-event** (q. v.) and *language gain* and, in part, "the New Quest of the historical Jesus." The best introduction to the NH is Paul J. Achtemeier's *An Introduction to the New Hermeneutic* (Philadelphia: The Westminster Press, 1969). (Note: The dominant interpretive principle of the NH is the Pauline-Lutheran doctrine of justification by faith alone. Hence, method, as a kind of justification by works of reason, is radically rejected. A more indigenously American approach to hermeneutics is currently underway among Process theologians; see, e.g.: David R. Griffin, *A Process Christology* [Philadelphia: The Westminster Press, 1973].)

Key terms in the hermeneutic discussion:

The hermeneutic problem, broadly speaking, is the problem of interpretation; it arises wherever meaning is in doubt. The history of hermeneutic reflection is therefore the history of the deepening perception of the problem of meaning. Linguistically, it exists particularly in cross-culture situations, as in the interpretation of texts whose language and culture have long since disappeared. It exists as well in the interpretation of everyday conversation (of special interest to Schleiermacher), in the interpretation of art and history (Dilthey), of dreams as expressions of humanity's inner psychic nature (Freud), of Being itself (Heidegger), and so on. The hermeneutical task, therefore, is that of discerning and transferring meaning from one time and place to another.

The hermeneutic circle (or spiral) refers to the path thought takes as it attempts to find meaning. Methodologically, it refers to the procedure which a translator follows as he turns from the parts of a sentence to the sentence as a whole and then, quite literally, from the whole back to the parts. Descriptively, the circle refers to that profound interrelationship which the words of a sentence have with the meaning of the sentence as a whole, and which a sentence has with the paragraph as a whole, and so on outward to the work as a unity, and then finally expanding to include all the elements contingent upon an adequate understanding of the text at hand. In short, the interrelationship of text and context. This we may call the horizontal dimension of the H. circle. As such it received its first articulation by Friedrich Ast (1778–1841), a noted German philologist. Another aspect of the circle, which we here call its vertical dimension, was introduced by Friedrich Schleiermacher and later developed by Wilhelm Dilthey and others. It is that subjective aspect which exists between the text, or rather the human psyche expressed in it, and the interpreter, wherein both text and interpretation are construed as manifestations of a larger whole, for example, the Universal Soul (Dilthey) or Being itself (Heidegger). In Bultmann's hermeneutical theory, the circle exists between the text's interpretation of existence and the existential questions which the interpreter puts to the text (e.g., "What must I do to be saved?"), or between the existential questions which the text puts to the interpreter (e. g., "Who do you say that I am?" [Mk. 8:29*b*]) and the answer by which the text in turn is interpreted. In the NH, the possibility of a "vertical circle" independent of a "horizontal" one is denied; there is no objective meaning in a text independent of the one for whom it is meaningful, viz., the interpreter.

The hermeneutic principle, or principle of interpretation, may be loosely defined as the key by which the interpreter gets into the circle of understanding. According to the traditional branch of hermeneutics, there are objective criteria or principles by which the meaning of a text is determined (so E. D. Hirsch, Jr., etc.). The Protestant Reformer Martin Luther was explicit in his use of the doctrine of justification by faith in his interpretation of the NT (see: *sui ipsius interpres*). The doctrine of **Verbal Inspiration** (q. v.) functions in similar fashion for conservative theologians. According to the other branch (see: *The New Hermeneutic* above), the understanding of texts occurs only by virtue of the fact that in some way, even negatively, the interpreter already understands or has a pre-understanding for the subject matter of the text. He must in some sense already be in the circle of understanding. That pre-understanding is the "key" or "principle" by which the process of understanding is initiated. In Bultmann's hermeneutical theory such "principles" are existentialist or existential in nature. The former are conceptual and objective such as the principle of **Demythologization** (q. v.) and the principle that existence is either authentic or inauthentic. The latter are existential and subjective; for example, the indispensable pre-understanding or interpretive principle for comprehending—or rather being apprehended by—the NT is consciousness of one's own sin (i. e., the awareness that one's life is inauthentic). In the NH these terms drop from use, replaced by a poetic emphasis on silence and the need for listening to the text.

Note: Structuralism by contrast sharply rejects the epistemological assumptions of Hermeneutic. S. consciously objectifies the text, suspends judgments of meaning, thereby purportedly distancing it from any subjective interests of the critic. It thus contends that the (vertical dimension of the) hermeneutic circle is circumventible by the deliberate neutralization of unconscious presuppositions such as attitudes and values as well as conscious ones, as in existentialist interpretation. Furthermore, S. generally tends to redefine the nature of the interdependence of the parts of an entity and the entity as a whole, arguing that the whole determines the nature and functions of the parts, not *vice versa.* —Thus S. claims methodological priority over Hermeneutic, just as H. claims to describe the inevitable processes of all understanding, Structuralism included.

Contemporary hermeneutical theory, particularly in France and the U.S. is dominated by the work of Paul Ricoeur, whose interest in Biblical interpretation is extensive. (See: *The Symbolism of Evil* [Boston: Beacon Press, 1969] and *Essays on Biblical Interpretation,* ed. Lewis S. Mudge [Philadelphia: Fortress Press, 1980].)

Hermetic Literature (also: Hermetica) arose in the 1st cent. B.C. to 2nd cent. A.D. within Greek theosophical circles superficially enamored with the gods and environs of Egypt. In content, HL is essentially Greek. The term comes from Hermes Trismegistus (meaning Thoth thrice greatest), who is (in the main) the reputed author of the various treatises. The standard edition of the literature is the *Corpus Hermeticum* by A. D. Nock and A. J. Festugière (Paris: Société d'édition "Les Belles lettres," 1945–54; 1962²), which contains: (1) the *Corpus Hermeticum,* also known as *Poimandrès* (18 tractates, poorly preserved), (2) a Latin recension of a speech by Hermes T. to Asclepius (the latter being the name by which it is known), and (3) 29 extracts of the writings of Stobaeus (23–27 recount the teachings of Isis to Horus; the 23rd extract is known as *Kore Kosmou*). In addition to this collection and also belonging to the Hermetica are the Coptic Hermetica from Codex VI of the Nag Hammadi texts, various Hermetically influenced letters, and other papyri. (Note: A new edition of the *Corpus Hermeticum* is in preparation by the Institute for Antiquity and Christianity of Claremont, California.)

These tractates, essentially devotional and occult in character, have the common themes of God, world, and humankind, their setting is mythical and fantastic, their symbolism dualistic (light-darkness, height-depth, birth-death), and in their dialogical character resemble the *Timaeus* and *Phaedo* of Plato, hence their characterization as "proletarian Platonism." For their relationship to the NT see esp., C. H. Dodd, *The Interpretation of the Fourth Gospel* (Cambridge: The University Press, 1953).

Hexapla, **hexaplaric** (Greek: sixfold). Specifically, the title of Origen's critical edition of the OT in which six texts were placed in parallel columns: Hebrew; a Greek transliteration; Aquila; Symmachus; LXX; and Theodotion. It was written with diacritical signs to restore the accuracy of the LXX from recensional error and to counter the Hebraicizing and anti-Septuagintal translations of Jews (esp. Aquila's translation) whose dislike for the LXX had grown with the Church's preference for it. In Textual Criticism, the adjective hexaplaric is a pejorative term denoting those MSS of the LXX which have been corrupted by readings from the *Hexapla.* Generally speaking, however, a *H.* refers to any volume with six parallel texts. See: **Aquila; Origen; Septuagint; Symmachus; Theodotion.**

Hieronymus. See: **Jerome.**

Hieros Logos (Greek: *hieros:* holy, sacred; *logos:* word, doctrine; Herodotus, LCL 2.81: sacred legend) is a t.t. used to denote that which is told *(logos)* about an event and/or place in explanation of its sacred *(hieros)* origin and significance. It is used in OT studies, for example, in reference to the instituting words *(hieros logos)* of the covenant (Joshua 24), the sacred legend concerning the sanctuary at Bethel (Gen. 28:10–17), and that concerning the ark at Jerusalem (1 Sam. 4:1–7:2; 2 Sam. 6–7). The appropriateness of the term in specific instances is an issue of debate.

Higher Criticism. See: **Lower Criticism.**

Historic, Historical. See: *Historie.*

Historical Critical Method (The) is a term often used loosely and somewhat erroneously as synonymous with the whole body of methodologies related to the discipline of **Biblical Criticism** (q. v.). This use is erroneous in that certain critical methodologies claim not to be historical in approach, such as Structuralism and linguistics; and with others the issue is debated, e.g., Form Criticism. Strictly speaking, the term HCM refers to that underlying principle of historical reasoning which came to full flower in the 19th cent., viz., that reality is uniform and universal, that it is accessible to human reason and investigation, that all events historical and natural occurring within it are in principle comparable by analogy, and that man's contemporary experience of reality can provide the objective criteria by which what could or could not have happened in the past is to be determined. There has of course never been *a* HCM, any more than there has ever been *one* view of reality. But the advocates of HCM in the 19th cent., under the aegis of "objectivity," strenuously tried to avoid any trace of dogma or theological bias. Carried to extremes, HCM resulted in **Radical Criticism** (q. v.). Throughout the 20th cent. the role and basic assumptions of HCM, as well as the constituent "methods" themselves have been energetically and constantly debated: If HCM by definition rules out the Divine as a causative factor in history, of what help can it be to the Church in understanding the Bible which views God and history precisely in that way? Further, if in fact every event in history is in some sense unique, of what value is the principle of analogy? And further still, is the meaning of an event reduceable to that which is objectively verifiable? And finally, does such a thing as "objectivity" in the interpretation of history (historiography) even exist anyway? (See Werner G. Kümmel, *The New Testament: The History of the Investigation of Its Problems* [Nashville: Abingdon Press, 1972; London: SCM Press, 1973]; Edgar Krentz, *The Historical-Critical Method* [Philadelphia: Fortress Press, 1975].)

See: **Biblical Criticism; Exegesis; Hermeneutics;** *Historie;* **Lessing.**

Historical Criticism. Same as HCM, above. Also: HC narrowly defined deals with the historical setting of a document, the time and place in which it was written, its sources, if any, the events, dates, persons, and places mentioned or implied in the text, etc. Its goal is the writing of a chronological narrative of pertinent events, revealing where possible the nature and interconnection of the events themselves. So defined, HC is distinguished from Literary Criticism as the analysis of a document in terms of its literary character. In recent years, however, scholars have found this distinction artificial, as evidenced by use of the hyphenated term, historical-literary criticism. If the two are separable at all, it is in terms of goal and not method; hence, for example, the older curricular division between "The History of Israel" and "The Literature of Israel" that formerly existed in colleges and seminaries.

Historie; Geschichte/geschichtlich; historisch (Ger.: history/historic; historical). In recent Biblical theology a distinction has been made between, on the one hand, history as objective fact, external and verifiable, and, on the other, history as significance, internal and non-verifiable. German theologians have used the word *Historie* to refer to the former; the word *Geschichte* to refer to the latter. That Jesus was a man who lived in the 1st cent. is an objective statement of a historical fact verifiable by the same canons of historical reason by which any fact of the past is verified. That he was the Son of God cannot be so verified; it is an interpretive statement about the significance of the man

88

Jesus, the validity of which is affirmed only by faith. This distinction permits the assertion that something (say the resurrection of Jesus) is "true" in terms of history-as-significance which is not "true" in the sense of history-as-fact, i. e., objectively verifiable.

English approximates the German usage in the two adjectives, historic *(geschichtlich)* and historical *(historisch)*. To say an event is historic is to note that it possesses great significance for a people; to say an event is historical is simply to note that it is a fact, without judgment concerning its significance. For the role of these terms and their meaning, see: Van Harvey, *The Historian and the Believer* (New York: The Macmillan Company, 1966; London: SCM Press, 1967).

Historiography (fr. Greek: to write history) is of especial concern to OT scholars, since the history presented in the OT extends from Creation to the Maccabean Revolt (ca. 167 B.C.); it is of less concern to NT scholars, since apart from the Gospels, only Acts purports to be a record of historical events, and it covers a span of less than 35 years, from the Ascension of Jesus to the imprisonment of Paul in Rome (ca. A.D. 60–62). (See: Ward W. Gasque, *A History of the Criticism of the Acts of the Apostles* [Grand Rapids: Eerdmans, 1975].)

As a narrative of past events, historiography is undoubtedly older than writing itself, initially taking the form of oral traditions in which saga, **myth** (q.v.) and history were interwoven without any awareness of the distinction between them. Modern H. attempts to make such a distinction, one which tries to distinguish between "what actually happened" and the supra- or a-historical causes and meanings attributed to it by the OT narrator(s). Historical methodology, which analyzes methods and perspectives employed in the interpretation of the texts and artifacts of history, is of primary interest to OT scholars. Four major approaches to OT history are said to exist at the present time:

(1) The Orthodox, or Traditional Approach assumes that the Bible is of supernatural origin and, in its original wording, free from error. The task of the Biblical scholar is therefore one of corroborating rather than questioning statements of Scripture. See: Harold Lindsell, *The Battle for the Bible* (Grand Rapids, Michigan: Zondervan, 1976).

(2) The Archaeological Approach contends that (a) the traditions of the OT embody historical memory and are in the main quite reliable, and that (b) archaeological remains provide an objective means for containing subjectivistic hypotheses whether literary, philosophical, or theological, regarding the history of Israel. This approach is most closely associated with **W. F. Albright** (q.v.) and his school. See: George E. Mendenhall, *The Tenth Generation* (Baltimore: Johns Hopkins Press, 1973).

(3) The Traditio-Historical Approach received its initial impetus in the

form-critical studies of **Hermann Gunkel** (q.v.) and is associated with the German scholars **Albrecht Alt** (q.v.), **Martin Noth** (q.v.), and **Gerhard von Rad** (q.v.). The T-H approach rests on certain principles of analysis deduced from the form-critical study of Scripture; these include the conviction that (a) OT traditions existed for centuries only in oral form, (b) the written documents found in the OT represent a late stage in the development of these traditions; (c) the traditions arose in specific settings in the life of the people and were shaped by generic and formal factors at the time; (d) such literary units or genres are the basic forms of the tradition; (e) the primary unit in the patriarchal traditions is the saga; (f) the function of the sagas was not historical but aetiological, that is, they were designed to explain the origin of shrines, cultic practices, ethnic relationships, customs, etc.; (g) the sagas were combined to form cycles of traditions; and (h) out of these came history writing in Israel. The consequence of these interpretive principles for the reconstruction of the history of Israel varies with each interpreter who employs them. For a description of the methodology and its history, see: D. A. Knight, *Rediscovering the Traditions of Israel* (Missoula: Scholars Press, 1973, 1975[2]).

(4) The Socio-Economic Approach applies the theories of sociology to the reconstruction of Israel's history and claims as its initiator the work of the sociologist Max Weber (1863–1920). The S-E Approach differs with the other views in that it sees the origins of Israel not in nomadic tribes of the Mesopotamian-Palestinian regions, but in a pastoral-peasant class in Canaan whose revolt against oppressive overloads produced a tribal-covenantal society which subsequently decayed into a monarchical state. For further discussion and bibliography, see: **Sociological Interpretation.**

For this typology and synopsis, see: John H. Hayes and J. Maxwell Miller, eds., *Israelite and Judaean History* (Philadelphia: Westminster Press, 1977). See: **Albright, Alt, Noth, Rad, Saga, Sociological Interpretation.**

History of Tradition. See: **Tradition Criticism.**

Holiness Code is the name applied by the German scholar A. Klostermann in 1877 to Lev. 17–26. As a literary entity the HC is distinguished by its hortatory style, by its prescriptions for moral conduct and cultic purity and, particularly, by its use of the divine first person, as in the statement, "You shall be holy for I the LORD your God am holy" (19:2; 20:26). It seems probable that the code evolved gradually within the cult, perhaps in stages and around chs. 19 and 21, finally serving as a catechism for use by priests and Levites. See: **Law.**

Holtzmann, Heinrich Julius (1832–1910). Born in Karlsruhe (Germany), H. was professor of NT in Heidelberg (1858–1873) and Strassburg

(1874–1904). H. is credited with establishing (in *Die synoptischen Evangelien,* 1863) the "Two Source Hypothesis" of the synoptic Gospels (Mk. and a common sayings source [Q] underlying Mt. and Lk.) which has been the basis of synoptic criticism ever since, notwithstanding numerous attempts, even in the last decade, to provide a more convincing and useful alternative. See: **Griesbach Hypothesis; Q; Two Source Hypothesis.**

Homoioteleuton; homoioarchton (Greek: similar ending; similar beginning) are technical terms in Textual Criticism which denote scribal errors in copying MSS, in which words, parts of words, or lines are omitted because the transcriber's eye fell to a subsequent and similar ending (or beginning), whether of a syllable, word, or line. According to B. H. Streeter there are 115 instances of omission by H. in Codex Sinaiticus.

In rhetoric, H. is the name given to a form of artistic prose based on the assonance of the final syllables of certain key words (BDF, para. 488). Its presence in the original languages of the Bible is almost always lost in translation. For example 1 Tim. 3:16 contains in the Greek a highly stylized form of H. with six aorist passive verbs, each ending with the same syllable of two letters. The RSV rendering of this passage, strictly speaking, retains H. only in the first two past participles, though much of the poetic power of the passage is preserved by other kinds of assonance. "He was manifested in the flesh, vindicated in the Spirit, seen by angels, preached among the nations, believed on in the world, taken up in glory." Cf. Rom. 12:15.

See: **Epiphora.**

Hort, Fenton John Anthony (1828–1892). Collaborator with B. F. Westcott, from 1870 to 1881, in editing the critical edition of the Greek NT which bears their names. Educated at Trinity College, Cambridge, where he was a Fellow (1852–1857), he taught at St. Ippolyts (1857–72) and Cambridge (1872–92; from 1887 as Lady Margaret Professor). See: **Critical Text; Textual Criticism; Westcott.**

Household Rules, governing the relationships of husbands and wives, parents and children, masters and slaves, are found in Col. 3:18–4:1; Eph. 5: 22–6:9; 1 Peter 2:13–3:7. The rules are based on a hierarchical and patriarchal structure cemented by the principle of obedience. As such, they represent a concession on the part of the early Church to the social ethic of the 1st cent. The term HR is the common translation of the German word *Haustafeln* (lit., "house tablets [of rules]"), a designation which dates back to Martin Luther (16th cent.). See: *Lasterkatalog;* **Paraenesis.** See: James E. Crouch. *The Origin and Intention of the Colossian Haustafel* (FRLANT 109; Göttingen: Vandenhoeck & Ruprecht, 1972).

Hymn (fr. Greek: *hymnos:* hymn, ode, song of praise). In OT form-critical studies since the work of Hermann Gunkel, the term H. (Ger.: *Hymne*) is used to designate a song of praise which glorifies God as God, in contradistinction for example to a song of thanksgiving, which praises God for some specific act of grace on behalf of the nation or the individual. Gunkel listed as Hs Pss. 8; 19; 29; 33; 65; 68; 96; 98; 100; 103; 104; 111; 113; 114; 115; 117; 135; 136; 145–150. To these he added Enthronement Songs (e. g., 93; 97; 99) and Songs of Zion (e. g., 46; 48; 76; 84; 87), which though hymnic in form constituted an identifiable subcategory in terms of content.

Form critics, however, have not agreed on terminology or on formal criteria for distinguishing between Hs, thanksgivings, prayers, and confessions. Claus Westermann has suggested that since Hs and thanksgivings are both songs of praise the respective designations "descriptive" and "declarative" psalms of praise are more appropriate.

Hs and hymnic themes are found outside the Psalter, e. g., Job 5:9–16; 9:5–12; 12:13–25; 26:5–14; 28; Prov. 1:20–33; 8; Sirach 1:1–10; 10:14–18; 16:18–19; 16:26–17:24; 17:29–30; 24:1–22; 39:12–35; 42:15–43:33; Wisdom of Solomon 6:12–20; 7:22–8:21; 11:21–12:22, etc.

In the NT, Hs are referred to in Col. 3:16 and Eph. 5:19 along with psalms and spiritual songs with no clear distinction between them. Among NT critics perhaps greatest unanimity concerns the following as early Christian hymns: Lk. 1:46–55 *(Magnificat);* 1:68–79 *(Benedictus);* 2:14 *(Gloria);* 2:29–32 *(Nunc Dimittis)*—although these may have originated in Judaism or in the Baptist movement; Christological hymns: Phil. 2:6–11; Col. 1:15–20; Heb. 1:(2)3(4); 5:5; 7:1–3; 1 Peter 3:18–22; Eph. 2:14–16; 1 Tim. 3:16; Rev. 5:9–13; the *Logos* hymn (also perhaps pre-Christian): Jn. 1:1–5, 9–14, 16; and, hymns to God: Rev. 4:8, 11; 7:10, 12; 11:17–18; 19:1*b*–3, 5, 6–8*a*. (See: Jack T. Sanders, *The New Testament Christological Hymns* [Cambridge: The University Press, 1971].)

See: *Benedictus;* **Gunkel;** *Magnificat; Nunc Dimittis;* **Ode; Psalms.**

Hypocoristicon is the abbreviation of a name or its modification by the addition of a diminutive. In OT studies in particular the term is applied to the ancient practice of dropping off the name of the deity suffixed to a person's name, such as Adon for Adonijah. However, H. by etymology (*hypo:* beneath, less than; *koros:* child) refers to the modification of names for children, e. g., Jonathan/Johnny.

Hypotaxis the opposite of *parataxis*, is a term used to describe "elaborate systems of grammatical subordination" (Eugene Nida, *Toward a Science in Translating* [Leiden: E. J. Brill, 1964], p. 210), a style of writing highly developed in the literary Greek of antiquity and in modern (esp. 19th cent.) German prose. H. is especially characteristic of the writings of the apostle Paul, but more due to the nature of his mind and temperament than to a desire for literary effect, e. g., Rom. 1:1–7; 1 Cor. 1:4–8; 1 Thess. 1:2–7.

IB. Common abbreviation of *The Interpreter's Bible*, ed. George Arthur Buttrick (New York: Abingdon Press, 1951–57); a twelve volume exegetical and expositional commentary containing introductory articles on each book as well as general articles on Biblical history, criticism, and theology. Though in many respects dated, the *IB* remains a valuable tool for study. It is often referred to as illustrating the difference between exegesis and exposition. See: **Commentary; Exegesis; Exposition.**

IDB. *The Interpreter's Dictionary of the Bible: An Illustrated Encyclopedia in Four Volumes,* ed. George Arthur Buttrick (New York: Abingdon Press, 1962) is the most authoritative Biblical dictionary in the English language. New and expanded articles appear in Vol. V, ed. Keith R. Crim (Nashville: Abingdon, 1976).

Idiom (Greek: one's own) may refer broadly to (a) the language peculiar to a people, or more narrowly to (b) an expression whose meaning cannot be derived from the customary meaning of the component words—also called in semantics an "exocentric expression" (the opposite of an "endocentric expression").

Idioms (b) abound in every language and can rarely be translated literally. In Scripture, e. g.: "to close one's bowels" = to be lacking in compassion (1 Jn. 3:17); to "heap burning coals upon his head" (RSV) = to make him ashamed (Rom. 12:20); "our mouth is open to you" (RSV) = we have spoken very frankly to you (2 Cor. 6:11); to be "before the LORD" (RSV) = "by the grace of the LORD" (Gen. 10:9—NJV), or "with the LORD's approval" (Gen. 27:7—NJV), or "by the will of the LORD." (Num. 3:4—NJV)

The uncertain Hebrew of Song of Songs 1:7b ("one who is veiled"—see RSV footnote ad loc.) becomes in the LXX, Latin Vulgate, and RSV "one who wanders," and in KJV "one that turneth aside"; but the NEB finds here the (ancient Hebrew?) idiom "that I may not be left picking lice"! Cf. JB: "wander like a vagabond."

Illustrative Story. A name frequently given in NT parable interpretation since the studies of Adolf Jülicher (1886) to those "parables" of Jesus which present models of behavior, i. e., narratives in which "the moral lies in the narrative itself" (Vincent Taylor)—rather than outside the story as in the true parable: e. g., the good Samaritan (Lk. 10:29–37), the rich fool (Lk. 12:13–21),

93

the rich man and Lazarus (Lk. 16:19–31), and the Pharisee and the publican (Lk. 18:9–14). No hard and fast line can be drawn between ISs and "parables," and in contemporary discussions the distinction is often ignored. See: **Parable.**

Inclusio (Latin: a shutting off, confinement) is a t.t. for a passage of Scripture in which the opening phrase or idea is repeated, paraphrased, or otherwise returned to at the close (also called a cyclic or ring composition), such as Psalm 1; 4:1*a*-3*b;* 8; 21; passim; Amos 1:3–5, 6–8, 9–15; Ezek. 25:3–7, 8–11, 12–17; Jer. 3:1–4:4 (cf. 3:1*d* with 4:1*a,* omitting prose insertions), etc. The presences of the *I.* can aid the critic in determining the limits of an idea or tradition, particularly in the analysis of material that is composite in nature such as the prophetic literature (see the Jeremiah passage above). See: **Rhetorical Criticism.**

Interlinear Greek NT is a NT written in Greek with an English translation placed according to the Greek word order between the lines of the text; e. g., *The Interlinear Literal Translation of the Greek NT with the Authorized Version* (with a critical apparatus from Elzevir, Griesbach, Lachmann, Tischendorf, Tregelles, Alford, and Wordsworth), by George Ricker Berry (Chicago: Wilcox and Follett, 1956 reprint). *The RSV-Interlinear Greek-English NT,* currently published by Zondervan Publishing House with a Nestle Greek Text, contains the RSV text in the margin with an interlinear English translation by Alfred Marshall (originally published in London by Samuel Bagster and Son, Ltd., 1958).

Internal Parallelism. See: **Parallelism.**

Interpolation. In Textual Criticism, the word I. denotes material inserted into the text in the process of scribal transmission, thereby altering the original reading. Interpolations in the text of the OT are difficult to ascertain because of the dearth of ancient MSS. In the NT the matter is different. Verses present in the later Byzantine MSS (used as the basis of the KJV) which are not found in the more ancient MSS of the NT are considered to be Is. Since most modern versions are based on the older MSS, the interpolated verses are often, but not always, omitted from the text and placed in a footnote. Over 70 verses or parts of verses contained in the KJV of the NT are Is.; over 40 of these are in the synoptic Gospels. E.g.: Mt. 1:16*a;* 6:13*b;* 12:47; 17:21; 18:11; 19:9*b;* 21:44; 23:14; 27:49*b.* See: **Gloss.**

Inverted Parallelism. See: Chiastic Parallelism under **Parallelism** (synonymous).

Ipsissima verba; ipsissima vox. Latin phrases meaning "the very words" and "the very voice" respectively, often used in the context of the quest for the historical Jesus. *Ipsissima verba Jesu* would be "the authentic sayings of Jesus" in contradistinction to those sayings, in the Gospels or elsewhere, attributed to Jesus by the Gospel writers themselves or by the early Church. *I. vox* makes a lesser claim: Though the words in question may not be the actual words of Jesus, they accurately express his mind and intention. Opinions vary widely in either regard and certainty is beyond the reach of any historical method. The same terms apply to OT study, particularly of the prophets. See: **Criteria of Authenticity.**

Irony (fr. Greek: *eironeia:* dissimulation). In the classical sense, I. is the statement of one thing with the intention of suggesting something else. The word and its original meaning derive from a stock figure in early Greek comedy, the *eiron,* who mocks and finally triumphs over his boastful antagonist *(alazon)* by feigning ignorance and impotence. In manner and method, Socrates is the personification of the *eiron;* hence, the "Socratic I." According to H. D. Betz, Paul's "dialogue" with the boastful charlatans of Corinth (2 Cor. 10–13) is an intentional satire, full of I. and sarcasm, in the Socratic tradition (see: *Der Apostel Paulus und die Sokratische Tradition* [Tübingen, J. C. B. Mohr, 1972]). In the OT prophets, as in Greek tragedy, I. dominates, as Israel, proud and wilful like Oedipus, remains blind to the doom that is at hand. Ironic incongruity underlies both the teachings of Jesus ("The last will be first and the first last" [Mt. 20:16]; "Blessed are you poor . . ." [Lk. 6:20]; etc.) and his fate (the crucifixion of the Messiah). As literature the Scriptures are also filled with dramatic I. in which the reader knows what the characters do not; e. g., David's self-condemnation (2 Sam. 12:5–6), Jonah's futile flight (Jonah), Peter's asseveration of faithfulness (Mk. 14:30), and Paul's appeal to Caesar (Acts 25:11*c*). For the use of I. as an intentional literary device see, Jn. 4:12; 7:35, 42; 8:22; 11:50. (See: Edwin M. Good, *Irony in the OT* [Naperville, Ill.: Alec R. Allenson, 1965].) See: **Meiosis.**

Itacism (or iotacism) is a t.t. in Greek phonology for certain vowels and diphthongs (*ι, ει, η* [*η*], *οι, υ* [*υι*]), all of which came to be pronounced like *i.* The process of leveling out the phonetic distinctions present in classical (Attic) Greek and its consequent effect on spelling began in the 2nd and 3rd cent. B.C. and is essentially complete in modern Greek. As a phenomenon of spelling it is frequent in NT MSS.

Itala. See: **Old Latin MSS.**

J (Yahwist) is the customary designation for one of the four major but hypothetical sources (with **E, D,** and **P**—q. v.) used in the composition of the Pentateuch or Hexateuch. The unknown author of this source is called the Yahwist, from the English spelling of the author's preferred name for God

J (Yahwist)

(Yahweh). The symbol J, however, comes from the German spelling of the same name *(Jahve)*. In English Bibles, Yahweh is translated LORD.

The existence, extent, date, and nature (whether written or oral) of the J source are widely debated. Nevertheless, the majority of scholars believe that it was composed from ancient folk traditions during the 10th or 9th cent. B.C. in Judah, perhaps during the reign of Solomon as a charter of national faith. In style and subject the document can be described as an epic, at once patriotic and religious (Pfeiffer). It ascribes the origin and well-being of Israel to Yahweh's promises to Abraham, viz., that his seed would become a great nation, that they would be a blessing to all nations, and that they would receive at the Lord's hand a land flowing with milk and honey (Gen. 12:1–4a, 7). It sketches the long journey to the land of promise, from the Patriarchs, to the vicissitudes in Egypt and in the wilderness, to the conquest of Canaan.

Most scholars are of the opinion that this source was supplemented with a later, northern tradition (E) by a redactor (R^JE) perhaps in the 8th cent. Others find an older tradition behind J, particularly in Genesis: Rudolf Smend used the symbol J¹ for this material; Otto Eissfeldt extended it to other books, using the symbol L; R. H. Pfeiffer found an S source differing from both J¹ and L, and so forth. The following reconstruction of the J source is therefore not the final word, but a widely accepted hypothesis by a noted OT scholar.

The "J-Document" according to Martin Noth: Gen. 2:4b–4:26; 5:29; 6:1–8; 7:1–(3a) 5, 7 (8–9), 10, 12, 16b, 17b, 22–23; 8:6a, 2b, 3a, 6b, 8–12, 13 b, 20–22; 9:18–27; 10:8–19, 21, 25–30; 11:1–9, 28–30; 12:1–4a; 12:6–13:5, 7–11 a, 13–18 (15:1–2*); 15:3b–4, 6*, 7–12, 17–21; 16:1b–2, 4–14*; 18:1–19:28, 30–38; 20:1a, 7, 20–24; 24:1–67 (25:1–4); 25:5–6, 11b, 21–26a, 27–34; 26:1–33; 27:1–45; 28:10, 13–16, 19; 29:1–35; 30:4–5, 7–16, 20–21, 24–43; 31:1, 3, 17, 19 a, 20–23, 25b, 27, 30a, 31, 36a, 38–40, 46–49, 51–53a; 32:3–13a, 22–32; 33:1–3, 6–7, 12–17, 18b; 34:1–31; 35:21–22a; 37:3a, 4–21, 25–28; 38:1–40:1; 41:34a, 35b, 41–45, 46b, 49, 55–57; 42:1b, 4–5, 8–11a, 12, 27–28a, 38; 43: 1–34; 44:1–34; 45:1, 4–5a, 16–28; 46:5b, 28–34; 47:1–5a, 6b, 13–26, 29–31; 50:1–10a, 14.

Ex. 1:8–12, 22; 2:1–22; 3:1–4a, 5, 7–8, 16–22; 4:1–9, 10–16, 19, 20a, 21–31; 5:1–6:1; 7:14–18, 20, 21a, 23–25; 8:1–4, 8–15a, 20–32; 9:1–7, 13–35; 10:1–11:8; 12:21–23, 27b, 29–39; 13:20–22; 14:5b, 6, 13–14, 19b, 20, 24, 25 b, 27a, 30–31; 15:20–21, 22b–25a; 16:4–5, 28–31, 35b, 36; 17:2, 4–16; 19:2b (7–9*), 11b–13, 18, 20–25; 24:1–2*, 9–11*, 12–15a; 32:1a, 4b–6, 15–20, 25– 35; 33 (problematic); 34:1–35.

Num. 10:29–32, 33–36; 11:1–35 (composite, older traditions); 12:1–16; 13:17b–20, 22–24, 27–31; 14:1b, 4, 11–25, 39–45; 16:1b, 12–15, 25, 26, 27b– 34; 20:19–20, 22a; 21:1–3, 4–9; 22:3b–8, 13–19, 21–37, 39–40; 23:28; 24:1–25; 25:1–5; 32:1, 16, 39–42.

Dt. 31:14–15, 23 (JE)*; (34:1b–5a, 6, 10 JE).

See Martin Noth, *A History of Pentateuchal Traditions* (Englewood Cliffs, N.J.: Prentice Hall, 1971), ch. 4 and Translator's Supplement. Passages marked with * indicate points at which, according to Bernhard Anderson, scholars deviate from Noth's analysis; parentheses indicate passages omitted by Noth.
See: **E: Elohist; P: Priestly Code; Noth; Tetrateuch.**

JB. Common abbreviation for The Jerusalem Bible (Garden City, N.Y.: Doubleday & Co., 1966), which is the English equivalent of *La Bible de Jérusalem,* a translation of Hebrew and Greek texts of the Bible with introductions and notes by the Roman Catholic Dominican Biblical School in Jerusalem, published by Les Editions du Cerf of Paris in 1956. The English text of the Bible, though in the main also a direct translation of ancient texts, is indebted to the French edition at many points; the introductions and notes of the JB are translations of those in the French edition, revised and updated under the general editorship of Père Roland de Vaux, O. P.

JBL. See: **SBL; CSR.**

Jehovah. See: *Tetragrammaton.*

Jerome (A.D. 340/350–420). The most learned Biblical scholar of the Latin Church, Eusebius Hieronymus, in English called J., was born in Strido in Dalmatia and died in Bethlehem, an ardent monastic and controversialist. He is noted for his translation of Scripture into Latin, which became known as the Vulgate. See: **Vulgate.**

Josephus, Flavius (A.D. 37/38–ca. 110). Jewish historian and apologist, though considered a traitor by his contemporaries. His histories of the Jewish revolt against Rome (A.D. 66–73; *De Bello Iudaico* [*The Jewish War*], covering the period from Antiochus IV [d. 164 B.C.] to the fall of Masada in A.D. 73) and of the Jews (*Antiquitates Iudaicae* [*Jewish Antiquities*], from the Creation to the outbreak of the war), as well as his defense of Judaism (*Contra Apionem* [*Against Apion*]) and his biography (*Vita* [*The Life*]) are of incomparable value for reconstructing the history of the Jews in the first centuries B.C. and A.D.—even though the works are replete with gossip and legend. Though a Pharisee and erstwhile military commander in Galilee early in the revolt, J. quickly sided with Rome, where he lived following the war under the patronage of Emperor Vespasian (whence his name Flavius). See: *Josephus:* The Loeb Classical Library (9 volumes; London: W. Heinemann; Cambridge, MA: Harvard University Press, 1926–65).

Jülicher, Adolf (1857–1938). Born in Falkenberg near Berlin, J. became a pastor in Rummelsberg (1882) and, on the basis of his book, *The Parables of*

Jesus (*Die Gleichnisreden Jesu,* 1888), was called to Marburg as Professor of Church History and NT (1888–1923), where he remained until retirement. All modern study of the parables begins with J's massive work (vols. I & II, 1899) of 970 pages (!); it marked the end of the allegorical interpretation of parables while committing the error of overstatement by reducing every parable to a single point, invariably one simple moral maxim. In addition to his *An Introduction to the NT,* trans. J. P. Ward (New York: G. P. Putnam's Sons, 1904), J. published important studies in church history and contributed to textual criticism by editing an Old Latin version of the Gospels. As a historian, Jülicher was incensed by both Albert Schweitzer's *Quest of the Historical Jesus* and Karl Barth's *Romans.* See: **Parable.**

Kaddish (Aramaic: "holy"). An ancient Jewish doxology now recited usually after the reading of Scripture in synagogal worship or elsewhere, and including a congregational response. Its eschatological character and phraseology show affinities with the Lord's Prayer (Mt. 6:9–13; cf. Ezek. 38:23). The doxology, without the response, reads:

> "Glorified and sanctified be God's great name throughout the world which He has created according to His will.

> May He establish His Kingdom in your lifetime and during your days, and within the lifetime of the entire house of Israel, speedily and soon; and say, Amen."

Kähler, Martin (1835–1912). Professor of NT and Systematic Theology at Halle (1867–1901), K. was "rediscovered" by Existentialist Interpretation and the New Hermeneutic at midcentury for his work, *The So-Called Historical Jesus and the Historic Biblical Christ,* trans. Carl Braaten (Philadelphia: Fortress Press, 1964; Ger.: 1892) in which he notes the theological character of the Gospels, the consequent futility and speculative character of the so-called historical "lives of Jesus," and the "trans-historical" character of the significance of Jesus Christ. His question to NT criticism remains: "How can Jesus Christ be the real object of faith for all Christians if what and who he really was can be ascertained only by research methodologies so elaborate that only the scholarship of our time is adequate to the task?" See: **Existentialist;** *New Hermeneutic* under **Hermeneutics; Quest of the Historical Jesus; Schweitzer.**

Kaige **Recension** (also: Proto-Theodotion recension). A version of the OT in Greek which arose either as a direct translation of the Hebrew/Aramaic Scriptures or as a revision of the Old Greek OT in the direction of the original. The name is derived from its unusual use of the Greek word *kaige* for the Hebrew word *gam* (also). A fragmentary scroll of this type containing portions of the Minor Prophets was found in 1952 at Naḥal Ḥever (Wadi Khabra) in the Judean wilderness; it dates from the beginning of the 1st cent. A.D. or before. The KR stands in the same text tradition as that of **"Theodotion"** (q. v.)

in the 2nd cent. A.D., hence it is commonly known as Proto-Theodotion.

Note: Recent study indicates that "Theodotion Daniel" (that is, the text of Daniel found in Theodotion's version of the Greek OT) may not be a part of the *Kaige* recension as heretofore believed, but a distinct and separate text-type. TD is the recension quoted in NT citations of Daniel. See A. A. Di Lella's article "Daniel" in *IDB,* Supplemental volume (V) (Nashville: Abingdon Press, 1976).

See: *Hexapla;* **Origen; Theodotion.**

Kaine Diatheke is Greek for "New Testament" or "New Covenant"; see Heb. 9:15.

Ḳal waḥomer (Heb.: light and heavy). See: *a minore ad majus.*

Kerygma (Greek: proclamation; preaching) is a Greek term which in Scripture and in modern Biblical theology and criticism may refer either to the content of what is preached or to the act of preaching; hence K. in 1 Cor. 1:21 may be translated: "It pleased God by the foolishness of *the preaching* [so Dodd; or, KJV: *"of preaching"*] to save them that believe."

The realization within Biblical criticism since the turn of the century that the Gospels were first of all apologetic and didactic and secondarily historical documents led to two diverse but related reactions: (1) the rise of Biblical theology within Protestant circles which rediscovered the Pauline and Reformation emphasis upon the preached word (the K.) and the decision of faith which the K. demands (so Martin Kähler, Karl Barth, Rudolf Bultmann, Emil Brunner, et al.); and, (2) the search for the earliest K. of the early Church. According to C. H. Dodd (*The Apostolic Preaching and Its Developments* [London: Hodder & Stoughton, Ltd., 1936; New York: Willett, Clark, and Co., 1937]) the K. is found in whole or in part in Acts 2:14–39; 3:13–26; 4:10–12; 5:30–32; 10:36–43; and 13:17–41; and in Paul's writings in Gal. 3:1*b;* 1:3–4; 4:6; 1 Thess. 1:10; 1 Cor. 15:1–7; Rom. 1:1–3; 8:34*a;* 8:34*b;* 2:16; 10:8–9. Here the K. opens with references to OT prophecy concerning the fulfillment of the age with Christ as its Lord, the fact of Jesus' powers and preaching, his crucifixion, resurrection, and exaltation, the promise of his coming, the call to repentance and the offer of forgiveness. The Gospel of Mark is the K. briefly elaborated, beginning with prophecy and ending with the promise of a Christophany.

Dodd's restrictive definition of the term K. served to point up again (1) the non-kerygmatic character of most contemporary preaching, and (2) the continuing riddle of the NT, viz., how Jesus who proclaimed the coming of the Kingdom became the proclaimed Christ-who-is-to-come (again) of the church.

The resistance of Biblical theologians and critics to leaving the riddle unsolved has caused the term K. to be more widely defined than Dodd's usage permits, nor have theologians wanted to permit the reduction of the K. to a doctrinal-like formula. Consequently, in its broader theological meaning the term K. has also come to connote "the saving message"—as for example in the phrase, "The K. of Jeremiah." Similarly, both "the New Quest of the Historical Jesus" and its theoretical counterpart, "The New Hermeneutic," sought to reestablish the historical origins of Christian faith in the person of Jesus, and in the process broadened the parameters of the term K.

Kethibh and Qere (Hebrew: "it is written"; "to be read" respectively) are terms employed in the study of Hebrew Bibles to distinguish the literal, uncorrected wording of the text (the Kethibh) from the corrected wording (the Qere), which was written in the margin of the text and was to be read in its place. The traditional text was thus "corrected" on various grounds: grammatical, aesthetic, or dogmatic. Such passages number over 1300. One example concerns the name for God, which out of reverence was never pronounced; hence, whereas YHWH appeared in the text, a different word meaning Lord (Adonai), was read in substitution. Since the word appears so frequently in the Bible, the Qere was not written in the margin. Instead, the vowel points of the word Adonai were added as a reminder to the four consonants (YHWH) of the text, making an impossible word in Hebrew but nevertheless translated since late mediaeval times as Jehovah. A Qere required but not written in the margin because of frequency is called a *Qere Perpetuum.*

Ketubim (also *Ketuvim;* lit., writings). See: **Hagiographa.**

Khirbet Qumran is the name given to the ruins of an Essene community (fanatic Jewish monastics) on the northwestern coast of the Dead Sea, first occupied around 150 B.C. and destroyed in A.D. 68–70 during the suppression of the First Jewish Revolt (A.D. 66–70) by Rome. In its vicinity the **Dead Sea Scrolls** (q. v.) were found in 1947–56. See: **Dead Sea Scrolls.**

Kittel, Gerhard (1888–1948). Son of Rudolf K.; professor of NT principally at Tübingen. Known for works on Tannaitic Judaism and early Christianity and as founder of the *Theologisches Wörterbuch zum Neuen Testament,* vols. I–IX (Abbrev.: *TWzNT;* 1933–73); English translation by Geoffrey W. Bromiley, *Theological Dictionary of the New Testament,* I–IX (Grand Rapids, Michigan: Wm. B. Eerdmans Publishing Company, 1964–1974).

Kittel, Rudolf (1853–1929). Professor of OT principally in Leipzig (Germany); known for his Hebrew edition of the OT, the *Biblia Hebraica* (1906, 1909^2, 1929^3) which bears his name.

KJV. Common abbreviation for the King James Version of the Bible published in 1611; though heeding the Hebrew and Greek texts at hand, it owed much of its English phrasing to antecedent translations and versions by Tyndale (1525); Coverdale (1535); Thomas Matthew (1537); as well as the Great Bible (1539); the Geneva Bible (1560); and the Bishop's Bible (1568). In England it is commonly known as the Authorized Version (AV). No single book has affected the language and culture of English-speaking peoples more than the KJV of the Bible.

Two major factors led to the revision of the KJV: (a) The discovery in the 19th and 20th centuries of MSS far older than the MSS used in 1611; and (b) the increasingly archaic and obsolete character of the Elizabethan English in which the KJV was written. (In re: [a] see: **Textual Criticism.**) The following are examples of KJV words whose meaning has changed from its usage in 1611: Acts 21:15: carriages = baggage; Acts 17:23: devotions = objects of worship; Mk. 6:8: script = wallet; 1 Tim. 5:4: nephews = grandchildren; Mk. 7:24: coasts = borders; 2 Thess. 2:7: let = restrain; 1 Thess. 4:15: prevent = precede; Mk. 6:25: charger = platter; James 3:13: conduct = conversation.

The New King James Bible (Nashville: Thomas Nelson; NT: 1979; OT to be published) attempts to modernize the KJV language by omitting archaic pronouns (thee, thou, thy, thine) and verb ends (-eth, -est), and by replacing archaic and obsolete words with modern equivalents. Although the participating scholars "signed a document of subscription to the plenary and verbal inspiration of the original **autographs** of the Bible" (q.v.), ironically they chose to follow the "traditional Greek text underlying the 1611 edition" rather than follow the Hebrew and Greek MSS found since 1611 and antedating the "traditional text" by as much as 1000 years and more. See: **Paraphrase; Version.**

Koiné **Greek** (or more appropriately: *Koiné dialektos:* Greek: common language) is the term used to designate the language most widely used by Greek-speaking peoples of NT times which came into being following the extension of Macedonian hegemony throughout the ancient Near East by Alexander the Great, 323 B.C. Also called Hellenistic Greek, KG arose as an amalgam of several dialects of which Attic, a minor member, proved dominant. The books of the NT were written in KG.

Kompositionsgeschichte is an alternate and less widely used term in Germany for *Redaktionsgeschichte* (redaction criticism) meaning "composition history/criticism," suggested by Ernst Haenchen (*Der Weg Jesu* [Berlin: Walter de Gruyter, 1968], p. 24); its English equivalent has been supported by some as preferable to redaction criticism, but is also less widely accepted. See: **Redaction Criticism.**

Kompositionskritik (Ger.: Composition Criticism). In some German OT scholarship a distinction is made between Literary Criticism and K. in which LC is narrowly defined as the analysis of single, usually brief literary units and K. as the analysis of those larger texts which are composed of at least two pre-existing (whether oral or written) units. So defined, "composition" can occur at any of three stages: (a) At an oral or written stage prior to adoption by a writer; (b) at the time when the writer himself joins the units together in the process of composition; or, (c) when a "redactor" reworks a text, adding material to a pre-existing literary unit. K. comes into play when a text shows that it has been formed by the joining together of partly literary and partly pre-literary units. It seeks to explain how such units were joined together and how the compositor made changes in the pre-existing material, and how and why he added his own. K. asks: What are the steps of composition? What is the function of the units within the composition? It may seek to determine the theological content of the various units, since they can vary greatly, along with perspective and intention. When K. investigates the redactional treatment of units or compositions and their function in larger works or books, it becomes virtually identical with *Redacktionskritik*. Examples of material studied include the Abraham and Jacob cycles, the narrative passages of the Pentateuch, 1 and 2 Kings, etc.

Redacktionskritik, by contrast, seeks to determine the extent and nature of the redactional elements in the text at hand. This can include marginal or interlinear glosses, the addition of larger units or parts of texts (such as the hymns in the book of Amos), the transposition of texts, or alterations within the texts themselves, including the loss of portions thereof (e.g., Amos 2:12). The Pentateuch/Hexateuch and the Deuteronomistic redaction remain the areas of greatest complexity and interest in this regard. (See, e.g.: Otto Eissfeldt, "Die Komposition der Sinai-Erzählung Exodus 19–34," in his *Kleine Schriften,* Vol. 4 [Tübingen: J. C. B. Mohr, 1968], pp. 231–37.)

Kore Kosmou. See: **Hermetic Literature.**

Kultgeschichtliche Schule (Ger.: Cult-history School). In German Biblical criticism, the term *KS* refers to the application of certain insights, perspectives, and funds of cultic knowledge from the field of comparative religions to the study of OT and NT traditions. While the term is not often used today except in historical surveys, it refers to two related but disparate formulations of the method, viz., to (a) the so-called "Myth and Ritual School" in England, and (b) the "Uppsala-School" in Scandinavia. The former is associated with the work of S. H. Hooke (*Myth and Ritual* [London: Oxford University Press, 1933]; also *Myth, Ritual, and Kingship* [Oxford: Clarendon Press, 1958]), Jane Ellen Harrison (*Ancient Art and Ritual* [New York: Henry Holt and Co., 1913]), et al. Throughout these works the ethnological studies of James Frazer's *The Golden Bough* (1890; 1911–15) is apparent. In Scandinavia, the chief representatives of this perspective (for which the term "school" is not particularly apt) are Wilhelm Grønbeck, Sigmund Mowinckel, Johannes Pedersen, Aage Bentzen, Geo Widengren, Ivan Engnell, Alfred Haldar, and A. S. Kapelrud; see e. g., Ivan Engnell, *Studies in Divine Kingship in the Ancient Near East* (Oxford: Basil Blackwell, 1943), and Sigmund Mowinckel, *The Psalms in Israel's Worship* (New York: Abingdon Press, 1962; Oxford: Basil Blackwell, 1963), the latter author being considered the most influential of all the Scandinavians.

The cult-historical method, as it is sometimes called, developed as a reaction to the limitations of literary criticism and to the evolutionistic rationalism typical of the **Wellhausen** School, which tended to reduce OT religion to matters of doctrine and ethics. In contrast, the C-H School, influenced by Form Criticism, lifted up the centrality of the cult, the communal and recurrent character of its sacred rites and festivals, and in particular the concept of sacral kingship and the role of the king in the cult drama.

Criticism of the C-H perspective as practiced among OT scholars—principally the Scandinavians—is directed primarily against its extreme emphasis on kingship, the cyclical aspects of the cult, and the isolation of these concepts and motifs from their specific cultural and religious contexts.

In his study of the Psalms, Mowinckel proposed the term cult-functional method as a corrective to the overemphasis of early Form Criticism on form alone, suggesting that psalms which outwardly appear to belong to different form categories nevertheless belong together, being governed by the same ideas, perhaps functioning as the psalms of a specific festival. In NT studies, the C-H critics analyzed NT documents centering on the formative influences which baptism and the Lord's Supper especially had on the traditions (particularly 1 Peter, Ephesians, the passion narratives, etc.).

See: **Form Criticism; Mowinckel; Tradition Criticism.**

Kunstprosa (German: artistic prose) is defined by Friedrich Blass as a writing which is "intended by an author technically trained in this regard, not only to instruct, nor merely to make an impression, but also to please" (BDF, para. 485). According to Blass, in the NT only the book of Hebrews fits the category of *K*.

Kunstspruch. See: *Volksspruch.*

103

Kyrios. In modern English there is no precise equivalent for the Greek *"K."* as used in the NT period: "Lord" or "lord" in the Elizabethan period and *"Herr"* in German are much closer approximations, meaning "master" (Mt. 13:27; 25:20; Lk. 13:8), "owner" (Mt. 20:8; 21:40), "Sir" (Mt. 25:11; Jn. 12:21), "lord" (1 Cor. 8:5), "Lord"—as a divine being (Acts 5:14; 9:10–11, 42; Rom. 12:11; Gal. 1:19, passim), and "God" (Mt. 5:33; Mk. 5:19; Lk. 1:6, passim). When the term appears untranslated as a t.t., to Biblical criticism it almost invariably means "Lord," referring to the lordship of Jesus Christ.

"L" is the symbol created by B. H. Streeter (1924) to designate material peculiar to Luke's Gospel alone, including such familiar passages as the parables of the good Samaritan (10:29–37) and the prodigal son (15:11–32) but excluding the infancy narratives (chs. 1–2), composed by Luke from traditional material around A.D. 60 in the province of Caesarea by the Sea.

In OT textual criticism, L is the siglum for Codex Leningradensis. Copied in Cairo in A.D. 1009 from a ben Asher MS of the OT, it was adopted as the base text for Kittel's *Biblia Hebraica,* 3rd Edition (1929). See: **Four Document Hypothesis; Griesbach Hypothesis; "M"; Q; Synoptic Problem; Streeter; Two Source Hypothesis.**

Lachmann, Karl; "The Lachmann Fallacy." Professor of German and classical philology in Berlin (1825–51) and known as the founder of the modern era of Textual Criticism for his publication of the first Critical Text based entirely on ancient MSS, L. (1793–1851) argued for the existence of a source antedating the synoptics whose order Mk. best preserved *(Urmarkus)* and of a second source (called *Quelle*) to explain the parallels between Mt. and Lk. The "LF" is a name in NT Source Criticism given to the argument that since Mt. and Lk. with few exceptions follow the order of Markan material and since wherever one disagrees with Markan order the other agrees, it follows that Mt. and Lk. are *dependent* on Mk. (or a document very much like it) while being *independent* of each other (a conclusion L. derived from other facts as well). Logically, however, the deduction is fallacious because it is but one of three possibilities, viz., that the order of dependence is (a) Mt. → Mk. → Lk., (b) Lk. → Mk. → Mt., or (c) Mk. → Mt. and Lk. L. himself did not commit this mistake of reasoning since he believed each of the Gospels to be dependent on a primitive Gospel (i. e., *Urmarkus*) but his contention that Mk. best preserved its order naturally led to the acceptance of the priority of Mk. once the hypothesis of an *Urmarkus* was abandoned. See: **Two Source Hypothesis;** *Urmarkus;* **Griesbach Hypothesis.**

Lacuna (pl.: lacunae; Latin: hole) is a technical term in Textual Criticism denoting a gap or missing portion of a text due to damage in the MS itself and caused by wear, decay, worms, mice, careless repair, or intentional alteration (e. g., cutting out illuminations). See: **Textual Criticism.**

Lament (Note: L. is occasionally used to translate the German word *Klage* in spite of its varied connotations in that language: 1. (a) complaint, (b) lament; 2. (a) grievance, (b) lawsuit, charge. In form-critical studies, the terms dirge (funeral song) and complaint are more precise than L.) For a critical analysis of the L. in the OT, see: Claus Westermann, *Praise and Lament in the Psalms* (Atlanta: John Knox Press, 1981). See: **Psalms; Qinah Meter.**

Language-event, Word-event (Ger.: *Sprachereignis, Wortgeschehen*) are synonymous t.ts. in the New Hermeneutic as developed by Ernst Fuchs (1903–) and Gerhard Ebeling (1912–) respectively. The concept of the LE, derived in part from German philosophers of language and existence, is based on the idea that language and reality are inseparably interconnected, that to human thought reality *happens*—comes into being—through language. Such events have an ongoing residual effect in and as language, called language-gain. The NT is evidence of the coming-into-language (language-gain) of the new reality known as Jesus Christ (language event). Cf. Jn. 1:1–14. See: **Hermeneutics;** *New Hermeneutic* under **Hermeneutics.**

Langue. See: **Structuralism.**

Lasterkatalog (Ger.: pl. *Lasterkataloge;* a catalog of vices) is a technical term in German NT studies frequently carried over into English without translation to designate the lists of vices enumerated by Paul and other NT writers in the context of ethical instruction (Rom. 1:29–31; 13:13; 1 Cor. 5:10–11; 6:9–10; 2 Cor. 12:20–21; Gal. 5:19–21; Eph. 4:31; 5:3–5; Col. 3:5, 8; Rev. 21:8; 22:15). The *Lk* constitutes a somewhat loosely delineable "gathering" or literary form which antedates Christianity, whether derived from the writings of Judaism (see Philo's *de sacr. Abelis et Caini* 22, 27; The Wisdom of Solomon 8:7; 14:25ff.; IV Macc. 1:19, 26; Jubilees 21:21; 23:14; Enoch 10:20; 91:6–8; Dead Sea Scrolls 1QS IV, 9–11) or the ethical discourses of Greek antiquity, especially the Cynic-Stoic diatribe, from which the asyndetic form of the *Lk* found in the NT probably comes (see e. g., Epictetus II 16, 45; Stobaeus, *ecl.* II 60, 9; Seneca, *de vit. beat.* VII, 3; X, 2; Lucian of Samosato's style is paratactic, e. g., *dial. mort.* X 4, 6, 8). Nag Hammadi Codex VI contains *Lke.*

Frequently coupled with *Lke* are catalogs of virtues *(Tugendkataloge).* See 2 Cor. 6:6; Gal. 5:22–23; Eph. 4:2–3, 32–5:2; Phil. 4:8; Col. 3:12; 1 Tim. 6:11; 2 Tim. 2:22; 1 Peter 3:8; 2 Peter 1:5ff.; also Epictetus I 29, 39; II 14, 8; III 5, 7; 20, 5, 14–15.

According to ancient Greek philosophy there were four cardinal virtues:

wisdom, righteousness (justice), manliness, and moderation (temperance); and four cardinal vices: folly, unrighteousness (injustice), cowardice, and licentiousness (intemperance). See: Victor Furnish, *Theology and Ethics in Paul* (Nashville: Abingdon Press, 1968).

See: **Diatribe.**

Late Judaism (fr. Ger.: *Spät-Judentum*) is a term used to designate the Judaism of the NT (and Talmudic) period. In spite of wide use, the term, which appears in anti-Semitic tracts of the Reformation and post-Reformation period (F. C. Grant), is inaccurate and misleading and should be dropped. It retains a tinge of anti-Semitism, implying either that Judaism faded away after the 1st cent. or that the Church and not rabbinic Judaism was the legitimate continuation of OT Israel. Preferred alternatives are "Ancient" or "early Judaism," or "Tannaitic Judaism," or simply "1st cent. Judaism," etc.

Latinism. Although the influence of Latin on the NT is not as great as that of Semitic languages, its presence is apparent in (a) military terminology: praetorium, legion, centurion, custodian; (b) legal and administrative language: Caesar, tax, colony, freedman, title; and, (c) measurements and coins: liter, mile, denarius, drachma, etc. E.g., see Mk. 12:42 ". . . two *lepta* [Greek coins] that is, a quadrans [Roman coin]." See: **Semitism; Septuagintism.**

Law. According to tradition Moses was the great lawgiver and at his hand the Torah (Pentateuch) was written. Literary Criticism has shown, however, that the laws of the OT, concentrated almost entirely in the first five books, vary in age, form, and historical setting, and are the product of more than 1000 years of social and religious development. In fact, it is not until the 6th cent. B.C., long after Moses' death, that the multiform civil and penal laws, cultic stipulations and prohibitions, moral and ethical commands, procedural rules, etc., were looked upon collectively as "Torah" or law (see Deut. 17:19; 27:3; 28:61).

Literary Criticism, prior to the advent of Form Criticism, identified five "codes" or collections of law: the Covenant Code (Ex. 20:22–23:33), the Decalogue (Ex. 20:2–17; Deut. 5:6–21), the Deuteronomic Code (Deut. 12–26), the Holiness Code (Lev. 17–26), and the Priestly Code (Ex. 25:31; 34:29–Lev. 16; and portions of Numbers). Form Criticism has since shown, however, that these codes are made up of individual laws and units of laws which often considerably antedate the period of their codification.

The antiquity of certain OT law is revealed by its similarity (and dissimilarity) with other ancient law codes discovered in the Near East: the Sumerian codes known as Ur-Nammu (*ca.* 2050 B.C.) and Lipit-Ishtur (*ca.* 1975 B.C.); the Akkadian codes known as Eshnunna (*ca.* 1700 B.C.) and the Hammurabi Code (*ca.* 1700 B.C.); Middle Assyrian codes (*ca.* 1450–1000

B.C.), Hittite codes (*ca.* 1500 B.C.), and Neo-Babylonian codes (*ca.* 600 B.C.). English translations of these codes can be found in J. B. Pritchard's *Ancient Near Eastern Texts* (Princeton: Princeton University Press, 1958, 1971⁵).

See: **Apodictic Law; Casuistic Law.**

Law, The. See: **Pentateuch; Torah.**

LB(P), LNT(P), with or without the parenthesis, are common abbreviations for *The Living Bible, Paraphrased* (Wheaton, Ill.: Tyndale House, 1971), and *The Living New Testament, Paraphrased* (Tyndale House, 1967) by Kenneth N. Taylor. The *LBP* is fundamentally a paraphrase of the King James Version and the American Standard Version of 1901, with only a limited indebtedness to the original languages. The *LBP* is not a standard translation approved by an authorized committee of scholars and churchmen (such as KJV, ASV, RSV, NEB, etc.) but an interpretive translation by an individual. Its working principle is that "when the Greek is not clear, then the theology of the translator is his guide . . ." ("Preface," *LNT*[*P*], 1967). Regrettably, interpretations often occur without notation. Elsewhere the *LBP* provides a footnote explaining the literal meaning of the text or suggesting that the new reading is implied. Involved may be historical assumptions (e. g., Lk. 23:5, 14; Jn. 13:23–26; 1 Peter 5:1; 1 Jn. 5:6–8) or theological ones (e. g., Lk. 4:19; 17:26; Mk. 10:12; Heb. 5:7; Gal. 1:6; Rom. 3:21–26; Rev. 1:1).

The theological point of view of the *LBP* is explicitly conservative. In the NT, for example, this means that the divine nature of Jesus is introduced or heightened at points or in ways not found in the Greek text (e. g., Mk. 1:2; 2:10; 8:38; Mt. 9:13; Jn. 8:59; 2 Tim. 2:8), that the Holy Spirit in the sense of a person of the Trinity appears where no such reference exists in the Greek (e. g., Jn. 4:21–23; Lk. 24:49; Rom. 8:4; Rev. 1:4; 4:5), that the concept of "scripture" is expanded to include either the Old Testament or the Bible as a whole when neither existed at that time in the modern sense of those terms (e. g., Mt. 5:17; 13:52; Lk. 24:27; 2 Tim. 3:16), and that the return of Christ (e. g., Lk. 17:26, 30), the role of Satan (e. g., Lk. 8:27ff.; 11:15; 1 Jn. 5:18–19), and salvation as "going to heaven" (e. g., Rom. 1:16; 3:21) are all introduced into the paraphrase or otherwise emphasized in a manner not found in the text itself. In short, the *LB(P)* often reads not as the original texts but as a 20th cent. conservative theologian wishes they had. Among linguists this type of translation (or paraphrase) is called a "cultural translation" because it introduces cultural ideas which are either absent in or foreign to the culture of the text.

For these reasons, the *LB(P)* serves the student of Scripture poorly and should always be used—if at all—in conjunction with one or more of the standard translations listed above.

See: **Paraphrase.**

Leben Jesu Forschung. See: **Quest of the Historical Jesus.**

Lectio difficilior probabilior is an old (Latin) rule in Textual Criticism dating from J. A. Bengel (1687–1752) and J. S. Mill (1645–1707) which states that when a choice is to be made between two or more renderings of a text "the more difficult reading is the more probable," i. e., more likely to be original. The logic of the rule is based on the assumption that subsequent copyists would attempt to eliminate from the text grammatical, historical, or theological errors or ambiguities. See: **Textual Criticism.**

Lectionary (Latin: a reader). A book containing brief selections (pericopes) of Scripture from the NT (except the book of Revelation) designed for use in services of worship or private devotion and arranged to fit the secular and the ecclesiastical year (Advent, Epiphany, etc.). The L. established for the secular (or movable) year is called the Synaxarion; the L. for the ecclesiastical (or fixed) year is called the Menologion. Ls may include readings for Sundays and Saturdays only, or for each day of the year. Since the use of Ls is ancient, following a Jewish tradition, and they have been highly resistant to change, they are an important source for Textual Criticism in ascertaining early variants of Scriptural texts. In Critical Apparatuses, they are given the *siglum* 1 followed by the number of the MS. See *Prolegomena to the Study of the Lectionary Text of the Gospels,* ed. E. C. Colwell and D. W. Riddle (Chicago: University of Chicago Press, 1933). See: **Textual Criticism.**

Legend (Lat.: *legenda:* "what is read"). Although the lines between them are fluid and permit no strict delineation, it is possible to differentiate between Ls, fairy tales (Ger.: *Märchen*), and myths. The last of these is discussed separately (see: **Myth**). Fairy tales are entertaining and fanciful creations that tell of "once upon a time in the land of make believe" where virtue is miraculously rescued from evil and all "live happily ever after." No narrative of Scripture falls totally within this genre. However, according to E. Jacob (*RGG³*), the miraculous rescues of Moses and of Elijah, the peril of great beauty (Sara, Rebecca), the victory of the weak over the strong (Joseph, Gideon, David), and the quarrel between two wives (Sara and Hagar) are "fairy-tale like" *(märchenhaft).*

The term L. appears in English-language form-critical study somewhat unhappily as a frequent translation of (a) the Latin technical term *legenda,* or (b) the Norwegian term *sagn,* or (c) the Norse "saga," or (d) the German *Sage.* Each of these terms denotes simply "what is said" (cf. **Tale**). In the Middle Ages, the term *legenda* referred to the lives of the martyrs and saints read in the context of worship or for purposes of private devotion; for this reason, attempts have been made to make a form-critical distinction between the L. proper and the saga, the former having inspirational and religious content, the latter having more generalized and popular content (see Mowinckel, *IDB*). Others suggest that such a distinction does not hold true of Biblical narratives, which combine both elements.

What must be remembered is that what is usually connoted by the English "L."—an inauthentic and unhistorical story—is not the intended connotation in the context of Literary or Form Criticism.

The following are loose categories since the subject matter in many instances can be discussed from another perspective and thus placed in a different category.

A. Etiological L.:

1. Natural Phenomena: the Dead Sea (Gen. 19), the salt "pillar" (Gen. 19), the stone of Makkedah (Josh. 10), the megalith of Bashan (Deut. 3), etc.
2. Persons or Place Names: the tower of Babel (Gen. 11), the tell of Ai (Josh. 7–8), the well of Kadesh (Gen. 16)—over forty-five such Ls are to be found in Gen. alone.
3. Cult Objects, -Practices, -Places. OT: the bronze serpent (Num. 21:4–9), the ark of God (1 Sam. 4–6; 2 Sam. 6), circumcision (Gen. 17; Ex. 4; Josh. 5), Passover (Ex. 1–15), Bethel—Jacob (Gen. 28; 35), Sinai—Moses (Ex. 19), Jerusalem—David (2 Sam. 5–7); NT: Eucharist (Mk. 14:22–26 pars.; 1 Cor. 11:23–25; also Mk. 14:12–16), Baptism of the Holy Spirit (Acts 2).
4. Culture Heroes: the originator of towns (Enoch, Gen. 4:17), tent dwelling and the breeding of cattle (Jabal, Gen. 4:20), musical instruments (Jubal, Gen. 4:21), blacksmithing (Tubal-cain, Gen. 4:22).

B. Ancestor or Ethnological L., explaining the origin or characterizing traits of a nation, tribe, or city: Cain (Gen. 4), Canaan (Gen. 9), Noah's sons (Gen. 10), Abraham (Gen. 12), Ishmael (Gen. 16), etc.

C. Hero Tales, containing perhaps historical kernels, e. g., stories of the Judges (see esp. Judg. 14–16), of Saul and David (esp., David and Goliath).

D. L. proper (so Mowinckel), i. e., a story with an "edifying devotional tendency" possessing a nucleus of historical fact: Elijah ("a masterpiece of epic art," 1 Kings 17ff.) and the more popularized accounts of Elisha (2 Kings). The latter may also properly be classified an aretalogy.

Ls of the NT dealing with persons can in the main be listed here: the accounts of Jesus' birth, the explanation of Mary's virginity (Mt. 1:18ff.), the Magi (2:1ff.), the slaughter of the children and the flight into Egypt may have originated with the School of Mt.; the Lukan narratives on the other hand show evidence of tradition reaching back to John the Baptist (Lk. 1:14–17).

The story of Jesus in the temple, the temptation, the accounts of the empty tomb and of the Emmaus disciples bear the same devotional motifs—whatever historical fact underlies them.

Persons surrounding Jesus are treated in a similar fashion by Lk., e. g., Mary and Martha (10:38–42), Zacchaeus (19:1–10), Peter (5:1–10; Acts 12:1ff.), Paul (Acts 9:1ff.), Paul and Silas (Acts 16:19–40), Stephen (Acts 7:54–60), Cornelius (Acts 10), etc.

In recent years attention has turned away from the nature and extent of L. as a literary category to larger genres, such as gospel and aretalogy. Obviously, as what are here termed Ls become more complex in literary structure and content (theological and otherwise), the more interesting and susceptible to varied interpretation they become. In some, historical content is less significant than religious function, both as a linguistic expression of perception (and thus as an object of investigation) and as a vehicle of expression (and thus as a medium of perception).

See: **Form Criticism;** *Gattung;* **Myth.**

Lessing, Gotthold Ephraim (1729–1781). In the area of Biblical criticism, L. is accorded notice for publishing posthumously portions of the writaing of H. S. Reimarus which, according to Albert Schweitzer at least, inaugurated the "Lives-of-Jesus Research" of the 19th cent.; for proposing an *Urevangelium* (q. v.) behind the synoptics to explain their interrelation-ships; and, in Biblical theology, for his axiom concerning the relationshipof history to revelation, called by L. "the ugly broad ditch [*garstige breite Graben*] which I cannot get across," viz.: "Accidental truths of history can never become the proof of necessary truths of reason . . ." (*"Zufällige Geschichtswahrheiten können der Beweis von notwendigen Vernunftswahrheiten nie werden"* ["On the Proof of the Spirit and of Power"]); for his argument that the *regula fidei* and not the Scriptures themselves were the source and norm of faith for the earliest Christians; and, for his insistence that a distinction had to be made between a miracle and a story about a miracle. In all these points L. remains one of the conversants in 20th cent. Christian theology. See: **Hermeneutics; Historical Critical Method; Reimarus;** *Urmarkus.*

Letter. As a literary form, none of the writings of the OT is a L.; several of the books contain letters, e. g., 2 Sam. 11:14–15; 1 Kings 21:8–11; and, 2 Kings 10:1–2. In the NT the situation is quite different; twenty of twenty-seven writings are, or bear semblances of, letters and two additional books contain letters (Acts 15:23–29; 23:26–30; and Rev. 2–3). None of the NT letters is, strictly speaking, private correspondence; all were intended for the larger community, even Philemon which deals with a personal matter. The typical Pauline L. contains an opening (including the name of the sender, the recipient, and a greeting; e. g., Rom. 1:1–7; Phil. 1:1–2); a thanksgiving or blessing (missing in Gal.; cf., Heb., Jas., et al.), which may include a prayer of intercession (e. g., Rom. 1:9–10) and an eschatological climax (e. g., 1 Cor. 1:8–9); the body of the L. with some kind of formulary opening (e. g., Rom. 1:13–15; Phil. 1:12–18), eschatological conclusion (e. g., Gal. 6:7–10), and a travelogue (e. g., Phil. 2:19–24); paraenesis (e. g., Gal. 5:13–6:10); and a closing, including greetings, a doxology, and a benediction (e. g., Phil. 4:21–22). See: William G. Doty, *Letters in Primitive Christianity* (Philadelphia: Fortress Press, 1973).

Lexeme. See: **Structuralism.**

Lexicon (pl.: lexica; Greek: word) has several connotations of which two are pertinent to Biblical criticism: (a) it is used most frequently to designate a dictionary of Hebrew, Greek, or Latin words found in the Scriptures or the Church Fathers, such as Brown-Driver-Briggs (OT Hebrew) or Bauer-Arndt-Gingrich (NT Greek); or (b) it may be used in a broader sense to denote any specialized vocabulary of a particular field of knowledge—this Handbook is in part a highly selective L. of Biblical criticism.

For details on these lexica see: **Exegesis:** Tools.

In addition to BDB see: *A Concise Hebrew and Aramaic Lexicon of the Old Testament,* ed. William L. Holladay (Grand Rapids: William B. Eerdmans Publishing House, 1971; 1974²); it is based on the 1st-3rd editions of the Koehler-Baumgartner *Lexicon in Veteris Testamenti Libros,* a German-English lexicon of the Hebrew and Aramaic OT.

Lex talionis (Latin: law of retaliation). "An eye for an eye and a tooth for a tooth" is the traditional expression of the *LT;* it is characteristic of the Code of Hammurabi and has its parallel in OT law (e. g., Ex. 21:23–25). An enlightened law, it was designed to *reduce* bloodshed by prescribing the extent of retaliation. See: **Law;** *Sätze heiligen Rechtes.*

Liber antiquitatum Biblicarum. See: **Pseudepigrapha.**

Liberal Lives of Jesus. See: **Quest of the Historical Jesus.**

Liddell-Scott is the common call name of *A Greek-English Lexicon,* compiled by Henry George Liddell and Robert Scott; revised and augmented by Henry Stuart Jones (2 vols.; Oxford: Clarendon Press, 1925–1940). *A Supplement,* ed. E. A. Barber, was published by Oxford in 1968. L-S is the standard Greek-English lexicon for classical and Hellenistic Greek; it appears also in an abridged, student edition. *A Patristic Greek Lexicon,* ed. G. W. H. Lampe (Oxford: Clarendon Press, 1961) contains the theological and ecclesiastical vocabulary of post-Biblical Greek Christian authors from Clement of Rome to Theodore of Studium (d. A.D. 826). See: **Exegesis.**

111

Lightfoot, Robert Henry (1883–1953). Born in Wellingborough, England, the son of an Anglican priest, L. was a Fellow of Lincoln College (1919–1921) and New College (1921–50), Oxford University, where he became Dean Ireland Professor of Exegesis and Holy Scripture (1934–49). An early English advocate of Form Criticism, he also recognized the necessity of giving place to the theological and literary tendencies of the Gospel writers (later called Redaction Criticism). See: *History and Interpretation in the Gospels* (Bampton Lectures for 1934; New York: Harper and Brothers, 1934); *The Gospel Message of St. Mark* (New York: Oxford University and Press, 1950); published posthumously by C. F. Evans, *St. John's Gospel* (New York: Oxford, 1956); he was editor of the *Journal of Theological Studies,* 1941–1953. See: **Redaction Criticism.**

Linguistics is the study of language; it seeks to describe and explain human speech in terms of its internal characteristics, its function and its role in society; it is both empirical and theoretical in that it gathers observable data and clarifies that data according to a general theory of linguistic structure. In recent decades, the field of L. has become exceedingly diverse and complex, since language in all its aspects can be subsumed under this one rubric. It includes the theoretical study of signs (Semiotics), communication theory (and media), language structure (see: **Structuralism**) and systems, social settings (sociolinguistics), psychological setting (psycholinguistics), geographical setting (dialectology, linguistic geography), language development, the characteristics of individual languages and their relationship to other languages (comparative linguistics) and the fundamental commonality of all languages.

The common subdivisions of L. include phonetics, phonology, morphology, syntax (grammar), semantics (semasiology, lexicology, lexicography, etc.), and pragmatics.

Whereas in earlier decades of this century, L. concentrated on the speech act, on rhetoric and stylistics, as well as on historical (diachronic) aspects of language generally, emphasis in recent decades has been on the structure of language (i.e., its synchronic aspects). The former is sometimes termed "classical L.," the latter, "modern L." Further, concentration on the sentence as the basic semantic unit has given way to increased attention to texts (text linguistics) and (more recently still) to complete "speech acts." This broadening of the scope of linguistics to macrosyntactic units, specifically to texts as such, has caused biblical critics and theologians (as well as sociologists, psychologists, neophysicists, etc.) to become interested in developments in modern linguistics. (See: Theodor Lewandowski, *Linguistisches Wörterbach* 2; Heidelberg: Quelle & Meyer, 1976[2].) Two journals joining the broad ranges of linguistics to biblical interpretation are *Semeia* (published by The Society of Biblical

Literature, 1974—) and *Linguistica Biblica* (ed. by Erhardt Güttgemanns; Bonn, W. Germany, 1970—).

Literal Inspiration. See: **Verbal Inspiration.**

Literary Criticism, as a term in the general field of Biblical criticism, has three major definitions according to its historical, technical, and contemporary usage: It may refer either to (1) a particular approach to the analysis of Scripture which appeared in systematic form in the 19th cent. (often called Source Criticism) and which, considerably refined, is still practiced as (2) that investigation of a text which seeks to explicate the intention and achievements of the author through a detailed analysis of the component elements and structure of the text itself (here the what and how of a writing rather than its whence or why, as in #1, is sought); or, quite broadly, to (3) any undertaking which attempts to understand Biblical literature simply as literature, often in a manner paralleling the interests and methods of contemporary literary critics generally, such as I. A. Richards, T. S. Eliot, Northrop Frye, et al.

The term C. in the sense here used dates only from the 17th cent.; the judgment it represents, however, goes back to ancient Greece and above all to Aristotle's *Poetics.* Early Greek scholars of the church practiced LC (#2) when they questioned the authorship of books of the Bible on the basis of linguistic and stylistic factors; e. g., on these grounds Origen (*ca.* 185–254) doubted the Pauline authorship of the book of Hebrews, and his pupil Dionysius of Alexandria disputed the common authorship of the Gospel of John and the book of Revelation. When Martin Luther in the 16th cent. called for the interpretation of Scripture according to its literal meaning (*Sensus Litteralis*), or when he called the Epistle of James an "epistle of straw" and wished the book of Revelation had never been written, he was making literary (value) judgments, although they included judgments concerning content (Ger.: *Sachkritik;* see: *Sachexegese*) and interpretation (see: **Hermeneutics**).

As the anticlerical, antidogmatic spirit of the 17th and 18th cents. (particularly in France and England) placed Scripture more and more under the scrutiny of reason, critical literary observations began to accumulate. Radical shifts in content, style, point of view, and vocabulary, the presence of contradictions, repetitions, and interjections, all within a single book (e. g., Genesis) pointed, it seemed, either to the use of multiple sources in composition, or to the hand of a later redactor or compiler. With the rise of historical reason, especially in the 19th cent. (see: **Historical Criticism; Historical Critical Method**), historical questions concerning the authorship, origin, and historical setting of the writings and their component parts were added to the above purely literary observations.

Since the answer to these historical questions was dependent upon the delineation of sources within Scripture, *Source Criticism* as a special focus of LC was developed, particularly with regard to the first five books of the Old Testament (the **Pentateuch**) and to the first three books of the New Testament (the synoptic Gospels). The 19th cent. solution to the origins of the Pentateuch was called the Documentary Hypothesis (see: **Graf-Wellhausen Hypothesis**); the solution to the synoptics was called the **Two Source Hypothesis** (q. v.). SC was eventually applied to virtually all the books of the Bible. Sometimes it was carried to absurd extremes, with multiple sources purportedly lying behind a single verse, but nevertheless lasting discoveries occurred (e. g., see: **Deutero-Isaiah; Q**).

19th cent. LC was shaped not only by historical methodology but by the philosophical idealism of the age, by ideas of individualism, moral progress, and social evolution. The author as a creative spirit was more the object of literary inquiry than the work he produced. Thus, LC of the OT, esp. as epitomized by Julius Wellhausen (1844–1918), functioned with two major assumptions no longer considered valid. First, that the redactor (editor) of the Pentateuch worked with written documents which were the literary products of singularly creative individuals; and, second, that the literature of Israel evolved through ever higher stages which reflected the evolution of Israelite religion itself. Both were erroneous. The sources behind the Pentateuch have been shown by 20th cent. **Form Criticism** and **Tradition Criticism** to be mainly ancient oral traditions which were preserved in a variety of forms (psalms, laws, creeds, sagas, etc.) and which stem from diverse situations in life.

NT studies during this period shared many of the assumptions of OT Literary Criticism, viz., that written documents lay behind and explained the relationship of the synoptic Gospels (see *Urevangelium; Urmarkus;* **Proto-Luke; Q**), that the development of NT literature could be explained along evolutionary lines (see: **Baur**), that the purpose of LC was to discover the author's aims and intentions (*Tendenzkritik,* see *Tendenz* **Criticism**), that the value of NT literature, e. g., the parables, lay in its moral perceptions and instructions, etc. None of these assumptions have remained unaltered.

Form Criticism and **Redaction Criticism** have shown, for example, that the Gospels are not simply primitive attempts at historical biography, as the 19th cent. thought (see: **Quest of the Historical Jesus**), but complex, theologically motivated interweavings of materials of varying age and origin, some perhaps from Jesus, some from the early Church, some from the Gospel writers themselves (see: **Criteria of Authenticity**). These studies have further shown that the form and content of literature cannot be easily separated, that linguistic images and forms have affective as well as cognitive content, and that such forms have theological as well as aesthetic significance.

LC in the 20th cent. has thus gone beyond the questions of the previous century. LC in the sense of #2 above is still pursued; it asks whether Paul wrote 2 Thess., or Ephesians, or Colossians. Elaborate statistical analysis is now even computerized. But in the main, LC (as #3 above) is now more attentive to the interests and methodologies of literary critics generally, to the philosophy of language and to **Structuralism** (q. v.). (Midwife to the birth of interest in "secular" literary criticism on the part of Biblical scholars has been Amos Wilder; see esp. his *Early Christian Rhetoric: The Language of the Gospel* [New York: Harper and Row, 1964; London: Harvard University Press, 1971].)

See: David Robertson, *The Old Testament and the Literary Critic* (Philadelphia: Fortress Press, 1977); Norman Petersen, *Literary Criticism for New Testament Critics* (Philadelphia: Fortress Press, 1978); and, Leonard L. Thompson, *Introducing Biblical Literature* (Englewood Cliffs, NJ: Prentice-Hall, Inc., 1978).

For additional discussion and relevant bibliography, see: **Biblical Criticism; Semiology; Structure.**

Litotes. See: **Meiosis.**

Lives of Jesus Research. (trans. of Ger.: *Leben-Jesu-Forschung*). See: **Quest of the Historical Jesus.**

Locus (pl.: loci; Latin: place; cf. Gk.: Topos; pl.: Topoi: place[s]). The term *loci* in its Greek form (see: **Topos, Topoi**) has a special meaning and function in rhetorical/literary studies and is discussed separately. The Latin term *loci* is primarily of historical interest, though in substance significant to exegesis.

The concept of *loci* (or *Topoi*) is derived from the notion that the mind is analogous to a spatial entity in which individual thoughts are separately located and pre-existent, ready at hand for use. This follows Plato's understanding of knowledge in which ideas are not created but remembered (anamnesis). Thoughts hidden in their various *loci* within the mind are called to remembrance through appropriate questions, as in the Socratic method.

According to Lausberg (pars. 40–41), the questions have been encapsulated since the 12th cent. in the following hexameter:

quis, quid, ubi, quibus auxiliis, cur, quomodo, quando? The questions, their corresponding *loci,* and their translations are:

a. quis	= locus a persona	—Who?
b. quid	= locus a re	—What?
c. ubi	= locus a loco	—Where?
d. quibus auxiliis	= locus ab instrumento	—By what means?
e. cur	= locus a causa	—Why?
f. quomodo	= locus a modo	—How?
g. quando	= locus a tempore	—When?

115

Although the Latin terms and the theory behind them are no longer in use, the questions themselves are still a part of an exegetical approach to a text, whether that approach be historical or rhetorical.

Locus classicus (Latin: classical source or place) is the academician's jargon for that passage of Scripture or literature generally most frequently cited as the best illustration or explanation of a subject; Rom. 3:21–26 is the *LC* of Paul's concept of justification by faith; Eccles. 3:1–9 of the Hellenized Jew's pessimistic view of history.

Logion (pl.: logia; Greek: a saying). In its singular form, L. means "a saying" and in its technical sense is almost always used in reference to an utterance of Jesus characterized by brevity and succinctness in contrast to longer sayings such as **parables** or **discourses** (as in Jn.'s Gospel). A "floating" or "migrant" L. is one which appears in a variety of settings in the Gospel tradition, due either to its location within the oral tradition or to the judgment of the Gospel writer. Two such "FL" are: "He who has ears to hear, let him hear" (Mk. 4:9, 23; Mt. 11:15; 13:9), and "The first shall be last and the last first" (Mt. 19:30; 20:1)

In its plural form (logia), the term usually refers to a hypothetical collection of sayings antedating the Gospels. According to Papias (*ca.* A.D. 60–130), Mt. compiled the "logia" of Jesus in Hebrew, but their precise identity has not been established. According to some scholars, the reference is to Q (*Quelle:* source), a collection of sayings and additional materials found in both Mt. and Lk. The Gospel of Thomas, which is not a gospel at all in the canonical sense, is a good example of logia, though in the main spurious; fragments of this gospel were found at Oxyrhynchus, Egypt, in 1897 and 1904 and were sometimes referred to subsequently as "the *Logia* of Jesus." See: **Q; Form Criticism.**

Loisy, Alfred (1857–1940). French Roman Catholic theologian and Biblical critic, excommunicated in 1908 for his views on Biblical criticism; called the father of the Modernist Movement in Roman Catholicism.

LORD. See: **J (Yahwist); Tetrateuch.**

Lower Criticism is an unhappy term, now of infrequent parlance, characterizing Textual Criticism in contrast to so-called "Higher" Criticism, i. e., all other forms of Biblical criticism. The term is falling into disuse because of its pejorative sound coupled with the increasing acknowledgment that Textual Criticism is both important and complex.

Lucianic Text. See: **Byzantine Text.**

Luke's Great Omission refers to Lk.'s apparent disuse of Mk. 6:45 (53)–Mk. 8: (21)26, which is to be explained either by (a) the *Urmarkus* hypothesis which states that the original form of the gospel used by Lk. lacked this section, or by (b) assuming the mutilation of Lk.'s copy of Mk., or by (c) Lk.'s intentional disuse of this material because of parallel materials, or by (d) Mk.'s being a recension of Lk. Of these (c) is most widely accepted. See: *Urmarkus.*

LXX (Seventy). See: **Septuagint.**

"M" is the symbol created by B. H. Streeter (1924) to designate material peculiar to Mt.'s Gospel alone, including the parables of the laborers in the vineyard (20:1–16), the hidden treasure and the pearl of great price (13:44–46), but excluding the infancy narratives (chs. 1–2). According to Streeter, it was composed in Jerusalem around A.D. 60 from traditions preserved by Jewish Christians associated with James the brother of Jesus. See: **Four Document Hypothesis; "L"; Streeter; Synoptic Problem.**

Magnificat is the traditional name of Mary's song of praise recorded in Lk. 1:46–55, from the opening word of the Latin text: *"Magnificat anima mea Dominum"* ("My soul magnifies the Lord"). The language of the hymn is styled after the Greek OT and hence offers one of the best examples of "Septuagintism" in the NT. See: *Benedictus;* **Hymn;** *Nunc Dimittis.*

Major Prophets is a designation based purely on length for the books of Isaiah, Jeremiah, and Ezekiel, as distinct from the shorter and therefore "Minor" prophets, which are: Hosea, Joel, Amos, Obadiah, Jonah, Micah, Nahum, Habakkuk, Zephaniah, Haggai, Zechariah, and Malachi. The terms have nothing to do with the significance of the writings themselves.

Makarism (or *Makarismos*) is a transliteration of the Greek word meaning "blessing" (cf. Rom. 4:6, 9; Gal. 4:15). It is sometimes used in form-critical studies as a technical term to denote sayings of this type. See: **Blessings.**

Manual of Discipline is the name of one of the most important of the documents known as the **Dead Sea Scrolls** (q. v.); it contains the rules by which the Essene community of **Khirbet Qumran** (q. v.) lived and a treatise about the community's theological beliefs. See: A. R. C. Leaney, *The Rule of Qumran and Its Meaning* (London: SCM Press, 1966).

Märchen (Ger.: fairy tale, legendary fiction). A literary genre within folk literature first studied as such principally by Wilhelm (1786–1859) and Jacob (1785–1863) Grimm (Germany) and Hans Christian Andersen (1805–75, Denmark). In German OT Form Criticism, the term is generally retained for those stories which are not identified with any specific person, place, or time;

Hermann Gunkel included Jonah, for example, in this category. According to some scholars, the term is best translated "folk tale." However, no complete uniformity of definition or translation exists. See: **Legend.**

Marcion (*ca.* A.D. 85–160). Called "the first Protestant" by Adolf von Harnack for his radical interpretation of the Pauline distinction between law and gospel, M. dismissed the God of the OT as a vengeful demiurge and proclaimed Jesus to be the non-carnate manifestation of the true, transcendent, and unknown God. M's rejection of the OT and the formation of his own canon of Scripture, made up of an abbreviated Gospel of Lk. (called the Gospel of M.) and ten edited letters of Paul (called the *Apostolikon*), contributed both to his expulsion from the church of Rome in A.D.144 and to the formation of a canon within orthodox Christianity. M's gospel and *Apostolikon* are important for source and textual criticism. See Adolf von Harnack, *Marcion: das Evangelium vom fremden Gott* (Leipzig: J. C. Hinrichs, 1921) and John Knox, *Marcion and the New Testament* (Chicago: Chicago University Press, 1942).

Mari Tablets, some 20,000 in number, were found in the palace archives of Zimri-Lin (*ca.* 1730–1700 B.C.) at Tell el-Hariri, the ancient dynastic city of Mari situated on the Middle Euphrates in Mesopotamia. The tell (or "mound") was excavated by the French archaeologist André Parrot between 1933–55. The tablets, which are written in Akkadian, contain contracts, diplomatic correspondence, inventories, lists of male and female workers, private letters, etc. They are of significant value in reconstructing the Amorite (Northwest Semitic) culture during the early centuries of the 2nd millennium B.C., the period of the Biblical Patriarchs as recorded in Genesis. For the original texts and French translation, see: *Archives royales de Mari,* Vol. 1–19 (Paris: Imprimerie Nationale, 1950–79); for a few texts in English, see *ANET.*

Mashal is a Hebrew word denoting a wide category of linguistic forms, such as: taunt (Isa. 14:4), riddle (Ps. 49:4), allegory (Ezek. 17:2–3), byword (Deut. 28:37), dirge (Micah 2:4), etc. In each case, the Greek version of the OT (the Septuagint) translates M. with parabolē. See: **Parable.**

Masoretic Text (abbrev.: MT) refers to the received text of the Hebrew OT as punctuated and furnished with vowel points by the Masoretes (or Masorites), the authoritative teachers of Scriptural tradition (Heb.: *Masorah*).

By A.D. 500, two schools of Masoretes had emerged, one in the West (Palestine/Tiberias), the other in the East (Babylonia/Sura). The consonantal text (without vowel points) was preserved from emendation by Masoretic notations in the margin *(Masora marginalis)* and at the end of books or at the end of the whole OT *(Masora finalis).* Marginal notes written at the side of the text are called *Masora parva* (Mp), while those at the top and bottom are called *Masora magna* (Mm). The rules governing the consonantal text were laid out in two tractates, *Sepher Tora* and *Sopherim*. It was not until the 9th and 10th centuries that the vocalization of the Hebrew Text practiced in the West by the leading Masoretic families of ben Asher and ben Naphtali became dominant. In the 14th cent. these two traditions were joined to form a kind of mixed text, called the *textus receptus* or "received text," on which the first two editions of the *Biblia Hebraica* were based. Subsequent editions follow the Leningrad Codex B 19ᴬ (*siglum* L), which dates from the first quarter of the 11th cent. See: **Kittel, Rudolf; Textual Criticism; Septuagint.**

Megillah (pl.: *Megilloth*) in Jewish tradition usually refers to the book of Esther, but applies as well to the *Megilloth* (or *Megillahs*) also called the Five Scrolls, including, with Esther, the Song of Songs, Ruth, Lamentations, and Ecclesiastes.

Meiosis (Greek: a lessening). In rhetoric, M. refers to understatement, of which litotes (a positive affirmation by the negation of an antonym or contrary expression) is a common type, e. g., "For Christ did not please himself" (Rom. 15:3*a*), or "For I am not ashamed of the gospel" (Rom. 1:16*a*). Thus, litotes is a form of periphrasis, usually for emphasis. Cf. 2 Cor. 11:21. See: **Diatribe; Irony.**

Messiah. See: **Christ.**

Messianic Prophecies. Passages in the OT that speak of a future bearer of salvation and traditionally interpreted by Christianity as referring to Christ, the Messianic King, are Gen. 49:9–10; Num. 24:17ff.; Isa. 7:14; 9:1–6; 11:1–5; Mic. 5:1ff.; Jer. 23:4; Ezek. 17:22–23; 34:23–24; Zech. 9:9–10; Pss. 2; 72; 110. See: **Christ.**

Messianic Secret refers to a discernible phenomenon in the Gospels, most especially in the Gospel of Mark, in which Jesus explicitly conceals his messianic character and power until the closing period of his ministry. The term MS. entered NT criticism with the epoch-making work of William Wrede (*Das Messiasgeheimnis in den Evangelien: Zugleich ein Beitrag zum Verständnis des Markusevangeliums* [Göttingen: Vandenhoeck and Ruprecht, 1901]; Eng.: *The Messianic Secret*, trans. J. C. G. Grieg [London: James Clarke, 1971]). Wrede argued that the MS., as it is found in Mark, is a product of Mk.'s own interpretive editing of traditional materials and therefore belongs to the history of theology and not to the life of Jesus. Key MS. passages in Mk. are (A) the demons' recognition of the Messiah (1:23–25, 34; 3:11–12; 5:2–19; 9:20) and (B) injunctions and acts designed to keep Jesus' Messiahship secret: (1) injunctions addressed to demons in cases involving exorcism (1:25, 34; 3:12); (2) injunctions following other miracles (1:43–45; 5:43; 7:36; 8:26); (3)

injunctions following Peter's confession (8:30; 9:9); (4) intentional acts to preserve Jesus' incognito (7:24; 9:30–31); and, (5) prohibitions by others (10:-47–48). Wrede further argued that, according to Mk.'s theory of the MS., Jesus' parables were purposely obscure in order to keep the MS. from all but the disciples (4:10–13, 33–34), who nevertheless did not readily comprehend who Jesus was, some not believing in spite of his resurrection from the dead. See: **Quest of the Historical Jesus; Schweitzer; Wrede.**

Metalanguage (adj.: metalingual or metalinguistic) refers to that part of language which is used to talk about language itself, such as sentence, clause, distich, anaphora, adjective, paronomasia, and pronoun.

Metaphor (Greek: transfer). A figure of speech in which a name or descriptive phrase is transferred to an object or concept which it does not literally denote in order to suggest comparison between them: "God is *light* and in him is no *darkness* at all." (1 Jn. 1:5*b*) Following I. A. Richards, it is customary to refer to the image (light/darkness) as the vehicle and the idea it conveys (truth/falsehood, etc.) as the tenor of the metaphor (see: C. K. Ogden and I. A. Richards, *The Meaning of Meaning* [New York: Harcourt, Brace & Co., 1938; London: Routledge & Kegan Paul, Ltd., 1949]).

Grammatically speaking, a M. is defined as "a simile without 'like' or 'as'." The difference between a simile and a M., however, lies in the disparity of their semantic power. For example, the figure, "Behold, I send you out as sheep in the midst of wolves; so be wise as serpents and innocent as doves" (Mt. 10:16) contains both M. and simile. The qualities which the images "serpents" and "doves" qualify (wisdom and innocence) are explicit and thus give less room for the imagination. The M. "sheep in the midst of wolves" startles; it even horrifies. The more oblique the relation between vehicle and tenor, the more likely clarification is needed. The M. in John's Gospel, "Behold, the Lamb of God," is properly corralled by the addition, "who takes away the sins of the world"; it intends to convey sacrifice and death, not something pleasant.

In *Metaphor and Reality* (Bloomington, Ind.: Indiana University Press, 1962), Philip Wheelwright suggests that there are two functions of M., which he terms epiphor and diaphor. The former bears the usual understanding of M. as the transference of something relatively well known to something less well known though of greater importance (the sacrifice of lambs//the sacrifice of Christ). The diaphoric M., though never really totally free of epiphor, refers to a semantic movement *(phora)* through *(dia)* certain data of experience "producing new meaning by juxtaposition." In the diaphor the relation between a pair of images is understood as presentational rather than representational. These two types of M. can be seen in the Song of Songs, diaphoric M.

120

particularly in 4:1–7; 5:10–16; 6:4–7; and 7:2–8 (see R. N. Soulen, "The Waṣfs of the Song of Songs and Hermeneutic," *JBL,* 86 [1967], pp. 183–190).

Note: If M. is "the best gift of the poet" as Aristotle says, it is the *sine qua non* of the theologian. The Transcendent eludes language; every reference is metaphorical (Creator, King, Judge, love, etc.). In ancient Judaism even his Name (the tetragrammaton YHWH) receded into silence (see *Bath Qol*) and a surrogate was pronounced in its place. It is in part this consciousness of the inherent limitation of theological language within the context of belief in a transcendent God that gave rise to the Christian doctrine of incarnation, the incipient form of which is found in Jn. 1:14: "And the *Word* became flesh." The paradox of God becoming man is now, in a time of women's liberation, faced with the metaphorical delimitations of *His* becoming *a* man.

Metaphrase. See: Paraphrase.

Meter (fr. Latin: to measure) refers to any specific form of poetic rhythm (OED).

The modern analysis of meter in early Hebrew poetry extends back two centuries and remains an issue of scholarly debate because (a) the current vocalization of the Hebrew text dates only from the early Middle Ages, and (b) the exact reading of the original consonantal Hebrew text is a matter of conjecture.

According to Douglas K. Stuart, four schools of thought concerning meter in early Hebrew poetry are discernible. The schools and their principal exponents are:

(1) The Traditional School: J. Ley, *Die metrischen Formen der hebräischen Poesie* (Leipzig: B. G. Tuebner, 1886); K. Budde, "Das Hebräische Klagelied," *ZAW* 2 (1882), pp. 1–52; and E. Sievers, *Metrische Studien I & II* (Leipzig: B. G. Tuebner, 1901 & 1904).

The TS argued that Hebrew meter is accentual rather than syllabic or quantitative, and that units of stress (called feet) may vary in content from one to six syllables. Most Hebrew poetry was observed to be written in two or three parallel lines (**bicolon/tricolon,** q.v.), the cola being either of equal (2+2; 3+3; 4+4, etc.) or unequal (2+3; 3+2; 3+4; 4+3; etc.) length. E.g.: Psalm 29 = 2+2; Job, Proverbs, and most Psalms = 3+3.

(2) The Semantic Parallelism School: Robert Lowth, *The Sacred Poetry of the Hebrews* (Latin: Oxford: Clarendon Press, 1753; Eng.: 1787; reprint: N.Y.: Garland Press, 1971); G. B. Gray, *The Forms of Hebrew Poetry* (London & New York: Hodder and Stoughton, 1915; reprint: KTAV, 1972); and T. H. Robinson, *The Poetry of the Old Testament* (London: Duckworth Press, 1947). The SP School suggested that the determining factor in Hebrew meter is to be found in the parallelism of semantic units rather than in phonetic

phenomena. The counter argument is that semantic parallelism is an element of style and not of meter.

(3) The Alternating Meter School: S. Mowinckel, "Zum Problem der hebräischen Metrik," *Festschrift Alfred Bertholet* (Tübingen: J. C. B. Mohr [Paul Siebeck], 1950), pp. 379–94; and S. Siegert, "Problems of Hebrew Prosody," *SVT* 7 (1960), pp. 283–91. The AM School, though not uniform, sees Hebrew poetry as characterized by a regular interchange of toned and untoned syllables, the basic Hebrew foot being iambic, occasionally trochaic. In most instances, AM theorists relied on the vocalization of the Masoretic text.

(4) The Syllabic School: P. Haupt, essays in *AJSL* 19 (1903), pp. 129–42; 20 (1904), pp. 149–72; 26 (1910), pp. 201–52; *Biblische Liebesliedes* (Baltimore: Johns Hopkins Press, 1907); W. F. Albright, *Yahweh and the Gods of Canaan* (Garden City: Doubleday, 1968; note bibliography). Though closely related to the Traditional School, the SS bases its approach on a syllabic scansion of the text and is not dependent on Masoretic vocalization. This method is relatively more exact, since it identifies cola according to precise numbers of syllables (four to thirteen or more) rather than simply noting them to be short (2 stresses) or long (4 or 5 stresses).

For an overview of these schools and an elaboration and defense of the last, see Douglas K. Stuart, *Studies in Early Hebrew Meter* (Missoula: Scholars Press, 1976).

See: **Parallelism, Qinah Meter.**

Metonymy is a figure of speech in which a word is substituted for the thing it is intended to suggest. Apocalyptic literature makes frequent use of M. and its close parallel, synecdoche, as do the prophets, Psalms, and Wisdom literature. In the book of Revelation, terms such as "head" or "crown" are pseudocryptic substitutes for Caesar (Rev. 13:3); similarly the use of Mt. Zion for Jerusalem, heaven for God, the bottomless pit for hell, or to say that one is reading Job or Mk. or Paul instead of saying "the book of . . . ," are all examples of M. See: **Synecdoche; Trope.**

Midrash (pl. Midrashim; fr. Heb.: *darash:* to search, inquire). In its generic sense, M. refers to the exegesis and interpretation of Scripture; more specifically it refers to a particular instance of Scriptural interpretation; and, more precisely still, to a literary work of Scriptural commentary, known in the plural as Midrashim. (See, e. g., 2 Chron. 24:27 and 13:22 in the Jerusalem Bible; cf. RSV). A M. may be either halakic (legal, procedural) or haggadic (nonlegal, illustrative, etc.) in content; exegetical, homiletical, or narrative in form.

However, it is always, explicitly or implicitly, commentary on Scripture and hence constitutes a literary genre. Examples of pre-rabbinic M. are the M. of the Passover *Haggadah* (see the *Encyclopaedia Judaica,* ad loc.), the several *"pesherim"* or commentaries in the Dead Sea Scrolls, the Wisdom of Solomon (chs. 11–19), and perhaps Jn. 6.

See: *Halakah.*

Minor Prophets. See: **Major Prophets.**

Minuscule denotes a MS written in small cursive or "running" letters, first used for codices of the Bible *ca.* A.D. 800. The style predominated after the 10th cent. and now constitutes more than nine-tenths of all known MSS. The earliest dated MS of the NT is a M. bearing the year A.D. 835. The most important Ms are the Lake group, known also as Family 1 (*siglum:* λ) and the Ferrar Group, known also as Family 13 (*siglum:* φ). Ms are designated by arabic numerals without a preceding zero, e. g., 1, 118, 131, 209, etc., extending at present to *ca.* 2700 for the NT. See: **Lectionary; Papyrus Manuscripts; Textual Criticism.**

Miracle Story. See: **Aretalogy.**

Mishna (fr. Heb.: *shanah:* to repeat, i. e., to learn). An authoritative collection of rabbinic halakic (legal and procedural) material developed within the oral traditions of pharisaic and rabbinic Judaism, and arranged and revised by Judah ha-Nasi in the first decades of the 3rd cent. The M. provides the foundation for and the structure of the Talmud. It is divided into six orders (or *sedarim*) containing a total of sixty-three tractates: (1) *Zeraim* (seeds), (2) *Moed* (set feasts), (3) *Nashim* (women), (4) *Nezikin* (damages), (5) *Qodashin* (holy things), and (6) *Tahoroth* (cleannesses). The most interesting of the tractates for Christians perhaps is the tractate *Pirkē Aboth* in *Nezikin,* but all are of great significance for understanding Judaism of the intertestamental and early Church period. ". . . one may say that just as the New Testament is represented by Christianity as the conception and fulfillment of the Old Testament, so the Mishnah is understood by Rabbinic Judaism as the other half of *Tanakh"* [q.v.]. See: Jacob Neusner, *Early Rabbinic Judaism* (Leiden: E. J. Brill, 1975) and J. Neusner, ed., *The Modern Study of the Mishnah* (Leiden: E. J. Brill, 1973). See: **Talmud;** *Halakah;* **Midrash.**

Monograph (Greek: a single writing). A scholarly, documented study of a specific and limited subject, in contradistinction to a general introduction, commentary, collection of essays, etc.; for an example of a M., see Reginald Fuller's *The Formation of the Resurrection Narratives* (New York: The Macmillan Company, 1980[2]; London: S. P. C. K., 1972). See: **Commentary; Exegesis;** *Festschrift.*

Morpheme (French: form + -*eme:* unit, thing). One of the two basic units of linguistic description (with phoneme), Ms can be loosely defined as "the smallest meaningful units in the structure of a language" (Gleason). Prefixes (a-, bi-, in-, etc.) and suffixes (-ed, -ly, -tion, etc.) as well as freestanding words (year, love, etc.) are all Ms, because they are indivisible units of meaning, indispensable to the sense of the utterance of which they are a part. (See, H. A. Gleason, Jr., *An Introduction to Descriptive Linguistics* [New York and London: Holt, Rinehart and Winston, 1955, 1961[2]].) See: **Phoneme; Structuralism.**

Morphology is the descriptive analysis of words; it is the study of morphemes and their arrangements in forming words (Nida). The combination of words into phrases and sentences is treated under syntax, but in some languages, word structure and phrase structure are almost impossible to distinguish. See: Eugene Nida, *Morphology* (Ann Arbor: The University of Michigan Press, 1949[2]).

Mowinckel, Sigmund Olaf Plytt (1884–1965). Born in Kjerringy, Norway, M. was from 1917 professor of OT in Oslo. Though he wrote on subjects ranging over the whole OT and its environment, he is especially noted for his studies of the Psalms and the prophets. Influenced by the form-critical studies of Hermann Gunkel and by the cult-centered studies of Wilhelm Grønbeck and Johannes Pedersen, M. combined both perspectives in his work on the cultic origin and setting of the Psalms and prophetic preaching. (See: *The Psalms in Israel's Worship* [Nashville: Abingdon Press, 1962; Oxford: Basil Blackwell, 1963]; *Prophecy and Tradition* [Oslo: I kommisjon hos J. Dybwad, 1946]; also, *He that Cometh* [New York: Abingdon, 1956; Oxford: Blackwell, 1956].) See: *Kultgeschichtliche Schule;* **Myth; Tradition Criticism.**

MS (MSS). Abbreviation for manuscript(s).

MT. Abbreviation for Masoretic Text.

Myth, Mythology. In popular usage the term M. connotes something untrue, imaginative, or unbelievable; or, in older parlance, "a purely fictitious narrative usually involving supernatural persons, actions, or events" (OED). (Deferring to this usage and to the Christian religion, standard Western encyclopedias of mythology omit from their discussion any reference to the narratives of the Bible.)

However, in the realm of Biblical studies and theology, just as in contemporary anthropology, philosophy, and literature, the term M. is employed in a largely positive and functional, if provisional, way. There is, however, no agreed-upon definition, whether in terms of its form (that is, its relationship to fairy tales, sagas, legends, tales, epics, etc.), or in terms of its content and function.

Some critics argue that the OT contains no real mythology, but only "faded out" myths (so Hermann Gunkel, defining M. in a strictly literary and narrow sense). Sigmund Mowinckel identified M. with *narrative belonging to a cult:* M. tells in epic form the "salvation" re-actualized and experienced in the cult. Israel "historicizes" M. by having the cult M. refer not to a time distinct from world time, as in Babylonian cult myths, but to the history of Israel itself. History, not nature, is the subject of the cultus. Here Yahweh is enthroned in power, is victorious over the gods of Babylonian and Canaanitic mythology (Leviathan, Baal, etc.), delivers Israel from bondage, leads her to the promised land, and so on (cf. Ps. 44:2; 74:12–17; 89:10ff.; Job 26:12–13; 7:12, etc.). M. is thus used to destroy M.; it becomes "iconoclastic, that is mythoclastic" (Wilder).

In NT criticism the concept of M. has played a dominant role since Rudolf Bultmann's program of **Demythologization** (q. v.). Here M. is defined as a way of speaking about the Transcendent in terms of the immanent; the world beyond in terms of this world. He suggested that Biblical myths need to be interpreted in terms of their understanding of existence if they are to be meaningful to contemporary man, for example hell is to be understood not as a place, but as a human condition connoting separation from God.

The function of myth in individual and corporate life has recently been summarized by Ian Barbour: Myths (1) order experience by providing a vision of the basic structure of reality, (2) inform humanity about itself, its identity, nature, and destiny, (3) express a saving power in human life, whether in the form of a redeemer, or a law, a ritual, or a discipline, (4) provide patterns for human actions, and (5) are enacted in ritual. (See Ian G. Barbour, *Myths, Models, and Paradigms* [London: SCM Press, 1974; New York: Harper and Row, 1974].)

The term mythology refers both to the study of myth and to the corpus of myths within a given religious tradition.

Myth and Ritual. See: *Kultgeschichtliche Schule.*

NAB (New American Bible). A Roman Catholic translation of the Bible, including the Apocrypha, by members of the Catholic Biblical Association of America, begun in 1944 and completed in 1970, based on a critical use of the best texts available. See: **Douay; JB; KJV;** *LB(P);* **RSV; TEV; Paraphrase; Version.**

Nag Hammadi Codices (abbrev.: NHC; older abbrev.: CG: Cairensis Gnosticus). A collection of Gnostic and other writings dating from the 4th cent. A.D. reportedly discovered in 1945–46 in an ancient tomb-cave near the modern town of Nag Hammadi, located on the Nile some forty air miles northwest of Luxor in Upper Egypt. Of the original library, consisting today of eleven codices (bound volumes), one tractate, and the fragments of a twelfth codex, somewhat less than 90% is intact, numbering over 1100 inscribed pages. Although some of the tractates were previously known in whole or in part, the find provides primary documentation of Gnosticism in late antiquity and is therefore of great importance for understanding a strand of religious development which was divergent from and competitive with both orthodox Christianity and Judaism.

The Facsimile Edition of the NHC is published by E. J. Brill (Leiden) 1972ff., under the auspices of the Department of Antiquities of the Arab Republic of Egypt and UNESCO, James M. Robinson, Secretary to the Editorial Board. For a bibliography of texts, translations, and secondary literature, see: David M. Scholer, *Nag Hammadi Bibliography 1948–1969* (Leiden: E. J. Brill, 1971), supplemented each year in *Novum Testamentum* (1971ff.).

The texts with brief introductions are available in translation in *The Nag Hammadi Library in English,* James M. Robinson, ed. (New York: Harper and Row, 1977). The collection includes related and previously known tractates of the Gnostics known as Papyrus Berolinensis 8502. Each codex contains several tractates, the current (1980) standard numbering, titles and abbreviations are as below. It should be noted that tractates bearing the same name may not be identical in content.

The codices and tractates are:

I,1	*The Prayer of the Apostle Paul*	*Pr. Paul*
I,2	*The Apocryphon of James*	*Ap. Jas.*
I,3	*The Gospel of Truth*	*Gos. Truth*
I,4	*The Treatise on the Resurrection*	*Treat. Res.*
I,5	*The Tripartite Tractate*	*Tri. Trac.*
II,1	*The Apocryphon of John*	*Ap. John*
II,2	*The Gospel of Thomas*	*Gos. Thom.*
II,3	*The Gospel of Philip*	*Gos. Phil.*
II,4	*The Hypostasis of the Archons*	*Hyp. Arch.*
II,5	*On the Origin of the World*	*Orig. World*
II,6	*The Exegesis on the Soul*	*Exeg. Soul*
II,7	*The Book of Thomas the Contender*	*Thom. Cont.*
III,1	*The Apocryphon of John*	*Ap. John*
III,2	*The Gospel of the Egyptians*	*Gos. Eg.*

III,3	*Eugnostos the Blessed*	*Eugnostos*
III,4	*The Sophia of Jesus Christ*	*Soph. Jes. Chr.*
III,5	*The Dialogue of the Savior*	*Dial. Sav.*
IV,1	*The Apocryphon of John*	*Ap. John*
IV,2	*The Gospel of the Egyptians*	*Gos. Eg.*
V,1	*Eugnostos the Blessed*	*Eugnostos*
V,2	*The Apocalypse of Paul*	*Apoc. Paul*
V,3	*The (First) Apocalypse of James*	*1 Apoc. Jas.*
V,4	*The (Second) Apocalypse of James*	*2 Apoc. Jas.*
V,5	*The Apocalypse of Adam*	*Apoc. Adam*
VI,1	*The Acts of Peter and the Twelve Apostles*	*Acts Pet. 12 Apost.*
VI,2	*The Thunder: Perfect Mind*	*Thund.*
VI,3	*Authoritative Teaching*	*Auth. Teach.*
VI,4	*The Concept of our Great Power*	*Great Pow.*
VI,5	*Plato, Republic 588b–589b*	*Plato Rep.*
VI,6	*The Discourse on the Eighth and Ninth*	*Disc. 8–9*
VI,7	*The Prayer of Thanksgiving*	*Pr. Thanks.*
VI,8	*Asclepius 21–29*	*Asclepius*
VII,1	*The Paraphrase of Shem*	*Paraph. Shem*
VII,2	*The Second Treatise of the Great Seth*	*Treat. Seth*
VII,3	*Apocalypse of Peter*	*Apoc. Pet.*
VII,4	*The Teachings of Silvanus*	*Teach. Silv.*
VII,5	*The Three Steles of Seth*	*Steles Seth*
VIII,1	*Zostrianos*	*Zost.*
VIII,2	*The Letter of Peter to Philip*	*Ep. Pet. Phil.*
IX,1	*Melchizedek*	*Melch.*
IX,2	*The Thought of Norea*	*Norea*
IX,3	*The Testimony of Truth*	*Testim. Truth*
X	*Marsanes*	*Marsanes*
XI,1	*The Interpretation of Knowledge*	*Interp. Know.*
XI,2	*A Valentinian Exposition*	*Val. Exp.*
XI,2a	*On the Anointing*	*On Anoint.*
XI,2b	*On Baptism A*	*On Bap. A*
XI,2c	*On Baptism B*	*On Bap. B*
XI,2d	*On the Eucharist A*	*On Euch. A*
XI,2e	*On the Eucharist B*	*On Euch. B*
XI,3	*Allogenes*	*Allogenes*
XI,4	*Hypsiphrone*	*Hypsiph.*
XII,1	*The Sentences of Sextus*	*Sent. Sextus*
XII,2	*The Gospel of Truth*	*Gos. Truth*
XII,3	*Fragments*	*Frm.*
XIII,1	*Trimorphic Protennoia*	*Trim. Prot.*
XIII,2	*On the Origin of the World*	*Orig. World*
BG,1	*The Gospel of Mary*	*Gos. Mary*
BG,2	*The Apocryphon of John*	*Ap. John*

BG,3   *The Sophia of Jesus Christ*   *Soph. Jes. Chr.*
BG,4   *The Act of Peter*   *Act Pet.*
    See: *Gnosis;* **Chenoboskion.**

Narratio.   See: **Rhetorical Analysis.**

Narrative, used as a noun (*"a* narrative"), is in the broadest sense an account of events, whether actual or fanciful, reported in any way for any reason. N., used as an adjective, may denote a part of such an account. According to some contemporary literary critics, N. in this latter sense may be distinguished from exposition and dialogue, though any one or two of these may be set within the other. In this view, N. is understood as that which advances action, whereas exposition informs the reader of what has already occurred as background to that action.

In OT Form Criticism, N. is commonly distinguished as a distinct literary type from law, prophecy, psalms, and wisdom. Initially, Form Criticism gave little effort to analyzing what constituted narrative; rather, as with the first important form critic, Hermann Gunkel (q. v.), interest centered on categorizing different narrative types, such as legends, fables, myths, novellas (stories), and sagas. Any given N. may of course incorporate non-narrative types (blessings, commands, laws, prophecies, etc.) or it may contain shorter narratives identifiable according to certain formal elements (dreams, visions, miracle stories, parables, etc.). Some scholars contrast poetic narratives (myths, legends, etc. above) to historical narratives (popular history, prophetic autobiography, reports of dreams and visions, etc.).

In NT Form Criticism initial interest among scholars also had to do with narrative types rather than with the elements which constitute N. As in OT criticism, there is unfortunately no common agreement as to the nomenclature or to the classification of narrative types. Rudolf Bultmann (q. v.) lists the following as Ns to be found in the synoptic Gospels: (a) miracle stories (miracles of healing, e. g., Mk. 5:1–20, and nature miracles, e. g., Mk. 4:37–41; these two sub-types are called paradigms and novellas *[Novellen]* respectively by the form critic Martin Dibelius [q. v.]), and (b) stories and legends, such as the infancy narratives, Ns dealing with the baptism to the triumphal entry, passion Ns and Easter Ns (called legends, passion stories, and myths by Dibelius). In a brief discussion of the elements of narrative, Bultmann lists the following: law of scenic duality, conciseness of duration and theme, treatment of a group as a unity, disregard of motives and feelings, use of direct speech, and the law of repetition. It should be noted that these characteristics pertain to the synoptic narratives only. (See: Bultmann, *The History of the Synoptic Tradition* [New York: Harper and Row, 1963; Oxford: Basil Blackwell, 1963], pp. 307ff.)

It is the question of the characteristic elements of narrative which occupies contemporary scholarship most actively today. The reason for this rests not in purely literary interests alone, but in theological and philosophical ones as well. For it is recognized that the narrative mode constitutes the founding medium of Christian religious perception, first in the metaphorical narratives (parables) of Jesus himself, then in the *kerygma* (proclamation) of the early Church and later in the Gospels. From such a perspective, the tendency among scholars is to define narrative as the relating of an event in which there is a buildup *(desis)* and a release (lysis) of tension, or, to define it as a plot with a beginning, a middle, and an end. (On narrative or "story" see: Amos Wilder, *The Language of the Gospel* [New York: Harper and Row, 1964]. The significance of narrative in the Judeo-Christian perception is suggested by his statement: "God is an active and purposeful God and his action with and for man has a beginning, middle and an end like any good story" [p. 64].)

See: **Apophthegm; Aretalogy; Autobiography; Bultmann; Dibelius; Form Criticism; Gunkel; Kerygma; Legend; Myth, Mythology; Parable; Peripeteia; Prophecy; Psalms; Structuralism.**

NAS (New American Standard Bible, 1963). See: **ASV.**

Naturweisheit (Ger.: knowledge of nature). See: **Onomasticon.**

NEB. Common abbreviation of the New English Bible, a new translation of the Bible from the original tongues by British scholars with C. H. Dodd as Director (1947–65) and as Joint Director with G. R. Driver from 1965, under the auspices of a Joint Committee of the non-Roman Catholic Churches of the British Isles (NT, 1961; OT and Apocrypha, 1970). See: **Version; Paraphrase; Exegesis.**

Nebiim (Heb.: prophets). See: *Ketubim;* **Pentateuch; Prophets; Tanak.**

Neofiti I. See: **Targum.**

Nestle, Eberhard (1851–1913). Born in Stuttgart, Germany, N. was professor of OT at Ulm for two periods (1883–89 and 1893–98), separated by an interlude as visiting professor of Semitic languages at Tübingen (1890–93); thereafter he accepted posts at the Evangelical Seminary at Maulbronn (1898–1913). After devoting his earlier years to the study of Syriac and the LXX, N. turned to editing a critical text of the Greek NT for which he is best known, commonly called the **Nestle Text** (q. v.).

Nestle Text. A critical text of the Greek NT by Eberhard Nestle (see above) based on prior editions by Tischendorf (1869) and Westcott and Hort (1881), which in turn followed primarily the text of Codex Vaticanus (B).

Nestle consulted a third scientific edition (R. H. Weymouth, 1886; from the 3rd edition on, Bernhard Weiss, 1894–1900) in order to get a majority reading in those cases where the editions of Tischendorf and Westcott-Hort differed. First published in 1898, the NT has continually been revised: 10th-21st editions (1914–52) by his son Erwin Nestle; 22nd-25th editions (1956–63) by Erwin Nestle and Kurt Aland. The twenty-fifth edition of the Nestle-Aland Text shows 558 variants from Westcott-Hort.

Neutral Text, The (also called: Alexandrian, Egyptian, or Beta Text). See: **Alexandrian Text.**

New Hermeneutic (The). See: **Hermeneutics.**

NIV is the common abbreviation of the New International Version of the Bible (NT, 1973; OT, 1978). The NIV was prepared by more than 100 scholars from more than a dozen conservative evangelical denominations in the US and abroad "united in their commitment to the authority and infallibility of the Bible as God's Word in written form" (Preface, 1978). The NIV "came into being as a result of the repudiation of the RSV by the majority of conservative Protestants" in the U.S. and in an effort to provide a translation of the Bible which might correct the perceived mistranslations or misleading translations of the RSV. Assuming, for example, the inerrancy of the Scriptures, the NIV frequently translates OT passages so as to conform to their rendering in the New Testament (e.g., Isa. 7:14 is made to conform to Mt. 1:23 and Ps. 16:10 to Acts 2:27, although there is no textual support for doing so). For a critical review article, see: *The Duke Divinity School Review* (Spring, 1979), 164–79. See: **KJV; LB(P); Version; Paraphrase; Textual Criticism.**

NJV is the common abbreviation for the New Jewish Version of the Hebrew Scriptures being prepared by the Jewish Publication Society and appearing piecemeal since 1962: *The Torah* (Genesis-Deuteronomy), 1962; *The Five Megilloth and Jonah* (Esther, Lamentations, Ruth, Ecclesiastes, and the Song of Solomon), 1969; *The Book of Psalms,* 1973; and *The Prophets-Nevi'im,* 1978. The remaining books of the *Kethubim,* or "Writings" (Job and Proverbs) are still to be published. For a critical review, see *The Duke Divinity School Review* (Spring 1979), 180–91. See: **KJV; NAB; NIV; JB; Version.**

Noth, Martin (1902–68). Born in Dresden, Germany, N. (pronounced Note) was *Privatdozent* at Greifswald and Leipzig before becoming Professor of OT at Königsberg (1930–44) and Bonn (1945–65); thereafter he was Director of the "Institute for the Study of the Holy Land" in Jerusalem until his death. A prolific writer, N. is best known for *The History of Israel* (Ger.: 1950; Eng.: New York: Harper and Row, 1958; London: A. and C. Black, 1960),

A History of Pentateuchal Traditions (Ger.: 1948; Eng.: Englewood Cliffs, N.J.: Prentice-Hall, 1971) and his commentaries on *Exodus* (Ger.: 1959; Eng.: Philadelphia: The Westminster Press, 1962), *Leviticus* (Ger.: 1962; Eng.: Westminster, 1965; London: SCM Press, 1965), and *Numbers* (Ger.: 1966; Eng.: Westminster, 1968; SCM, 1968). Two of his theories received the greatest attention: (1) that "Israel" came into being as a tribal "amphictyony" which followed the invasion of Canaan by the tribe of Joseph, and that no reliable information concerning its prehistory, including the figure of Moses, exists, and (2) that the book of Deuteronomy is to be understood as a kind of preamble to the historical books of the OT (Joshua–2 Kings) and not as an addendum to the Tetrateuch (Genesis–Numbers). See: **E: Elohist; J (Yahwist); P: Priestly Code; Tradition Criticism, Deuteronomist(ic) History.**

Novelle (Ger.: novelette, short story) is a word employed by Martin Dibelius as a form-critical term, translated by the English word "tale" (*From Tradition to Gospel* [Ger.: 1919, 1933²; Eng.: London: Ivor Nicholson and Watson, Ltd., 1934; repr. James Clarke, 1971; New York: Charles Scribner's Sons, 1935]).

In OT Form Criticism the term is used perhaps in a manner more consistent with its original sense, that is, a novelette or short story. Gerhard von Rad, for example, contends that the story of Joseph in Genesis is more appropriately called an *N.* rather than "Saga" (Ger.: *Sage*) as some form critics had earlier suggested. (von Rad, "Biblische Joseph-Erzählung und Joseph-Roman," *Neue Rundschau,* 76 [1965], pp. 546–559.)

See: **Tale; Form Criticism; Dibelius.**

Nunc Dimittis is the traditional name of Simeon's prayer uttered according to Lk. at the dedication of the infant Jesus in the temple, recorded in Lk. 2:29–32, from the first two words of the Latin text: "*Nunc dimittis servum trium Domine . . .*" ("Lord, *now lettest* thou thy servant *depart* in peace . . ."). See: *Benedictus; Magnificat.*

Ode (Greek: song). A poem intended to be sung, expressive of the poet's feelings, and generally possessing an irregular metrical form. In the LXX and in the Greek NT, the term refers to a song of praise to God (e. g., Ex. 15:1) or to Christ (Rev. 5:9; 14:3). That the "odes" mentioned in Eph. 5:19 and Col. 3:16 are qualified as "spiritual" suggests that not all odes were sacred. In the LXX, thirty-six Psalms are identified as odes in their title (4; 17; 29; 38; 44; 47; 64–67; 74; 75; 82; 86; 87; 90–92; 94; 95; 107; 119–133). Its usage in the LXX is somewhat arbitrary perhaps since it is not used as the exclusive translation of any one Hebrew term.

OED. Oxford English Dictionary.

Old Latin MSS (also called Itala; *siglum:* it). The name given to approximately 30 MSS that antedate or are otherwise independent of the Latin Vulgate (*siglum:* vg) which Jerome completed in A.D. 405. The OL texts are highly divergent, and no single MS contains the whole NT. The oldest, Codex Vercellensis (*siglum:* a), dates from the 4th cent. The *sigla* for OL MSS are lower-case letters: a, b, c, etc.

Onomasticon (pl.: -a; Greek: consisting of names) is a learned term for a list of names, particularly of the proper names within a given culture as a philological aid to their meaning and etymology, as found for example in Plato's *Cratylus.* The *O.* of Julius Pollux (2nd cent.) is a ten-volumed lexicon containing the most important words related to a wide range of subjects (music, theater, politics, nature, crime, religion, etc.) with short explanations, illustrated with quotations from ancient writers. It is suggested that Oa were used in Wisdom writing, e. g., Job 28; 38–39; 41; Wisdom of Solomon 7:17–23; Sirach 43, etc. Cf. the *O.* of Amenemope (*ANET,* 421–425). Each of these deals with knowledge of the wonders of nature (*Naturweisheit,* Ger.: knowledge of nature). The O. of Eusebius, published about A.D. 328, is a treatise on the names and places of the Bible; it was translated into Latin by Jerome.

Onomatopoeia (Greek: lit., "to make a name"). Strictly speaking, O. is the creation of a word in imitation of a sound (whack, swish); in rhetoric, however, it refers to the use of words whose sound is used for its own effect or which suggests the intended sense (e. g., the Hebrew words *thohu wavohu* in Gen. 1:2 suggest to the ear what the English translation communicates only conceptually: "without form and void").

Oracle (Latin: *oraculum,* which denoted both a divine message and the place or medium by which it was communicated). In OT literary criticism the term has often been used broadly as any oracular communication of God *to* man, in contrast to prayers in which man communicates *with* God. Omens (e. g., Gen. 30:27; 44:5; Num. 17:1–11; 2 Sam. 5:22–24), dreams, and visions are not classed as oracles, although the accounts of dreams or visions may be incorporated into the body of a prophetic oracle.

A distinction was formerly made between the priestly O. and the prophetic O.; recent scholarship, however, generally ties both prophet and priest closely to the cult, although the question of the prophet's setting in the life of Israel is still debated. It may be that originally the cultic (or priestly) O. was little more than a "yes" or "no" reply to specific inquiries of the deity by a priest, in Israel principally through the use of lots called Urim and Thummim (see: 2 Sam. 23:2, 11; 28:6). Eventually, the mechanical use of lots seemed a poor substitute for the word of an inspired man (prophet) of God; nevertheless, the use of lots did not entirely disappear with the rise of prophecy (see: Jer. 3:16; Acts 1:26).

The earliest account of a prophetic oracle is recorded in the autobiographical narrative of Wen-Amon, an official in the court of the Egyptian god Amon at Karnak. It dates from the 11th cent. B.C. (See: *ANET,* 25–29, "The Journey of Wen-Amon to Phoenicia.")

By the 9th cent. B.C., the prophetic O. attained such distinction in style and content as to be preserved in written form as an identifiable genre, although at times incorporating other rhetorical forms, such as parable, vision, dialogue, song, etc. After the classical period of prophecy in the 8th–6th cent. B.C., the prophetic O. slowly disappeared, giving way to the priestly prayer and the apocalyptic vision.

See: **Prophecy.**

Oral Tradition refers to any body of material handed down from generation to generation by word of mouth, or to the process thereof; the stories of creation and of the Patriarchs in Genesis, of the Exodus and Moses in the Pentateuch, the deeds and teachings of Jesus in the Gospels, and the accounts of the rise of the early Church in Acts were all shaped by the laws of oral tradition, explication of which is one of the goals of Form Criticism. Theories concerning the nature of oral tradition have occupied Scandinavian scholars in particular; see: Birger Gerhardsson, *Memory and Manuscript* (Uppsala, 1961); Sigmund Mowinckel, *Prophecy and Tradition* (Oslo: I kommisjon hos J. Dybwad, 1946); and Eduard Nielsen, *Oral Tradition* (Chicago: Alec R. Allenson, 1954). See: **Form Criticism; Q; Synoptic Problem; Tradition Criticism.**

Origen (*ca.* A.D. 185–251/254). Born in Alexandria, Egypt, of Christian parents, O. is generally recognized as the most brilliant Biblical scholar and theologian of early Christianity, even though his views were later condemned by the Council of Constantinople (553). His chief works include his monumental *Hexapla,* his *De Principiis* (*ca.* 230), the first great systematic presentation of Christianity, and his *Against Celsus* (*ca.* 247), a reply to the Platonist Celsus in defense of Christian beliefs. O. died, probably in Caesarea, as a result of persecution initiated by the Roman Emperor Decius (249–251). See: *Hexapla.*

Ostraca (Greek: shell) in textual criticism refers to small pieces of pottery, usually fragments of vases, pots, plates, etc., used in antiquity for writing brief notes, letters, receipts, school exercises, religious maxims, hymns, etc. Written mostly in Greek, but also in Coptic and Latin, O. are more important for gaining knowledge of the early Church, its liturgy and its milieu, esp. Coptic, than for restoring the original text of the NT. See: **Textual Criticism.**

Otto, Rudolf (1869–1937). Professor of Systematic Theology at Göttingen, Breslau, and Marburg in Germany, O's influence in NT criticism and interpretation came primarily from his books, *The Idea of the Holy* (1917; Eng.: London: Oxford University Press, 1923) and *The Kingdom of God and Son of Man: A Study in the History of Religion* (1934; Eng.: London: Lutterworth Press, 1938); the former harks back to Schleiermacher, to the experience of the numinous and to God as the "Wholly Other"; the latter rejects the radical skepticism of Bultmann and attempts to reconstruct the self-consciousness of Jesus as the suffering servant of Isaiah.

Oxymoron (Greek: pointedly foolish) is the immediate juxtaposition of contradictory terms for effect, such as Jesus' reference to "living water" (Jn. 4:10, 11, 14), or Paul's proclamation of "Christ crucified" (1 Cor. 1:23); Martin Dibelius' description of Mark's Gospel as a "book of secret epiphanies" is a modern example.

Oxyrhynchus Papyri. A treasure trove of ancient papyrus fragments, numbering in the thousands, first discovered by B. P. Grenfell and A. S. Hunt (1897–1907) at Oxyrhynchus, near Behnesa in Upper Egypt. The papyri, dating from 2nd cent. B.C. to 7th cent. A.D. and written in Greek, Latin, Egyptian, Coptic, Hebrew, and Syriac, contain all varieties of texts, including fragments of the OT and NT and apocryphal literature, such as the Gospel of Thomas, the last being found intact at Nag Hammadi in 1946. See: **Nag Hammadi Codices; Papyrus.**

P: Priestly Code, Priestly Document, Priestly Narrative, Priestly Writer. According to the majority of OT scholars, P represents the latest stratum of material used in the formation of the Pentateuch (or Hexateuch), deriving its name from the Hebrew priests whose traditions and theological point of view it contains.

The existence of this tradition, later designated "P", was first proposed in 1853 by Hermann Hupfeld who thought it the earliest rather than the latest material in the Pentateuch as subsequently proposed by the **Graf-Wellhausen** [Documentary] **Hypothesis** (q. v.) later in the same century. In the documentary view, which stresses the creative individuality of an unknown author, the P Code is described as a product of historical and legal (cultic) erudition, as evidenced by its concern for genealogies, tables of nations, dates and measurements, cultic ordinances, and literary formulae (e. g., Gen. 2:4*a;* 5:1; 6:9; 10:1; 11:10, 27; 25:12, 19; 36:1; 37:2), and in its repetitious and judiciously exact diction (e. g., Gen. 1:11–12; Ex. 7:9–10; 8:1–2, 12–13, etc.). In content, the P Code sketches the origins of the people of God, their sacred institutions and cultic laws from the creation of the world (Gen. 1:1–2:4*a*) to the settlement of the promised land, a history divided into four great periods marked by the revelation of divine law first to Adam, then to Noah, to Abraham, and finally, to Moses. One representative of the traditional view has thus called the P Code "the charter of Judaism" or "the constitution of a theocratic state" (R. Pfeiffer).

In recent decades, however, the precise nature, date, and content of P, and the age and origin of the traditions it contains, have been heatedly debated. A modification of the documentary hypothesis is found in the work of Martin Noth whose traditio-historical criticism, though affirming a final literary stage in the Exilic period (586–539 B.C.), stresses the *preliterary* history of the traditions. Noth suggests that P is but one of three (not four) distinct literary strands in the Pentateuch (apart from Deuteronomy), that it is principally a *narrative* which forms the framework of the Pentateuch and into which (older?) *legal* material (e. g., Lev. 1–7) was subsequently added. The narrative emphasizes the establishment of the cult at Sinai (Ex. 25–31; 35–40; Lev. 8–9) and the formation of the twelve-tribe confederacy (Num. 1–9).

According to Noth, the content of P is (with minor omissions):

Gen. 1:1–2:4a; 5:1–28, 30–32; 6:9–22; 7:6, 11, 13–16a, 18–21, 24; 8:1–2a, 3b–5, 7, 13a, 14–19; 9:1–17, 28–29; 10:1–7, 20, 22–23 (24), 31–32; 11:10–27, 31–32; 12:4b–5; 13:6, 11b–12; 16:1a, 3, 15–16; 17:1–27; 19:29; 21:1b–5; 23:1–20; 25:7–11a, 12–17, 19–20, 26b; 26:34–35; 27:46; 28:9; 31:18; 33:18a; 35:6, 9–13, 15, 22b–29; 36:1–14; 37:1–2; 41:46a; 46:6–27; 47:27–28; 48:3–6; 49:1a, 29–33; 50:12–13.

Ex. 1:1–7, 13–14; 2:23–25; 6:2–7:13, 19, 20a, 21b, 22; 8:5–7 (16, 19); 9:8–12; 11:9–10; 12:1–20, 28, 40–51; 14:1–4, 8–10*, 15–18, 21–23, 26, 28–29; 15:22a, 27; 16:1–3, 6–27, 32–35a; 17:1; 19:1–2a; 24:15b; 25:9–31:18; 35:1–40:38.

Lev. (chs. 1–7 are additions to P) 8:1–10:20 (chs. 11–15 are additions); 16:1–34 (chs. 17–27 are additions).

Num. 1:1–4:49 (chs. 5–6 are additions); 7:1–89 (8:1–4* is an "isolated piece"); 8:5–10:28; 13:1–17a, 21, 25–26, 32–33; 14:1a, 2–3, 5–10, 26–38; 16:1a, 2–11, 16–24, 27a, 35–50; 17:1–18:32 (ch. 19 is an addition); 20:1–13, 22b–29; 22:1 (25:6–18* may be an addition to the completed Pentateuch; 26:1–27:11, an addition to P); 27:12–23 (chs. 28–36, except 32:1, 16, 39–42 [J] are additions to P).

Dt. (other scholars add: 32:48–52) 34:1a (5b), 7–9.

See: Martin Noth, *A History of Pentateuchal Traditions* (Englewood Cliffs, N.J.: Prentice-Hall, 1972); this volume contains a helpful "Analytical Outline of the Pentateuch" by the translator, B. W. Anderson.

Asterisk (*) marks major passages which, according to B. W. Anderson, are disputed by other scholars.

Paleography is the study of ancient writing, its history and development, as a means of deciphering and dating ancient texts; used in textual criticism to date Biblical MSS and to determine their place of origin.

Palestinian Talmud. See: **Talmud.**

Palimpsest. In Greek P. literally means "rubbed (smooth) again" and denotes a MS of parchment from which the original text has been erased and a second text placed on top of it. The earlier and sometimes more significant text is recoverable by various means, particularly infrared or ultraviolet photography. Codex Ephraemi Rescriptus (C) is a palimpsest with parts of the OT and NT dating from the 5th cent.; the upper writing is a 12th cent. Greek translation of the homilies of Ephraem Syrus (a Syrian Church Father who died in A.D. 373). There are over 50 P. MSS of the NT earlier than the 11th cent.

Papyrus (Latin: *Cyperus papyrus*) is a perennial plant of the Nile Delta whose long triangular stems (known in Greek as *papyros* and *byblos*) were cut into thin strips and glued together to form sheets for writing. Papyrus, known also as the paper-reed or paper-rush, was widely employed for writing throughout the Mediterranean from the 4th cent. B.C. to the 7th cent. A.D.

Papyrus Manuscripts. The P. MSS of the NT are its earliest extant witnesses and are therefore of great significance for the early history and restoration of the original text. Discovered primarily in the 20th cent. in Egypt, they now number 81, each bearing the *siglum* P plus a numerical identification. The oldest fragment (P^{52}), found in a mummy cartonage, contains a small portion of Jn. 18 and is dated *ca.* 125. Several P. MSS come from *ca.* 200: P^{32} (fragment of Titus), $P^{64/67}$ (fragment of Mt. 3; 5; and 26), P^{46} (sections of Rom. 5ff.; Heb., 1 and 2 Cor., Eph., Gal., Phil., Col., and 1 Thess.—all with lacunae), and P^{66} (*ca.* 2/3 of John). P^{75}, also *ca.* 200 now in the Bodmer Library (Geneva), contains most of Lk. and more than half of Jn. P^{45}, P^{46}, and P^{47} constitute the so-called Chester Beatty Papyri, purchased by Beatty in Egypt in the 1930s. Together they contain fragments of all the books of the NT. Of more recent discovery are the Martin Bodmer papyri (P^{66}, P^{72}, P^{74}, P^{75}—above), which have been published since 1954. There are also P. MSS of the OT and of many "literary" works from antiquity (of which Homer is the most frequently attested). See: **Minuscule; Textual Criticism; Uncial.**

Par.(s). In NT criticism, par. is an abbrev. meaning "and its parallel" and refers to a passage of Scripture to be found in two or more of the synoptic Gospels; in general usage, however, par(s). (*or* para.) is the abbreviation for paragraph(s).

Parable; Parabolic Sayings (Greek: *parabolē*). Broadly speaking, parabolic sayings constitute a type of figurative speech involving a comparison which is distinguishable from the simple metaphor on the one hand and allegory on the other, yet which contains, or may contain, elements of both, particularly the "shock" quality of the metaphor and, occasionally, several points of comparison (see: *Tertium comparationis*) as in the allegory. The parabolic sayings of Jesus (our focus here) are usually categorized as the "similitude" (an "extended metaphor" or "metaphor extended into a picture"), the "parable proper" (a metaphor extended into a story—so C. H. Dodd), and the "example story," which are often omitted from discussions of Ps though sometimes called a P. in Scripture, e. g., "The rich fool" (Lk. 12:16–20). The images employed are drawn from nature and everyday life. Some scholars suggest that the similitude relates typical, recurrent events, the parable proper particular and therefore non-recurring ones (so Jülicher, Via); however, no general agreement exists.

The use of the term *parabolē* in the Septuagint and in the Greek NT offers no help in definition; it is used to translate the Hebrew word *mashal* (q.v.) which, being a very broad term refers to a variety of linguistic forms, such as: taunt (Isa. 14:4), riddle (Ps. 49:4), allegory (Ezek. 17:2–3), byword (Deut. 28:37), dirge (Micah 2:4), proverb (Lk. 4:23), etc. Until the late 18th cent., the Ps of Jesus were universally treated as allegories, following Mk. 4:10–12, 13–20 pars. The scientific basis of all modern criticism was laid by Adolf Jülicher (*Die Gleichnisreden Jesu,* 1888, 1899), whose study brought an end to allegorical interpretation.

Because the Ps are thought to provide the best access to the historical Jesus, the study of their interpretation since Jülicher is highly illuminative of the changing perspectives and methodologies of NT criticism. The Ps have been interpreted as (a) vehicles of moral teaching, (b) weapons of self-defense, (c) calls to decision, (d) witnesses to Jesus' faith, (e) gifts of time, (f) invitations to a new reality, etc. See esp. C. H. Dodd, *The Parables of the Kingdom* (1935; London: Nisbet, 1955; rev. ed., New York: Charles Scribner's Sons, 1961); Joachim Jeremias, *The Parables of Jesus* (Scribner, 1970[8]; London: SCM Press, 1972); Dan O. Via, Jr., *The Parables: Their Literary and Existential Dimension* (Philadelphia: Fortress Press, 1967); and, John D. Crossan, *In Parables: The Challenge of the Historical Jesus* (New York: Harper and Row, 1973). For a structuralist approach see *Sēmeia* I (1974), ed. Robert W. Funk (Missoula, Mont.: The Scholar's Press).

The following is Jülicher's listing of parabolic sayings. Most of Jülicher's *Gleichnisse* are now considered simple metaphors or similes. Jülicher's terminology is in parenthesis.

137

A. Similitudes and Similes *(Gleichnisse)*

[1. Concerning Salt	Mt. 5:13;	Mk. 9:49–50;	Lk. 14:34–35
**[2. Concerning Light(s)	Mt. 5:14, 16;	Mk. 4:21;	Lk. 8:16; 11:33
[3. The Eye as the Light of Life			
	Mt. 6:22–23;		Lk. 11:34–36
4. Concerning the Fig Tree	Mt. 24:32–33;	Mk. 13:28–29;	Lk. 21:29–31
5. The Servant's Wages			Lk. 17:7–10
6. The Playing Children	Mt. 11:16–19;		Lk. 7:31–35
[7. The Petitioning Son	Mt. 7:9–11;		Lk. 11:11–13
[8. The Pupil and His Teacher	Mt. 10:24–25;		Lk. 6:40
[9. The Blind Leading the Blind			
	Mt. 15:14;		Lk. 6:39
[10. On What Defiles a Man	Mt. 15:10–20;	Mk. 7:14–23	
[11. On Revealing What Is Hidden	Mt. 10:26–27;	Mk. 4:22;	Lk. 8:17; 12:2–23
[12. Concerning Two Masters	Mt. 6:24;		Lk. 16:13
[13. The Tree and Its Fruit	Mt. 7:16–20; 12:33–37;		Lk. 6:43–45
[14. The Householder	Mt. 13:51–52		
[15. The Eagles	Mt. 24:28;		Lk. 17:37
*16. The Watchful Householder	Mt. 24:43–44;		Lk. 12:39–40
17. The Faithful and Wise Servant	Mt. 24:45–51;		Lk. 12:41–48
18. The Coming of the Householder		Mk. 13:33–37;	Lk. 12:35–38
[19. On Healing Oneself			Lk. 4:23
[20. The Physician and the Sick	Mt. 9:12–13;	Mk. 2:17;	Lk. 5:31–32
[21. The Bridegroom	Mt. 9:14–15;	Mk. 2:18–20;	Lk. 5:33–35
[22. Old Cloth and Old Wine Skins	Mt. 9:16–17;	Mk. 2:21–22;	Lk. 5:36–39
23. On Building Towers and Going to War			Lk. 14:28–33
[24. On Beelzebul	Mt. 12:22–30, 43–45	Mk. 3:22–27;	Lk. 11:14–26
25. On the Way to the Judge	Mt. 5:25–26;		Lk. 12:57–59
26. Places at the Feast			Lk. 14:7–11, 12–14
[27. On Crumbs under the Table			
	Mt. 15:26–27;	Mk. 7:27–28	

Key: [Metaphor or Simile omitted by Jeremias from the category "Parable."
(Added by Jeremias
** Treated as two separate *Gleichnisse* by Jülicher.
* Parallels in the Gospel of Thomas: #16: 85:7–10; 98:6–10. #33: 98:22–27. #36: 93:1–18. #37: 92:10–35. #43: 83:3–13. #44: 85:15–19. #46: 81:28–82:3. #47: 84:26–33; 97:2–6. #48: 98: 31–99:3; 94:14–18. #52: 92:3–10.

B. Parables Proper *(Parabeln)*

	Mt.	Mk.	Lk.
28. A House Built on Sand	Mt. 7:24–27;		Lk. 6:47–49
29. The Importunate Friend			Lk. 11:5–8
30. The Unjust Judge			Lk. 18:1–8
31. The Two Debtors			Lk. 7:36–50
32. The Unmerciful Servant	Mt. 18:21–35		
*33. The Lost Sheep and Lost Coin	Mt. 18:10–14;		Lk. 15:1–10
34. The Lost Son			Lk. 15:11–32
35. The Two Sons	Mt. 21:28–32		(Lk. 7:29–30)
*36. The Wicked Tenants	Mt. 21:33–46;	Mk. 12:1–12;	Lk. 20:9–19
*37. The Great Supper (2)	Mt. 22:1–10 (11–14);		Lk. 14:15–24
38. The Unfruitful Fig Tree			Lk. 13:6–9
39. The Ten Virgins	Mt. 25:1–13		(Lk. 13:23–30)
40. The Laborers in the Field	Mt. 20:1–16		
41. The Pounds	Mt. 25:14–30;		Lk. 19:11–27
42. The Unjust Steward			Lk. 16:1–12
*43. The Sower	Mt. 13:3–9, 18–23;	Mk. 4:3–9, 14–20;	Lk. 8:5–8, 11–15
*44. The Seed Growing Secretly		Mk. 4:26–29	
45. The Wheat and the Tares	Mt. 13:24–30, 36–43		
*46. The Dragnet	Mt. 13:47–50		
*47. The Mustard Seed and the Leaven	Mt. 13:31–33;	Mk. 4:30–32;	Lk. 13:18–21
*48. The Treasure and the Pearl	Mt. 13:44–46		
(49. The Last Judgment	Mt. 25:31–46		

C. Example Stories *(Beispielerzählungen)*

	Lk.
50. The Good Samaritan	Lk. 10:29–37
51. The Pharisee and the Publican	Lk. 18:9–14
*52. The Rich Fool	Lk. 12:16–21
53. The Rich Man and Lazarus	Lk. 16:19–31

See: **Allegory;** *Bildhälfte;* **Dodd; Eschatology; Jülicher; Metaphor;** *Tertium comparationis.*

Paradigm (adj.: paradigmatics; Greek: pattern, model, example). Of increasing parlance, the word P. (pronounced paradime) commonly means "model," as in "a P. of literary craftsmanship" *(JBL).* The student of language finds it used as an example of a conjugation or a declension demonstrating a word in its various inflected forms.

As a t.t. used by Martin Dibelius in his form-critical study, *From Tradition to Gospel* (Ger.: 1919; Eng.: London: Ivor Nicholson and Watson, Ltd., 1934; repr. James Clarke, 1971; New York: Charles Scribner's Sons, 1935). P. is defined as "a short illustrative notice or story of an event, not more descriptive than is necessary to make the point for the sake of which it is introduced" (p. xii). According to Dibelius, the "setting-in-life" of the P. was the sermon. Ps were the early Christian preacher's "material" by which he illustrated a point, often a saying of Jesus with which the P. is concluded. Dibelius discovered, in all, eighteen Ps, including eight of "noteworthy purity" in Mk.: "The Healing of the Paralytic" (2:1ff.); "The Question of Fasting" (2:18–19); "Plucking Wheat on the Sabbath" (2:23ff.); "The Healing of the Withered Hand" (3:1ff); "The Relatives of Jesus" (3:31–35); "Blessing the Children" (10:13–16); "The Tribute Money" (12:13–17); and "The Anointing in Bethany" (14:3–7).

See: **Apophthegm; Form Criticism; Pronouncement Story.**

Paradosis (Greek: that which is handed down or delivered) is usually translated "tradition" (so e. g., Mk. 7:5, 8, 9, 13; Mt. 15:2, 3, 6; Col. 2:8, etc.). In English the verbal forms of P. are rendered by "deliver" (RSV), "passed on" (Phillips), "handed on" (NEB), etc., translations which have the disadvantage of losing the connotations surrounding the more technical term "tradition." See: **Oral Tradition; Double Tradition; Triple Tradition.**

Paradox (fr. Greek: beyond or contrary to expectation; unbelievable). An apparent contradiction; that is, a statement which though to common opinion is false may be profoundly true. In Christian theology, and in Pauline thought particularly, the crucifixion of the Christ is the foundational paradox (1 Cor. 1:22–25); it is presented as the resolution of prior paradoxes pertaining to the nature of God, viz., that God is both just and merciful, that although he makes absolute moral demands upon humankind (Ex. 20; Mt. 5:20–48), his forgiving love is also infiinte (Hosea; Lk. 15) as seen particularly in Christ (Jn. 3:16). Jesus' teachings are filled with paradoxes (Mk. 8:35; Lk. 18:14; Mt. 5:3–5, etc.). Paul often cites paradoxes (e. g., 1 Cor. 7:22; 2 Cor. 4:8–11; 5:17; 12:10b; Phil. 3:7); cf. the paradoxical antitheses of 2 Cor. 6:9–10 with Epictetus II 19, 24–26: "Show me a man who though rich is happy, though in danger is happy, though dying is happy, though condemned to exile is happy, though in disrepute is happy. Show him! By the gods, I fain would see a stoic . . . which to this very day I have never seen." See: **Irony.**

Paraenesis (also parenesis; Greek: exhortation, advice, counsel) is a t.t. in Form Criticism, principally introduced by Martin Dibelius in his studies of the epistle of James, to denote a text containing a series of admonitions, usually ethical and eclectic in nature and without any reference to concrete situations. The paraenetic passages of the NT outside Jas. are varied: In 1 and 2 Thess.; Gal. 5–6; Rom. 12–13; Col. 3–4; and Eph. 4–6, P. follows a theological discussion; Paul admonishes the believers to become what the faith declares him to be already in Christ (cf. Rom. 6:1–14; 8:12–13; 1 Cor. 5:7–8; 6:9–12,

15–20, etc.); in 1 and 2 Cor. and Phil., the P. contains concrete pastoral advice for specific situations.

The epistle to the Hebrews which moves back and forth between theological reasoning and P., is by its own author called a "word of exhortation" (RSV), i. e., its main purpose is paraenetic. In 1 Peter, P. finds its setting in a baptismal homily (cf. also 1 Cor. 5:9; Eph. 2:1–10; 5:1–21; Col. 3); in 1 Jn., Jude, and 2 Peter in the dangers of heresy; in the Pastoral Epistles in the responsibilities of the various church orders. For a hypothesis concerning the role of P. in the formation of the gospel tradition, see Dibelius, *From Tradition to Gospel* (London: Ivor Nicholson and Watson, Ltd., 1934; repr. James Clarke, 1971; New York: Charles Scribner's Sons, 1935), chap. IX.

The place of paraenesis, in the sense of homiletic exhortation, is also important in OT studies, particularly in regard to that tradition surrounding or otherwise related to the covenant renewal festivals in Jerusalem. Gerhard von Rad interprets Deuteronomy, for example, as basically a collection of sermons ostensibly in the form of a single sermon by Moses but in fact attributable to Levitical circles active prior to the Exile. P., as a "summons to obedience" reaches its high point in the commandment to love Yahweh "with the whole heart and with the whole soul and with all one's might" (Deut. 6:4–5; cf. 10:12; 11:13; 13:4, etc.). P. is also found in the prose sections of Jeremiah; whether patterned after or serving as a pattern for the Deuteronomic paraenetic style is a matter of debate. Elsewhere, cf. also Prov. 8:1–21, 32–36, etc.

Paralipomenon (pl.: -mena; Greek: thing[s] left out). The Septuagint and Latin Vulgate name for the two books of the OT otherwise known in English as 1 and 2 Chronicles; the term, which implies that the works are supplementary to 1 Samuel–2 Kings, is still used by the Roman Catholics and Eastern Orthodox churches.

Parallel, A. See: **Synopsis.**

Parallelism *(parallelismus membrorum)* is a word used to designate a formal characteristic of Hebrew poetry, though it is found somewhat in Greek, particularly Greek influenced by Semitic idiom as in the NT. P. (or *parallelismus membrorum,* the Latin technical term first employed by Robert Lowth [1753] meaning "parallelism of members") takes three major forms: synonymous, antithetic, and synthetic.

1. Synonymous P. describes a couplet or distich (two stichs or half-lines of a poem and occasionally three lines or tristich) in which the idea expressed in the first line is repeated in the second (or third) with equivalent but different words. Ps. 114 contains this form throughout; note e. g., the two distichs of vss. 3–4:

141

> The sea looked and fled,
>   Jordan turned back.
> The mountains skipped like rams,
>   the hills like lambs.

According to C. F. Burney (*The Poetry of Our Lord* [Oxford: Clarendon Press, 1925], p. 17), SP is most perfectly exemplified in those instances in which the subject, verb, and object of the first line are paralleled in the second; e. g., Ps. 19:1:

> The heavens are telling the glory of God;
>   and the firmament proclaims his handiwork.

In Hebrew the parallel members are expressed: a.b.c.d.: a'.b'.c'.d'; in English the line reads: a'.b'.d'.c'. So also: Ps. 94:9, 16; 101:7; Num. 23:7–10. SP appears in prophetic literature: Amos 5:21–24; Isa. 40:29–31; 55:6–7, passim. It should be noted that P. of this type can vary greatly in degree of completeness.

It is a curiosity of Mt.'s description of Jesus' entry into Jerusalem that he fails to recognize the SP of the OT passage he is quoting: Zech. 9:9; see Mt. 21:4–7. For SP in Jn. see 2:11; 4:36; 6:35; 55; 7:34; 13:16.

2. Antithetic P. describes a P. of thought in which the second line is posed as a contrast to the first. For example: Ps. 1:6; 10:16; 11:5; 20:8, etc. The form is especially frequent in Wisdom literature:

Prov. 10:12: Hatred stirs up strife, but love covers all offenses.

Prov. 10:20: The tongue of the righteous is choice silver; the mind of the wicked is of little worth.

Cf. 1 Cor. 7:29b–31, 32–34; 9:19–22; 10:6–10; 12:15–26, etc.; also Jn. 3:18; 8:35; 9:39.

3. In Synthetic P. (also called formal, numerical, or constructive P.) the P. involved is not of thought but of form and is in part discernible by identity of rhythm marked off by a clear break between distichs; in its thought, however, the second line is seen to supplement or complete that of the first (Burney, p. 21). E. g., Ps. 3:2, 4 (in Hebrew, 3:3, 5); 14:1–2; 40:1–3 (in Hebrew, 40:2–4); Prov. 6:16–19, etc. In NT, Jn. 8:44.

Step P. is a type of synthetic P., usually of three or more stichs, in which the thought of the unit is advanced with each line. Since one or more members of the initial line is often repeated, step P. bears a resemblance to synonymous P. as well, e. g., Ps. 29:1–2; 3:1–2. In NT, Jn. 1:1–5, 10–12, 14; 6:37; 8:32; 13:20; 14:21.

A P. which exists within a distich or tristich (2 or 3 lines) is sometimes called internal P.; a P. which exists between two or more di- or tri-stichs is called external P.

See: *Chiasmus;* Colon.

Paraphrase. Commonly, a P. is a free rendering of the sense of a difficult passage or text into another form in the same language.

Within the context of Bible translation, P. generally refers to a style of translation in which clarity is given precedence over fidelity to the original phrasing and vocabulary. The word P., its meaning and proper use, however, is a frequent subject of debate. Some argue that all translation is P.; others, that a P. is an interpretive translation while *metaphrase* is a slavishly literal translation—good, faithful translation being somewhere in between. J. B. Phillips *(The New Testament in Modern English)* admits to an occasional P. "because a literal translation of the original Greek would prove unintelligible" ("Translator's Foreword"), but his translation is nevertheless usually termed a paraphrase.

The Living Bible, Paraphrased defines P. "as a careful restatement of the author's thoughts," which "does not attempt to translate word by word, but rather thought by thought." The *LB(P)* calls itself an "interpretive translation"—a description which Phillips explicitly rejects for the *NTME*.

Cf. Jn. 1:1*a* in RSV: "In the beginning was the Word"; Phillips: "At the beginning God expressed himself"; *LB(P):* "Before anything else existed, there was Christ."

See: *LB(P);* **Version; Exegesis.**

Parataxis (Greek: to place beside). In grammar generally P. refers to the coordination of clauses without indicating their syntactic relation; in NT study it more often refers to the simple coordination of words, clauses, sentences, or paragraphs with "and" *(kai)*. P. is especially characteristic of Semitic style and, in the NT, is the most distinguishing characteristic of Mark, of whose 88 sections (as found in the Westcott-Hort Greek text) 80 begin with "and" (Hawkins, p. 151). Asyndetic P. refers to the conjoining of parallel syntactic elements (whether words, phrases, or sentences) without a connective (such as and, but, or therefore). The opening verse of Ps. 23 is an example of asyndetic P. and can be properly translated "Since the Lord is my shepherd, I shall not be in need" (Eugene Nida, *Toward a Science in Translating* [Leiden: E. J. Brill, 1964], p. 210). See: **Hypotaxis; Prostaxis.**

Parchment. See: **Vellum.**

Parole. See: **Structuralism.**

Paronomasia broadly defined is a play on words, a pun; in a more technical sense it is "the recurrence of the same word or word stem in close proximity" (BDF, p. 258). P., whether appearing in the Hebrew OT or the Greek NT, is usually lost in translation, as e. g., in the NT: Mt. 21:41; 2 Cor. 4:8 (NEB:

143

"Hard-pressed on every side, we are never hemmed in"); Phil. 3:2–3 (see KJV and the circumlocution of NEB). Other NT *P.* include Mk. 5:26; Rom. 1:23, 25, 27, 28; 5:16, 19; 12:3, 15; 13:7; 14:22–23; 1 Cor. 8:2–3; 9:19–22; 11:31–32; 13:6; 15:50; 2 Cor. 3:2; 7:5; 9:8; 8:22; Acts 21:28; 23:3, etc. In Hebrew *P.* is natural and ubiquitous. For example, Gen. 1:2 describes the earth as *"thohu wavohu";* here by onomatopoeia the sense of chaos is conveyed; in Gen. 2:7, Adam is made of Adamah (ground), an etiological pun; Gen. 4:1; 19:30–21:24; Job 3:25, etc., are etymological puns (or *figura etymologica*), in which substantives are derived from verbs.

Related to P. is *antistasis:* the use of a word twice in close proximity with a sharp shift in meaning, e. g., Mt. 10:39: "He who finds his life will lose it, and he who loses his life for my sake will find it." Cf. 1 Cor. 1:21; 2:16, etc. Similarly: *antanaclasis,* in which the shift in sense is not so sharp, e. g., Mt. 8:22; 13:9 (KJV); Lk. 10:16; 13:30, etc. Though neither term is current, the phenomena they describe are worth noting.

Parousia (Greek: presence). In primitive Christianity, P. referred to the "second coming" of Christ at the end of time (see the prayers in 1 Cor. 16:22 *b* and Rev. 22:20; cf. 22:7, 12). The expectation of Jesus' return, coupled with his non-appearance (called "the delay of the P."), had a profound effect upon the life and thought of the NT church (see e. g., 2 Pet. 3:3–13; 2 Thess. 2:1–12; Lk. 21:7–9; Mk. 13; Mt. 24), the nature and extent of which is a subject of Biblical criticism and theology. See: **Apocalyptic; Eschatologize; Eschatology.**

Partitio. See: **Rhetorical Analysis.**

Pasce oves pericope (Latin: Feed [my] lambs; pericope: Greek: passage). See: Jn. 21:15–17.

Pastoral Epistles consist of 1 and 2 Timothy and Titus in the NT; the title is derived from the "pastoral" advice which the author is writing to the recipients. The epistles are thought by many to be pseudonymous (or eponymous) though perhaps containing fragments of authentically Pauline letters. See: **Catholic Epistles; Deutero-Pauline.**

Pedersen, Johannes Peder Ejler (1883–   ). Born in Illebolle, Denmark, P. was lecturer in OT Exegesis at the University of Copenhagen (1916–22) and later Professor of Semitic Philology (1922–50). His major work (*Israel: Its Life and Culture,* vols. I–IV [Eng.: 1926–40]) greatly influenced subsequent OT research, particularly in Scandinavia, for its descriptive rather than historical approach to Israelite religion and for its emphasis on the role of the cult and primitive psychology in the formation of OT traditions. See: *Kultgeschichtliche Schule.*

(6) Post-Reformation (17-18th cen.) .... Confessional

(7) Modern (19-20th cen.) .... Critical/Existential

3. Two causes for non-natural interpretation:

a. Growth of religious rites and practices. The Scriptures are forced to support these: Pharisees, Talmud, Papacy.

b. Adoption of pagan philosophical systems: Philo, Aristotle/Plato, Papacy, Bultmann, Fundamental Evangelicalism(?).

PERIOD 1: RABBINIC INTERPRETATION

RABBINIC	HELLENISTIC	QUMRAN
Palestine	Alexandria, Egypt	N.W. Dead Sea
Practical and Pastoral, overliteral exegesis, Tradition	Allegorical & Mystical, Attempted to combine Platonic Philosophy with Biblical interpretation	Monastic, Messianic, and eschatological: Pesher-- manipulating or applying texts to contemporary situations
Midrash & Talmud	LXX = Septuagint	Dead Sea Scrolls
Hillel (and other Pharisees)	Philo	Essenes
Hedge about the Law (Oral Law). Concentration on words and phrases to the neglect of context	Allegory: Subjective, arbitrary & artificial	Bibliolatry. Atomistic and relativistic interpretation through Pesher

I. Jewish Interpretation

A. The Bible was seen as part of Jewish Nationality.

Pentateuch is a name derived from Greek for the first five books of the OT commonly known in Hebrew as the *Humash* ("the five fifths"); it is the first of three divisions of the Jewish Scriptures and is also called the Law or the Torah. See: **Prophets**; *Tanak; Torah; Hagiographa;* **E: Elohist; J (Yahwist); P: Priestly Code; D: Deuteronomic Code; Graf-Wellhausen Hypothesis.**

Pericope (Greek: lit., "cut around") appears as a t.t. in Hellenistic rhetoric (3rd cent. A.D.) for a short section or passage of a writing and is carried over into Latin by Jerome to designate portions of Scripture; use of the term in this way preceded the division of Scripture into chapters (the Pentateuch first being divided into 175 pericopes) and subsequent to that, the P. came to be used as a "lesson" for reading in public worship and later as the unit for preaching. In Biblical criticism, the term is often used to refer to any self-contained unit of Scripture.

Pericope de adultera refers to Jn. 7:53–8:11, the account of the woman caught in adultery, which is absent from all MSS of Jn.'s Gospel prior to *ca.* A.D. 350. See: **Deuterocanon; Pericope; Textual Criticism.**

Peripeteia (also peripetia, peripety) is a Greek technical term used in literary criticism to denote a sudden or unexpected turn of events or reversal of circumstances in a literary work; as in 2 Sam. 12:1–15; Lk. 12:13–21; Mk. 8:27–33, etc.

Peroratio. See: **Rhetorical Analysis.**

Pesher (pl.: *pesherim;* Heb.: interpretation, commentary). A t.t. from Hebrew meaning commentary and applied as a descriptive designation to certain documents among the Dead Sea Scrolls: the *pesherim* on Habakkuk (1QpH), Nahum (4QpNah), Isaiah (1QpIsa), etc. The P. of the DSS are haggadic midrash, that is, Scriptural commentary of a non-legal nature; they are, however, commentaries of a special character in that they view the prophetic books of the OT as containing divine mysteries which pertain to the last days in which the Qumran sectarians believed themselves to be living and which therefore call for divinely illuminated interpretation. The Aramaic equivalent, *peshar,* is used 31 times in the Aramaic portions of the book of Daniel, the great apocalyptic interpretation of history of the 2nd cent. B.C. See: **Dead Sea Scrolls;** *Halakah;* **Midrash.**

Peshitta (syp; also Peshitto: "simple"). The authorized Bible of the Syrian Church, dating from the latter 4th or early 5th cent. and traditionally ascribed to Rabbula, Bishop of Edessa (d. 435). Omitted from early MSS of the P. are

145

2 Peter, 2 and 3 John, Jude, and Revelation, which the Syrian Church did not accept as canonical.

Philo of Alexandria (*ca.* 20 B.C.–A.D. 45). A Hellenistic-Jewish philosopher of religion of the first century, who lived in Alexandria, Egypt, the member of a wealthy and influential family and, significantly, a contemporary of Jesus (d. *ca.* A.D. 30) and Paul (d. *ca.* A.D. 65). Called a "man of two worlds," the Jewish world of the (Greek) OT and the Hellenistic world of philosophy, P. devoted his life to the adaptation of the former to the latter. By way of allegorical exegesis, P. interpreted the Pentateuch in terms indigenous to Platonic and Stoic philosophy. In the NT, the Gospel of John (esp. Jn. 1.1–18) shows greatest affinity to his thought. P.'s writings, in some instances preserved only in translation and fragmentarily, and usually cited according to their Latin name, here provided with the English translation of *The Loeb Classical Library* (Cambridge, MA: Harvard University Press; London: William Heinemann, Ltd.; *Philo,* Vols. I-X [with two Supplementary Volumes], 1929, 1962⁴):

1. *Apologia pro Iudaeis (Hypothetica)*
2. *De Abrahamo (On Abraham)*
3. *De Aeternitate Mundi (On the Eternity of the World)*
4. *De Agricultura (On Husbandry)*
5. *De Cherubim (On the Cherubim)*
6. De Confusione Linguarum (On the Confusion of Tongues)
7. *De Congressu quaerendae Eruditionis gratia (On the Preliminary Studies)*
8. *De Decalogo (On the Decalogue)*
9. *De Ebrietate (On Drunkenness)*
10. *De Fuga et Inventione (On Flight and Finding)*
11. *De Iosepho (On Joseph)*
12. *De Legatione ad Gaium (On the Embassy to Gaius)*
13. *De Migratione Abrahami (On the Migration of Abraham)*
14. *De Mutatione Nominum (On the Change of Names)*
15. *De Opificio Mundi (On the Creation)*
16. *De Plantatione (On Noah's Work as a Planter)*
17. *De Posteritate Caini (On the Posterity and Exile of Cain)*
18. *De Praemiis et Poenis (On Rewards and Punishments)*
19. *De Providentia (On Providence)*
20. *De Sacrificiis Abelis et Caini (On the Sacrifices of Abel and Cain)*
21. *De Sobrietate (On Sobriety)*
22. *De Somniis (On Dreams)*
23. *De Specialibus Legibus (On the Special Laws)*
24. *De Virtutibus (On the Virtues)*
25. *De Vita Contemplativa (On the Contemplative Life)*

26. *De Vita Mosis (Moses)*
27. *In Flaccum (Flaccus)*
28. *Legum Allegoriae (Allegorical Interpretation)*
29. *Questiones et Solutiones in Genesiu (Questions and Answers on Genesis)*
30. *Questiones et Solutiones in Exodum (Questions and Answers on Exodus)*
31. *Quis Rerum Divinarum Heres (Who Is the Heir)*
32. *Quod Deterius Potiori insidiari solet (The Worse Attacks the Better)*
33. *Quod Deus immutabilis sit (On the Unchangeableness of God)*
34. *Quod Omnis Probus Liber sit (Every Good Man Is Free)*

See: Samuel Sandmel, *Philo of Alexandria: An Introduction* New York: Oxford University Press, 1979);*also Studia Philonica* (published by the Philo Institute, Chicago) dealing with "Hellenistic Judaism in general and with the works of Philo Judaeus in particular."

Phoneme (Greek: sound). In linguistics a P. is "the maximum feature of the expression system of a spoken language . . ." According to H. A. Gleason there are forty-six phonemes in the English language: 24 consonants, 9 vowels, 3 semivowels (including two consonants), 1 open transition, 4 stresses, 4 pitches, and 3 clause terminals—each of which is an indispensable part of the English system of verbal communication. See: H. A. Gleason, *An Introduction to Descriptive Linguistics* (New York and London: Holt, Rinehart and Winston, 1961²). See: **Morpheme; Structuralism.**

Pleonasm (Latin: more than enough) is a technical term denoting a real or apparent redundancy of expression. The repetition of an idea by way of synonyms, particularly in poetry, is characteristic of Hebrew not duplicated in precise manner or extent in Greek. Consult a synopsis of the Gospels and note the following pleonasms in Mk. which (assuming the priority of Mk.) are eliminated in the Matthaean parallel: Mk. 2:25; 3:26; 4:2; 7:15, 21; 9:2; 14:1, 61; 15:26. Some pleonastic formulations may be for precision, see Mk. 1:28, 32, 35, 38, passim. See: **Synopsis.**

Pneumatophany. See: **Epiphany.**

Poimandrès. See: **Hermetic Literature.**

Polyglot is a Greek word meaning "many tongues" or "languages." As a noun it is used most frequently in reference to a Bible with the text in several languages placed in parallel columns.

Pre-Pauline. The term is perhaps self-explanatory, except that it is frequently misunderstood by the tyro in NT criticism, for in normal use it refers to doctrines, formulas, ideas, etc., which were in existence within the Church

147

prior to Paul's *use* of them, rather than being prior to Paul himself or to his conversion. See: **Deutero-Pauline; Tradition Criticism.**

Primitive Christianity. See: **Early Church, The.**

Probatio. See: **Rhetorical Analysis.**

Prolepsis (adj.: proleptic; Greek: a taking beforehand; anticipation; preconception). In literary criticism, P. is a t.t. for that type of prophetic speech which treats as past that which in fact is only a future possibility. For example, in Amos 5:1–3 the prophet laments the fall of Israel as an accomplished fact though it is yet to occur and in Mt. 23:38 Jesus laments the fall of Jerusalem which does not take place until 40 years after his crucifixion. However, the latter may be a *vaticinium ex eventu* (q. v.) placed on the lips of Jesus by the Gospel writer.

Pronouncement Story is the name given by English scholar Vincent Taylor (*The Formation of the Gospel Tradition* [London: Macmillan and Co., 1933]) to 35–40 brief narratives in the synoptic tradition which embody as their raison d'être a pronouncement-type saying of Jesus. An example of the PS "at its best" concerns tribute to Caesar (Mk. 12:13–17). Taylor's PS is essentially equivalent to what Dibelius termed "paradigms" and Bultmann "apophthegms." In English scholarship the term PS has perhaps gained the greater currency. In contrast to Dibelius, Taylor did not believe that these narratives were primarily the product of the early Church's need for sermonic illustration; in contrast to Bultmann, he did not believe the narrative settings of the pronouncement sayings were "ideal" or "fictitious" but, in large measure at least, historical. See: **Apophthegm; Form Criticism; Paradigm.**

Prooemium. See: **Rhetorical Analysis.**

Prophecy (Greek: *prophēteia*) is an utterance, whether originally oral or written, of a prophet (Greek: *prophētes,* lit.: "one who speaks for another"). In Biblical tradition, a prophet (Heb.: *nābî'*) was one who proclaimed the will or mind of God—whether to an individual (such as the king; see: 2 Sam. 12; 1 Kgs. 21:17–24) or to the nation, even if he spoke falsely (1 Kgs. 22:13–36; esp. vs. 23) or was in service to false gods (such as Baal; see 1 Kgs. 18:22). Since the prophet's interpretation of divine will often pertained to the future, the identification of P. with foretelling future events naturally followed. (1 Sam. 9:9 states that "he who is now called a prophet was formerly called a seer" [Heb.: *rô'eh*].) This aspect of P., however, is generally considered a secondary and later characteristic. In any case, it is certain that OT prophecy normally saw the future not as predetermined by divine foreordination but as a just

148

consequence of past and present actions on the part of the individual or of Israel as a whole.

The origins of P., its relation to divination and sorcery, its role in the cult, and the role of ecstasy in prophetic inspiration are to some extent uncertain due to the fragmentary and ambiguous evidence of Scripture itself. 1 Sam. 10:6 identifies prophecy with an ecstasy and frenzy which caused the spirit-possessed person to change "into another man." Ecstatic utterances by their very nature, being formless, are without rational content and therefore cannot be preserved in writing. OT prophecy in the classical sense (see below) is by contrast rational speech, poetic in form, and thus susceptible to repetition, reinterpretation, and reapplication. P. as rational speech also explains the rise of schools of prophets, with master-disciple relationships, which in turn accounts for the collection, redaction, and preservation of the great prophetic oracles and traditions. The period of prophecy appears to have run from the 11th to the 2nd cent. B.C. The classical period of P. occurred during the 8th to the 6th cent. B.C. and is represented predominantly by the OT books of Amos, Micah, Hosea, Isaiah, Jeremiah, and Ezekiel. The book of Daniel (ca. 165 B.C.), though numbered among the minor prophets, marks the ascendancy of a new world view and a new literary mode divergent from that of classical prophecy and known as **apocalyptic** (q. v.).

In OT Form Criticism, P. constitutes a separate category of literature distinct from narrative, law, psalms, and wisdom. P. is not a strictly formal category, however, since the *means* by which a prophet received a divine revelation (dreams, visions, ecstasies, or mystical experience) did not necessarily determine the *form* by which the prophecy itself was to be communicated. P. could take the form of symbolic names (e. g., Isa. 7:3), a play on words (apparent only in Hebrew; e. g., Amos 8:1–3; Jer. 1:11–12, etc.), a song (Isa. 5:1–7; 23:16), a symbolic act (Hosea 1; 3; Isa. 20:1–6; Jer. 32:6ff.), a funeral elegy (Isa. 14:4a–21; Amos 5:1–2; Ezek. 19, etc.), an allegory (Ezek. 16; 20; 23), a report, such as an account of a vision or dream (Amos 7:1–9; 8:1–3; Jer. 13:1–11, etc.), and so on.

Early form-critical studies, especially that of Hermann Gunkel (q. v.), concentrated on the analysis of prophetic sayings; later Form Criticism turned to the study of prophetic narratives. The latter have been divided into three major forms: (A) autobiography or "private oracle," such as (1) reports of visions (see above), of which a special type in terms of content is the prophet's call (Isa. 6; Jer. 1; Ezek. 1–2, etc.), and (2) accounts of symbolic acts (in addition to the above, see: Isa. 7:3; 8:1–4; Jer. 16:1–9, etc.); (B) biographies of the prophets (Jer. 26–28; 36–45, etc.); and, (C) legends about the prophets, e. g., Ahijah the Shilonite (1 Kgs. 11:29ff.), Samuel (1 Sam. 3:1–18, etc.), Elijah (1 Kgs. 17:1–16, 17–24, etc.), and Elisha (2 Kgs. 2:19–22, 23–24; 4:1–7, etc.).

Form critics have identified two major types of prophetic sayings (speeches or oracles): (a) the prophecy of judgment (or disaster) and (b) the prophecy of salvation. According to Claus Westermann, the former can be divided between the "Judgment-speech to the individual" (e. g., 1 Kgs. 21: 18–19; 2 Kgs. 1:3–4; Amos 7:14–17; Isa. 22:15–25; 37:22–29; Jer. 20:1–6; 22:10–12, 13–19, and passim) and the "Judgment-speech to the nation" (e. g., Amos 4:1–2; Hos. 2:5–7; Isa. 8:5–8; 9:7–11, 17–20; 22:8–14; 28:7–13; 29:13–14; 30:12–14, 15–17; Mic. 2:1–4; 3:1–2, 4, 9–12; Jer. 5:10–14, and passim). Westermann further suggests that such oracles have a set structure which includes (1) an introduction (e. g., "Hear," "Woe"), (2) an accusation (oppression, harlotry, etc.), (3) a development of the accusation, (4) a messenger formula, such as "Thus says the LORD" (e. g., Amos 1:3, 6, 9, 11, 13; called a *kôh'ā mar* formula); or "The word of the LORD came to me, saying . . ." (e. g., Jer. 1:4, 11, 13; 2:1, and passim); or simply, "Therefore" (Hosea 2:6; Isa. 8:7), (5) an announcement of God's intervention (e. g., "the days are coming upon you," Amos 4:2), and (6) the results of intervention (e. g., "Jerusalem shall become a heap of ruins," Mic. 3:12). The early form critic Hermann Gunkel considered (2) and (3), and (5) and (6) to be two originally separate and distinct prophetic types, the former called a "reproach" or "invective" (Ger.: *Scheltrede*), the latter called a "threat" (Ger.: *Drohrede*). Westermann's study now shows this not to be the case.

A variant or secondary form of the prophetic oracle of judgment is the Woe-oracle (Heb.: *hôy*), which has been identified by Westermann and others in Amos 5:18–20; 6:1–7; Isa. 5:8–23; 28:1–31:9; Hab. 2; Mic. 2:1–4, etc. (See: Claus Westermann, *Basic Forms of Prophetic Speech,* trans. Hugh Clayton White [Philadelphia: The Westminster Press, 1967].)

According to Klaus Koch, the prophecy of salvation bears a structure similar to that of the prophecy of judgment; it may be found in Jer. 28:2–4; 32:14–15, 36–41; 34:4–5; 35:18–19; 1 Kgs. 17:14; 2 Kgs. 3:16–19, etc. (See: Koch, *The Growth of the Biblical Tradition,* trans. S. M. Cupitt [New York: Charles Scribner's Sons, 1969; London: A. and C. Black, 1969].) In addition to the prophecy of salvation, Westermann further distinguishes between the oracle of salvation (e. g., Isa. 41:8–13, 14–16; 43:1–4, 5–7; 44:1–5) and the proclamation of salvation (e. g., Isa. 41:17–20; 42:14–17; 43:16–21; and 49: 7–12), the former dealing with the present, the latter with a distant future, the former connected with a priest in the setting of individual lament, the latter with a prophet and community lament.

Note: It has recently been suggested that the origin of apocalyptic eschatology is to be traced to the joining of the prophetic oracle of salvation (blessing) with the oracle of judgment (curse). This salvation-judgment oracle (e. g., Isa. 58:1–12), it is said, constitutes a new genre and corresponds to the apocalyptic outlook that part of Israel would be saved, part damned with the coming of the Day of Yahweh (see: Paul Hanson, *The Dawn of Apocalyptic* [Philadelphia: Fortress Press, 1975]).

Form critics have identified other forms among the prophetic speeches of the OT which may be borrowed from various settings within the culture. These "secondary" forms, which help shape the content and meaning of the passage in question, include the "trial speech" patterned after Israel's legal procedures (e. g., Isa. 1:18–20; 3:13–15; Mic. 6:1–5; Hos. 2:4–17; 4:1–3, 4–6; 5:3–15, etc.); the "disputation" or "controversy" (Ger.: *Streitgespräch;* e. g., Mic. 2:6–11; Jer. 2:23–25; 3:1–5; 8:8–9, etc.); the "parable" (e. g., Isa. 5:1–7; 2 Sam. 12); the "lament" (e. g., Amos 5:1–3; Jer. 8:4–7, 18–23; 9:17–21; 10:19–20; 12:7–13; 13:18–19; 15:5–9; 18:13–17, etc.); and the "prophetic torah" (e. g., Isa. 1: 10–17; 8:11–15; Jer. 7:21–23). (See: Westermann, op. cit., pp. 199ff.) The form receiving the greatest attention in recent years is the *rîb* or "covenant lawsuit" (see: *Rîb* **Pattern**).

For an overview of the status and history of the form-critical study of OT prophecy, see: *Old Testament Form Criticism,* ed. John H. Hayes (San Antonio, Texas: Trinity University Press, 1974).

The presence of prophets and the phenomenon of prophecy in the early Church is abundantly attested to by the NT. Both John the Baptist and Jesus are called prophets (Lk. 1:76; Mt. 14:5; 21:26//Mt. 16:14; 21:11, 46; Mk. 8:28; Lk. 7:16, 39; 9:19; cf. Jn. 1:21, 25; 6:14, etc.). The apostle Paul lists prophecy among the gifts of the Spirit (1 Cor. 14; cf. 1 Tim. 1:18; 4:14) and he names prophets along with apostles and teachers as a ministry appointed by divine calling (1 Cor. 12:28–29). But later NT writers warn of false prophets (e. g., Mt. 7:15; 24:11; 1 Jn. 4:1; Rev. 2:20; 16:13; 19:20; 20:10) and Paul himself is compelled to contrast the edification which comes from true prophecy with the pandemonium (1 Cor. 14:23) of speaking in tongues (1 Cor. 14), intimating the close connection between ecstasy and prophetic inspiration (Acts 2:4ff.; 19:6). According to Paul, the function of Christian prophecy is essentially pastoral; it is one of the means by which the Lord says to the church what he has to say. In this sense, it is suggested, chapters 2 and 3 of the book of Revelation and chapter 22:6–19, which proclaims the nearness of the parousia, are appropriately termed prophecy; by contrast, the remainder of the book of Revelation is apocalyptic in character. Other examples of early Christian prophecy have been identified by Ernst Käsemann in 1 Cor. 3:17; 14:38; 16:22, etc. (see: *Sätze heiligen Rechtes*).

The nature and incidence of Christian prophecy and its relation to apocalyptic are widely debated; so, too, is the question of the relationship of Jesus' proclamation of the kingdom of God to the prophetic and to the apocalyptic world views. Prophecy sees the future as the divinely ordered consequence of man's past and present actions; apocalyptic sees the future in basic discontinuity with the present, as the divine breaks into and thus totally dissolves the human sphere.

See: **Allegory; Apocalyptic; Eschatology; Form Criticism; Glossolalia; Gunkel; Legend; Major Prophets; Oracle;** *Rîb* **Pattern;** *Sätze heiligen Rechtes.*

Prophetic Eschatology. See: **Eschatology.**

Prophetic Lawsuit. See: *Rîb* **Pattern.**

Prophets, The. In Judaism: the second of the three divisions of OT Scripture, known in Hebrew as the *Nebiim* and comprising the Former Prophets (Joshua, Judges, 1 and 2 Sam., 1 and 2 Kings), and the Latter Prophets (Isaiah, Jeremiah, Ezekiel, Hosea, Joel, Amos, Obadiah, Jonah, Micah, Nahum, Habakkuk, Zephaniah, Haggai, Zechariah, and Malachi).

In Christian tradition, the P. (construed as singular) refers to the above, but excludes the so-called historical books of Joshua–2 Kings; as in Judaism, they are divided into the Major P. (Isa., Jer., and Ezek.) and the twelve Minor P. (Hos.–Mal.).

See: **Tanak.**

Propositio. See: **Rhetorical Analysis.**

Prostaxis is a term in linguistics used to identify "a particular way of combining clauses into long strips of relatively coordinate expressions" (Eugene Nida, *Toward a Science in Translating* [New York: W. S. Heinman Imported Books, 1964], p. 210). Formally speaking, such clauses are co-ordinated by the use of continuative particles (such as "and"), but semantically speaking these serve to mark the divisions between clauses and therefore "function more like periods than conjunctions." According to Nida, P. can be found in both Biblical Hebrew and Greek. In Hebrew, "the clause initial *waw* is often merely a signal of a clause beginning, and does not really link the clause in any coordinate way to the previous clause" (ibid.). In Greek, the opening verses of Mark may also be an example of P., since, it can be argued, the *kai* ("and") forms are not used to construct one long sentence of many clauses but function to set the clauses off from each other. See: **Hypotaxis; Parataxis.**

Protasis. In a conditional sentence, the conditional clause is called the protasis and in English usually begins with "If." The main clause, called the apodosis, states a conclusion conditioned on the fulfillment of the supposition stated in the subordinate (conditional) clause; e. g., Gal. 1:10*b*: "If I were still pleasing men [protasis], I should not be a servant of Christ [apodosis]." See: *A minore ad majus.*

Protoevangelium (Greek: the first, or earliest form of, the gospel) in Catholic tradition always refers to Gen. 3:15, in which God announces that the offspring of Eve will in the future crush the offspring of the serpent, interpreted to be a sign of ultimate victory over evil. See JB note ad loc.

Proto-Lucian. See: **Septuagint.**

Proto-Luke, meaning "the earliest form of" Luke, denotes a hypothetical document proposed by B. H. Streeter (*The Four Gospels* [London: Macmillan and Co., 1924]) composed of Q and "L" only, exclusive of any Markan materials and of Lk. 1–2; it was deduced to account for the verbal differences between Q as found in Mt. and Lk. and to establish a source equal in antiquity and authenticity to Mk. yet independent of it. The hypothesis lacks general acceptance. See: **Four Document Hypothesis; Streeter; Q; "L"; "M"; Two Source Hypothesis.**

Proto-LXX. See: **Septuagint.**

Proto-Theodotion. See: *Kaige* **Recension.**

Psalms (Greek: songs) is a five part collection of 150 hymns, prayers of confession, psalms of thanksgiving, trust, and complaint, dating from the period of the twelve-tribe confederacy to the post-Exilic period (*ca.* 1100–400 [200] B.C.). The divisions are (after Ps. 1) I: 2–41; II: 42–72; III: 73–89; IV: 90–106; V: 107–150. The division between the Pss. in the Hebrew OT (MT) is not identical with the Greek OT (the Septuagint, *siglum:* LXX) here in ( ): MT 1–8 (1–8); 9/10 (9); 11–113 (10–112); 114–115 (113); 116:1–9 (114); 116:10–19 (115); 117–146 (116–145); 147:1–11 (146); 147:12–20 (147); 148–150 (148–150). Ps. 14 is essentially identical with Ps. 53; Ps. 40:13–17 with Ps. 70; Ps. 108 with Ps. 57:7–11 and Ps. 60:5–12.

The following categorization is based on Hans Joachim Kraus' *Psalmen*, vols. I–II (Neukirchen Kreis Moers: Neukirchener Verlag, 1960). Psalms in parenthesis ( ) are of mixed form or otherwise of tentative classification. No single system of classification has met with universal acceptance.

    I. Hymns
        A. To Yahweh: 8; 19; 29; 33; 65; 66; 100; (103); 104; 105; 111; 113; 114; 117; 135; 145–(147)–150.
        B. To Yahweh as King: 47; 93; (95); 96; 97; 98; 99.

II. Individual Psalms of Complaint (or Lament; Ger.: *Klage*), Thanksgiving, and Trust
   A. Complaint: 3; 5–7; (12); 13; (14); 17; 22; 25–28; (31); 35; (36); 38; 39; (40); 41–43; 51; (52); (53); 54–57; (58); 59; 61; 63; 64; 69; 70; 71; (77); 86; 88; (94); 102; 109; 120; 130; 140–143.
   B. Thanksgiving: 9/10; 18; 30; 32; (34); 92; (103); (107); 116; 138.
   C. Trust in *Yahweh:* 4; 11; 16; 23; (27); 62; 131.
III. Community Psalms of Complaint, Thanksgiving, and Trust
   A. Complaint: (44); 60; 74; 79; 80; 83; 85; 90; (94); (123); (126); 137.
   B. Thanksgiving: (66–68); (75); (91); 124; (126); (139).
   C. Trust in Yahweh: 46; 125; 129.
IV. Enthronement Psalms (or Hymns): 2; (18); 20; 21; 45; 72; 89; 101; 110; 132; 144:1–11.
V. Songs (or Hymns) of Zion: (46); 48; 76; 84; 87; 122; (132).
VI. Psalms of (Salvation) History: 78; (105); 106; 136.
VII. Torah Psalms: 1; 19; 119.
VIII. Wisdom Psalms: 34; 37; (49); 73; (78); 112; 127; 128; 133.
IX. "Liturgies" or portions thereof: 15; 24; (40); (107); (110); (115); 118; (132); 134; (136).
X. Covenant Renewal Psalms: 50; 81.
XI. Cult Prophecy: 82.

Pivotal works available in English are: Hermann Gunkel, *The Psalms: A Form-Critical Introduction,* trans. Thomas M. Horner; Introduction by James Muilenburg (Philadelphia: Fortress, 1967, 1972³); and Sigmund Mowinckelru*The Psalms in Israel's Worship,* trans. D.R. Ap-Thomas, 2 vols. (New York: Abingdon, 1962; Oxford: Basil Blackwell, 1962); Claus Westermann, *Praise and Lament in the Psalms,* tr. Keith Crim and Richard N. Soulen (Atlanta: John Knox Press, 1981).

Pseudepigrapha (Greek: falsely entitled). In Protestant tradition since the 17th cent., the term P. has been used to designate those ancient Jewish and Hellenistic Jewish writings not in the OT canon or in the Apocrypha. Since the content of the Apocrypha in fact varies according to ecclesiastical tradition, and even within a given tradition, no universally accepted listing of P. exists. Some scholars would include writings found among the DSS as well as certain books sometimes numbered among the Apocrypha. The potential group includable numbers over 100 texts or text fragments.

The criteria currently employed (see James H. Charlesworth below) are: (1) the work must be at least partially Jewish or Jewish-Christian; (2) it should date from the period 200 B.C. to A.D. 200; (3) it should claim to be inspired;

(4) it should be related in form or content to the Old Testament; (5) it ideally is attributed to an Old Testament figure.

The following titles and their abbreviations are of texts chosen to appear in an English edition of the Pseudepigrapha, to be translated by an international team of scholars, and edited by J. H. Charlesworth. The publisher is Doubleday and Co.

1.	Apocalypse of Abraham	ApAb
2.	Testament of Abraham	TAb
3.	Apocalypse of Adam	ApAdam
4.	Life of Adam and Eve	LAE
	(Apocalypse of Moses)	ApMos
5.	Ahigar	Ah
6.	An Anonymous Samaritan Text	AnonSam
7.	Letter of Aristeas	LetAris
8.	2 (Syriac) Baruch	2 Bar
9.	3 (Greek) Baruch	3 Bar
10.	4 Baruch	4 Bar
	(*Paraleipomena Jeremiou;* sometimes called The Rest of the Words of Baruch, 2 Baruch, 3 Baruch, Christian Baruch)	
11.	Apocalypse of Elijah	ApEl
12.	1 (Ethiopic) Enoch	1En
13.	2 (Slavonic) Enoch	2En
	(Book of the Secrets of Enoch)	
14.	3 (Hebrew) Enoch	3En
	(Sepher Heikhalot)	
15.	Apocalypse of Ezekiel	ApEzek
16.	4 Ezra (4, 5, 6 Ezra; 2 Esdras, 4 Esdras, Apocalypse of Ezra)	4 Ezra
17.	Greek Apocalypse of Ezra	GkApEzra
18.	Questions of Ezra	QuesEzra
19.	Vision of Ezra	VisEzra
20.	Fragments of Historical Works	FrgsHistWrks
21.	Testament of Isaac	TIsaac
22.	Ascension of Isaiah	AscenIs
	Martyrdom of Isaiah, Treatment of Hezekiah, Vision of Isaiah)	
23.	Ladder of Jacob	LadJac
24.	Testament of Jacob	TJac
25.	Jannes and Jambres	JanJam
26.	Testament of Job	TJob

27.	Joseph and Asenath	JosAsen
28.	Prayer of Joseph	PrJos
29.	Jubilees	Jub
30.	3 Maccabees *(Ptolemaika)*	3Mac
31.	4 Maccabees	4Mac
	(Concerning the Supreme Power of Reason)	
32.	Prayer of Manasses	PrMan
33.	Assumption of Moses	AsMos
	(Ascension of Moses, Testament of Moses)	
34.	Pseudo-Philo	Ps-Philo
	(Liber Antiquitatum Biblicarum)	(LAB)
35.	Pseudo-Phocylides	Ps-Phoc
	(Poiēmo Nouthetikon) Ps-Phoc	
36.	Fragments of Poetic Works	FrgsPoetWrks
37.	Lives of the Prophets	LivPro
	(Deaths/Triumphs of the Prophets,	
	Pseudo-Epiphanius)	
38.	Apocalypse of Sedrach	ApSedr
39.	Treatise of Shem	TrShem
	(Book of Shem)	
40.	Sibylline Oracles	SibOr
41.	Odes of Solomon	OdesSol
42.	Psalms of Solomon	PssSol
43.	Testament of Solomon	TSol
44.	Five Apocryphal Syriac Psalms	5ApocSyrPss
	(Five Psalms of David, Psalms 151–155)	
45.	Testaments of the Twelve Patriarchs	T12P
46.	Apocalypse of Zephaniah	ApZeph
	(Apocalypse of Saphonias)	
47.	Apocalypse of Zosimus	ApZos
	(Narrative/Testament of Zosimus, The	
	Abode of the Blessed)	

For bibliography, see: James H. Charlesworth, *The Pseudepigrapha and Modern Research* (SBLSCS 7; Missoula: Scholars Press, 1976; *Supplementary Volume* [proj.]; also see: *Bulletin of the International Organization for Septuagint and Cognate Studies,* esp. Vol. 10 (1977) and Vol. 11 (1978).

Pseudo-Jonathan. See: **Targum.**

Pseudonymity (Greek: lit., using a false name). The practice of ascribing a writing to someone other than its real author. In the OT (e. g., Daniel and certain Psalms), in the Pseudepigrapha (Wisdom of Solomon, Additions to Esther, etc.), in the NT (Jn. [?], 2 and 3 Jn. [?], the Pastorals, 1 and 2 Peter, Jas., Jude), and in the NT Apocrypha, the pseudonym is always of some ancient worthy or of a leading apostle. P. in these instances is probably not to be thought of from a modern (cynical) point of view as a means of gaining authority and wide circulation for a work, but rather as a product of the sincere conviction that truly inspired Scripture was not of one's own doing but God's, or the Holy Spirit's, and must therefore be attributed to an acknowledged instrument of revelation. In the NT period, the pseudonymous writings stand between the anonymous Gospels and Acts (to which names were affixed subsequently) and the apologists of the 2nd cent. who defended the gospel in their own name.

Pseudo-Pauline. See: Deutero-Pauline.

Psychological Reconstruction is a pejorative term in contemporary Biblical criticism which refers to the attempt to reconstruct the thought processes of a historical personage (Jesus, Paul, Jeremiah, etc.) on the basis of conjecture and a modern psychological theory of personality or of human behavior. Although no book influenced the diminution (not the demise) of the PR of Jesus more than did Albert Schweitzer's *The Quest of the Historical Jesus* (Ger.: 1906), it, too, succumbed to the temptation to go beyond what a historian can reasonably know or justifiably assume. See: **Hermeneutics; Historical Critical Method; Quest of the Historical Jesus.**

Q (also called "sayings source"; Ger.: *Redenquelle;* and simply: The Double Tradition), from the German word *Quelle* meaning "source," is the symbol used loosely to mean (a) all the material held in common by Matthew and Luke but not found in Mark, or more specifically, (b) a hypothetical *written document* lying behind and accounting for material which Mt. and Lk. have in common and including certain passages found also in Mk., or, finally, (c) a variation of the preceding, including theories concerning stages of oral and written tradition, translations of earlier sayings collections to account for differences, etc. The Q-hypothesis rests on two main arguments: (1) The degree of verbal agreement between Lukan and Matthaean non-Markan material is so high that it can be explained only by the use of a common source; and (2) The order of this non-Markan material is so often the same that only a (written?) common source can account for it.

According to the Two Source Hypothesis, Q antedates Mark. There is, however, no universal agreement as to its origin, date, or content. The following are proposed reconstructions of its content as found in Luke.

Q

A. Hawkins	B. Streeter	C. Schulz
Lk. 3:7–9	Lk. 3:2a-9	Lk. 3:7–18
	(10–14)	
17	16–17	
	21–22	
4:3–13	4:1–16a	4:1–13
6:(20–21)	6:20–49	6:20b–23
22–23		
27–49		27–49
7:1–3	7:1–10	7:1–10
6–9		
18–19	18–35	18–28
22–28		
31–35		31–35
9:57–60	9:(51–56)	9:57–60
	57–60	
	(61–62)	
10:2–9	10:2–16	10:11–16
12–15	(17–20)	
(16)		
21–24	21–24	21–24
11:2–4	11:9–52	11:9–26
9–14, 16		
19–20, 23–26		
29–32		29–35, 39
34–35		
39, 41–42		42–44
(44)		
46–51		46–52
12:2–9	12:1a–12	12:2–11
22–31	22–59	22–31
33–34		33–34
		39–40
		42b–47

A. John C. Hawkins, *Horae Synopticae: Contributions to the Study of the Synoptic Problem* (Oxford: Clarendon Press, 1909²), pp. 108f.
B. Burnett H. Streeter, *The Four Gospels: A Study of Origins* (London: Macmillan and Company, 4th rev. ed. 1930), p. 291.
C. Siegfried Schulz, *Q: Die Spruchquelle der Evangelisten* (Zürich: Theologischer Verlag Zürich, 1972).
See also Richard A. Edwards, *A [Greek] Concordance to Q* ("Sources for Biblical Study 7"; Missoula, Mont.: The Scholar's Press, 1975) and idem, *A Theology of Q* (Philadelphia: Fortress Press, 1975).

51–53		51–53
58–59		57–59
13:20–21	13:18–35	13:18–21
(25–29)		23–24
		26–29
34, 35		34–35
14:11; cf. 18:14	14:11	14:11; cf. 18:14
		16–24
(26–27)	26–27	26–27
	34–35	34–35
15:4–5, 7		15:4–7
16:13, 16–17	16:13, 16–18	16:13, 16–18
17:1, 3(4, 6)	17:1–6	17:3–6
24, 26–27	20–37	23–24
		26–27, 30
34–35, 37		33–36
	19:11–27	19:12–27
(22:28, 30)		22:28–30

See: **"L"; "M"; Proto-Luke.**

Qinah **Meter** (Heb.: *Qinah:* lament) is the name given to the rhythmic pattern 3 + 2, because of its dominance in the book of Lamentations, and because the imbalance in the lines seems to capture the tension of extreme emotion like grief (but also joy, e. g. Psalm 65). The meter is usually lost in translation, but cf. "My eyés are spént with weéping/my sóul is in túmult." (Lam. 2:11–RSV) The interpretation of the *"Qinah* meter" is debated. (See: N. K. Gottwald, "Poetry, Hebrew," *IDB.*)

Qoh.   Abbrev. for Qoheleth, or Koheleth; better known by the Greek name: Ecclesiastes, or "The Preacher."

Quellenkritik (Ger.: Source Criticism). See: **Literary Criticism.**

Qere.   See: **Kethibh.**

Quest of the Historical Jesus (The); Leben-Jesu Forschung; Liberal Lives of Jesus; The New Quest.

The *QHJ* is the English (1910) title of Albert Schweitzer's critical history of 19th cent. biographies of the life of Jesus, entitled in German *Von* [*H. S.*] *Reimarus zu* [*William*] *Wrede* (1906).

Since Schweitzer's epoch-making work, the various attempts to write a historical biography of Jesus, whether of the 19th or 20th cent., have been referred to, sometimes pejoratively, as *Leben-Jesu Forschung* ("Lives of Jesus

Research"), which is a phrase taken from the German subtitle. The phrase is however also used broadly to refer to any search for the historical Jesus, however fragmentary and tentative the expected results might be.

Schweitzer (1875–1965) characterized those works written after **D. F. Strauss'** [q. v.] final "Life of Jesus" (1864) as the "Liberal Lives of Jesus," because they attempted to limit the explanation of Jesus' actions and the events of his life to natural, psychological causes and motivations and completely ignored the profoundly eschatological setting of Jesus' teachings and actions (see: **Eschatology**). The term "Liberal Lives of Jesus" is frequently expanded to include studies of Jesus' life by the American social movement through the 1930s, including Shailer Mathews' *Jesus on Social Institutions* (New York: The Macmillan Co., 1928), and Shirley Jackson Case's *Jesus: A New Biography* (Chicago: University of Chicago Press, 1927).

Two key assumptions of the 19th cent. quest were (a) the objective recoverability of the past by critical historiographical means and (b) the adequacy of the synoptic Gospels as sources for the historical reconstruction of the life of Jesus, at least of his public ministry. Schweitzer himself largely accepted these assumptions for his own sketch of the life of Jesus (*QHJ*, ch. XIX). Building on Johannes Weiss' *Jesus' Proclamation of the Kingdom of God* (Philadelphia: Fortress Press, 1971; London: SCM Press, 1971; Ger.: 1892) and William Wrede's notion of the **Messianic Secret** (from Wrede's *The Messianic Secret* [Naperville, Ill.: Alec R. Allenson, 1972; Ger.: 1901]), Schweitzer proved to most of the scholarly world that Jesus' eschatological outlook determined his actions and teachings. Thus placed squarely in the thought-world of the 1st cent., Jesus becomes "as One unknown" to the 20th (p. 403). This portrait of Jesus as an eschatological preacher replaced that of 19th and early 20th cent. Liberalism, if not wholly, then at least with the rise of **Form Criticism** first in Germany (1920s) and subsequently in English-speaking lands (1930–   ). But it is one of the ironies in the history of Biblical criticism that Schweitzer's own picture of Jesus as a religious fanatic who died disillusioned on a cross merely became an additional witness to the erroneous assumptions on which such "Lives" were based (see above) and to the inevitable failure of any quest built on similar grounds. In Germany, then, the original quest thus ended with Schweitzer's book and was not initiated again for fifty years, and then on different grounds. The two major factors contributing to this giving up of the quest were: (a) historical skepticism, arising from Source and Form Criticism, as to the authenticity of the Gospel records, and (b) theological disinterest toward the historical Jesus for purely dogmatic reasons, both on the side of dogmatic theology itself (esp. Karl Barth) and on the side of existentialist theology (Rudolf Bultmann). In Protestant scholarship outside Germany, however, the matter was quite different; here the so-called quest continued.

160

A *New Quest of the Historical Jesus* designates one of two interrelated but distinct approaches by which students of Bultmann in Germany and Switzerland sought to reestablish historical and theological (or, more accurately, philosophical) grounds for identifying the Jesus of history with the Christ proclaimed by Christian faith. It was coined by the NT scholar James M. Robinson and is the title of his sketch of the discussion and contribution to it, The *NQHJ* (London: SCM Press, 1959). Bultmann had argued that the only identity between the two was the "fact" itself which faith alone made. Students of Bultmann and critics alike were dissatisfied with this answer. The *NQHJ*, therefore, pertains primarily but not exclusively to the historical critical side of this issue. It has sought criteria for judging the authenticity of sayings attributed to Jesus as an objective basis for saying something specific about him (see: **Criteria of Authenticity**). This aspect of the NQ is associated with Ernst Käsemann (*Essays on New Testament Themes* [London: SCM Press, 1964]), Günther Bornkamm (*Jesus of Nazareth* [New York: Harper and Row, 1961; London: Hodder & Stoughton, 1973]), and more recently outside Germany, Norman Perrin (*Rediscovering the Teaching of Jesus* [New York: Harper and Row, 1967; London: SCM Press, 1967]), and a host of others.

The philosophical and theological side of the effort to explain how the crucified Jesus came to be proclaimed as the risen Lord is more commonly known as the New Hermeneutic (q. v. under **Hermeneutics**). In brief, the NH addresses the problem from the standpoint of a phenomenology of language, the assumption being that there is a connection between historical statement on the one hand and theological assertion on the other. It suggests that there is an identity between the *event* of faith which came to expression in the acts and teachings of Jesus as recorded in the Gospels (see: **Language-event**) and the event of faith which is articulated in Christian proclamation about Jesus. Here the New Quest and the New Hermeneutic overlap. See Gerhard Ebeling's *Word and Faith* (Philadelphia: Fortress Press, 1963), Ernst Fuchs' *Studies of the Historical Jesus* (London: SCM Press, 1964), and Robert W. Funk's *Language, Hermeneutic, and Word of God* (New York: Harper and Row, 1966), et al.

Although in the last decade this discussion has dissipated into a countless number of delineable problems and discussions, its American continuation is most clearly discernible in the field of parable interpretation.

Note: Major works of the 19th cent. quest and other notable studies of Jesus are being published in the Lives of Jesus Series, General Editor, Leander E. Keck, by Fortress Press, Philadelphia.

See also: Existential Interpretation under **Existentialist; Hermeneutics; Parable.**

Qumran. See: **Khirbet Qumran.**

Rad, Gerhard von (1901–1971). Born in Nürnberg, he studied theology at Erlangen and Tübingen, becoming in 1925 a curate in the *Landeskirche* (Lutheran Church) in Bavaria. Disturbed by the anti-OT sentiments of the German Christian Church, he turned to OT studies and became one of the leading OT theologians of the mid-20th cent. He taught at Erlangen (1929; tutor), Leipzig (1930–34; *Privatdozent*), Jena (1934–45; Prof.), Göttingen (1945–49), and Heidelberg (1949–67). He maintained that the compiler of the Hexateuch joined two streams of tradition (a Sinai tradition and an Exodus-Conquest tradition) into a unified theology of history *(Heilsgeschichte),* of which the cultic credo in Deut. 26:5–11 is the most succinct formulation. His major works include *Deuteronomy* (London: SCM Press, 1966; Philadelphia: The Westminster Press, 1966), *Genesis* (Westminster, 1961; 1973; SCM, 1972), *Old Testament Theology* (2 vols.; New York: Harper and Row, 1962–64), *The Problem of the Hexateuch* (New York: McGraw-Hill Book Co., 1966), and *Wisdom in Israel* (London: SCM Press, 1972). See: **Tradition Criticism.**

Radical Criticism. According to W. G. Kümmel, a distinction is to be made between "the radically historical approach" to the Bible (which characterized the work of Wellhausen, Wrede, Bousset, Goguel, Loisy, Gunkel, et al.) and the totally ill-founded "RC" of Bruno Bauer and of those Dutch, French, German, and English scholars at the turn of the century who denied both the existence of Jesus and the Pauline authorship of almost all the letters ascribed to him. See: **Biblical Criticism; Historical Criticism; Historical Critical Method.**

Ras Shamra Texts discovered in 1929 in the ruins of the royal palace and temple environs of ancient Ugarit, a Phoenician city on the Syrian coast, bearing the modern name RS, which means "Hill of Fennel." These Ugaritic and Akkadian texts, numbering in the hundreds, are unexcelled in their importance for understanding Canaanitic culture and hence the milieu of Hebrew history and religion in the second millennium B.C. In addition to providing knowledge of the Canaanitic pantheon (El, Baal, Anath, Dagon, Mot, etc.) and the ritual myths that surrounded them, the texts disproved Wellhausen's evolutionary theory of cultic development which gave a post-Exilic date to the Priestly Code. For a translation of some of the religious texts, see *ANET;* further, Ps. 29 has a parallel in Ugaritic literature, with the name Baal appearing in place of Yahweh.

Reading. In Textual Criticism a R. is a variant version of a given passage of Scripture as it is found in a particular text, e. g., a variant and less ancient R. of Mt. 5:22 adds "without cause" to "everyone who is angry with his brother . . ." (cf. KJV with RSV) and thereby provides an effective escape from the harsher command.

Realized Eschatology is a t.t. coined by C. H. Dodd (*The Parables of the Kingdom* [London: Nisbet & Co., 1935]) to characterize the ministry of Jesus in which "the *eschaton* has moved from the future to the present, from the sphere of expectation into that of realized experience" (p. 50). Dodd argued that in the unprecedented and unrepeatable events of Jesus' life "the powers of the world to come" are present and made real. See: **Eschatology; Existentialist; Parable; Quest of the Historical Jesus.**

Recension (Latin: a review, reassessment). Meaning "an editorial revision of a text," the term was first used in the text-critical studies of Karl Lachmann (d. 1851); it is sometimes applied more generally to any handwritten copy of a text in the broad sense that every MS is a "recension" of the original autograph and is not identical with it. The recension of the book of Acts in Codex D is one-tenth longer than that of Codex G; explaining and evaluating the differences in these Rs is in part the task of Textual Criticism.

Reception Theory (Reception Analysis; Ger.: *Rezeptionsasthetik*) is the name applied to that field of literary research emerging since the 1960s, principally in Germany and Czechoslovakia, which focuses on the reception (interpretation) of a work rather than on the historical factors giving rise to it (historical criticism), or on the work itself as an a-historical, autonomous entity (structuralism). It does so on the theory that "the historical and cultural reality which we call the 'literary work' is not exhausted in the text. The text is only one of the elements of a relation. In fact, the literary work consists of the text (the system of intra-textual relations) in its relation to extra-textual reality: to literary norms, tradition and the imagination" (J. M. Lotman). Such a theory requires that a distinction be made between the text as written document ("Text₁," or "artefact") and the "metatext" ("Text₂" or "aesthetic object") which is created within the consciousness of the recipient as the "meaning correlate" of the text.

The basic assumption here is that the meaning of a text is open and, by virtue of its autonomy as a linguistic entity, indeterminant; that the indeterminancy of the text is closed—is replaced with meaning—only in the act of reading. As these "readings" of the text are concretized in new texts, or "interpretations (Text₂)," they become the subject matter of a history of reception (Ger.: *Rezeptionsgeschichte*). By contrast, the *empirical study of reception* analyzes the contemporary reception of a work with the help of questionnaires. In this approach, the object of study (Text₂; the aesthetic object) results from the relation between Text₂ and the reader's "syndrome" or "horizon of expectations" at the time of reading. According to W. Bauer (*Text und Rezeption;* Frankfurt: Athenäum, 1972), components of this syndrome of expectations are: (1) linguistic experience, (2) experience in dealing with texts, and

(3) individual experiences (emotional, socially determined, and cultural).

The historical study of reception, the dominant form of RT, deals with texts which are themselves the interpretations of prior texts. Both the original text (Text$_1$) and its interpretation (Text$_2$) thus become the object of interpretation. (The problem thus arises, as R Theorists are aware, that a given textual interpretation is a Text$_2$ in relation to the original text, but to the researcher it becomes a new artifact. It is a problem overcome fully neither in theory nor in practice.) Because of this focus on texts, however, RT employs the insights of all other text-oriented methodologies. *It is important to note that rather than being an autonomous method in itself, RT is viewed by its practitioners as "a partial reflection on method which is open to additions and dependent on cooperation with other disciplines"* (H. R. Jauss). These include **historical criticism, hermeneutics, structuralism,** and **semiotics.**

RT shares with historical criticism its acknowledgment of the historicity of the text. But rather than seeking the causative factors giving rise to the text, it sees the text as a sign system (phonological, lexical, syntactic or thematic) related to other contemporaneous synchronous systems outside the text which locate and define the text in its epoch. RT is structuralist by virtue of this concept of relation; it is semiotic by virtue of its application of the sign concept to the text and its recognition of a plurality of codes within the system (linguistic, social, ethical, etc.). RT differs with model structuralism in its effort to locate the text in its epoch, mentioned above, and in its emphasis upon the historicity of the researcher whose value judgments make the text (as artefact) what it is perceived to be (the aesthetic object). At this point RT sides with recent hermeneutical theory against both historical criticism and structuralism which viewed the interpreter as an a-historical entity. But whereas hermeneutical theory (e.g., H. G. Gadamer) effaced the distinction between text and interpreter in the concept of a "fusion of horizons" *(Horizontsverschmeltzung),* RT attempts to reassert a measure of objectivity by suggesting that the text, though "open," has a horizon of expectations which, though multivalent, is not panvalent. Further, that the reader as well comes to the text with an identifiable horizon of expectations. However, it is a fundamental assumption within RT that the "hermeneutical difference" (or "historical distance") between previous and present interpretations of a text bears witness to the multivalence of the text on the one hand and the historical relativity of the interpretive norms on the other. It is this continual shifting of the text as aesthetic object (Text$_2$, virtual text—Iser) that has given rise to the term "dynamic- (rather than "model-) structuralism."

For this description of RT and an extensive bibliography, see: D. W. Fokkema and Elrud Künne-Ibsch, *Theories of Literature in the Twentieth Century* (London: C. Hurst and Co., 1977).

Redaction Criticism (fr. Ger.: *Redaktionsgeschichte*) is a method of Biblical criticism which seeks to lay bare the theological perspectives of a Biblical writer by analyzing the editorial (redactional) and compositional techniques and interpretations employed by him in shaping and framing the written and/or oral traditions at hand (see Luke 1:1–4).

RC, which in NT study pertains above all to the synoptic Gospels, is generally conceived as a logical and therefore methodological correlative to **Form Criticism** (q. v.), the latter dealing with the identification of formal elements in a composition, the former with their use and interpretation within the total literary unit as a coherent and meaningful whole. Form Criticism, which in NT studies began in the 1920s, fragmented the synoptic Gospels into a multitude of disparate linguistic forms (e. g., parables, miracle stories, sayings, etc.) in an effort to distinguish between "redactional" elements on the one hand and earlier traditional forms on the other which were then considered to be of greater historical value. Consequently, FC tended to treat the synoptic writers as mere "collectors," "editors," or "traditionists," who were "only to the smallest extent authors" (Martin Dibelius, *From Tradition to Gospel* [London: Ivor Nicholson and Watson, Ltd., 1934; repr. James Clarke, 1971; New York: Charles Scribner's Sons, 1935], p. 3). The author's use of his materials was thus disregarded. Interest centered on rediscovering the hypothetical setting within the life of the Church (see: *Sitz-im-Leben*) which purportedly gave rise to the forms themselves. The literary setting given to the traditions by the Gospel, their functions, and their meaning, were all passed over as irrelevant. RC, however, deals positively with the redactional framework into which the traditions have been placed; it therefore provides a corrective to the methodological imbalance of Form Criticism. It is the evangelist's use, disuse, or alteration of the traditions known to him that is in view, rather than the form and original setting of the traditions themselves. The redaction critic asks, for example: Why does Luke alter the Markan tradition concerning John the Baptist as Elijah? (Cf. Mk. 6:15–16 with Lk. 9:7–9; Mk. 6:17–29 and 9:9–13 are absent from Lk.) Why does he have Satan present at the beginning and end of Jesus' ministry and not during it? (Lk. 4:1–13; 22:3, but cf. Mk. 8:31–33 with Lk. 9:21–22.) Why does he restrict the appearances of the risen Lord to Jerusalem and its environs? (Cf. Mk. 16:7 with Lk. 24:6–7, 46–49; Acts 1:4.) In answering these questions and countless others like them, redaction critics have effectively restored the synoptic writers to their rightful place as theologians of the early Church. They are, in one scholar's words, the "earliest exegetes" of the Christian tradition, not merely its first editors.

RC functions, then, only where identifiable sources are present within a composition, such as the Gospels and the book of Acts in the NT or Deuteronomy and Judges in the OT. It is important to note that RC as applied to the synoptic Gospels is based on the **Two Source Hypothesis** (q. v.) which names Mark and Q as sources in the writing of Mt. and Lk. Should the priority of Mt. be established, as some suggest (see: **Synoptic Problem**), the redaction-critical analysis of the synoptics would have to begin all over again.

The term *Redaktionsgeschichte* was coined by Willi Marxsen (1954), and his book, *Mark the Evangelist* (Nashville: Abingdon Press, 1969; Ger. 1956) is one of its earliest exemplars, along with *Tradition and Interpretation in Matthew* by Günther Bornkamm, Gerhard Barth, and H. J. Held; trans. Percy Scott (Philadelphia: The Westminster Press, 1963; London: SCM Press, 1972; Ger.: 1948), and Hans Conzelmann's *The Theology of St. Luke,* trans. Geoffrey Buswell (New York: Harper and Row, 1961; London: Faber & Faber, 1971; Ger.: 1954). RC, as represented by these inaugural works, is not without its antecedents in both OT and NT scholarship. In NT studies historians point to William Wrede's *The Messianic Secret* (see the entry: **Messianic Secret**) and R. H. Lightfoot's *History and Interpretation in the Gospels* (Bampton Lectures for 1934; New York: Harper and Brothers, 1934), as well as to Adolf Schlatter's studies in Matthew. (See esp.: Norman Perrin, *What Is Redaction Criticism?* [Philadelphia: Fortress Press, 1969]; and Joachim Rohde, *Rediscovering the Teaching of the Evangelists* [Philadelphia: The Westminster Press, 1969, 1974²; London: SCM Press, 1969; Ger.: 1966].)

Antecedents in OT research, which included the perspectives and concerns of RC in fact if not in name, include Gerhard von Rad's work in the Pentateuch and Martin Noth's studies in Deuteronomy and the Former Prophets (Joshua–2 Sam.). Strictly speaking, *Redaktionsgeschichte* as the *"history* of redaction" applies as a term more appropriately to OT research than to NT research, since the Gospels (except perhaps John) are the work of one redactor and not several redactors over a period of time as is the case with some OT writings. (See: Wolfgang Richter, *Exegese als Literaturwissenschaft* [Göttingen: Vandenhoeck and Ruprecht, 1971].)

See: **Form Criticism; Synoptic Problem; Tradition Criticism.**

Redaction History. See: **Redaction Criticism.**

Redactor. One who arranges, revises, edits, or otherwise shapes oral and literary materials into a final composition. See: **Redaction Criticism.**

Redaktionsgeschichte (Ger.: redaction/composition criticism). See: **Redaction Criticism.**

Refutatio. See: **Rhetorical Analysis.**

Reimarus, Hermann Samuel (1694–1768), teacher of oriental languages in Hamburg, is treated as the initiator of "Lives of Jesus Research" by

Schweitzer and accorded special honor by him for recognizing that Jesus' thought-world was essentially eschatological, a fact overlooked until the end of the 19th cent. The portions of R's study on Jesus which were published were done so posthumously by G. E. Lessing in 1774–78 as "Fragments by an Unknown Author." While demurring at Schweitzer's exalted assessment, W. G. Kümmel acknowledges that R. saw the need to distinguish between the proclamation of the historical Jesus and the proclamation of the Early Church and to ask to what extent Jesus himself is the origin of his followers' break with Judaism. See: **Lessing; Quest of the Historical Jesus.**

Reitzenstein, Richard (1861–1931). Born in Breslau, Germany, where in 1888 he became a Privatdozent for classical philology, R. taught in Rostock (1889–1892), Giessen (1892–1893, becoming a full professor), Strassburg (1893–1911), Freiburg i. Br. (1911–1914), and Göttingen (1914–1931). As a leading member of the "Comparative Religions School" *(Religionsgeschichtliche Schule)*, R. contributed significantly to the understanding of the hellenistic mystery religions, Gnosticism, and Mandaism and thus to the cultic background of the New Testament generally. His continued importance for NT study is reflected in the re-publication of his major works in Germany (1962–66) and by the appearance in English of his major work, *Hellenistic Mystery-Religions: Their Basic Ideas and Significance,* tr. John E. Steely (Pittsburgh Theological Monograph Series, 15; Pittsburgh, Pa.; The Pickwick Press, 1978). For a bibliography, see: *Festschrift Richard Reitzenstein zum 2. April 1931,* ed. by E. Fraenkel et al. (Leipzig and Berlin; B. G. Tuebner, 1931).

Religionsgeschichte (**adj.**: *religionsgeschtliche); Religionsgeschichtliche Schule.* *Rg.* is a German term without a single English equivalent. It is translated most accurately and literally as "the history of religion(s)." In broadest terms, it refers to the application of the historical method of analysis, as developed in the late 19th cent., to the study of religion. As such it can be differentiated (though often now only loosely and with difficulty) from phenomenology-, psychology-, sociology-, and philosophy of religion. *Rg.* is also frequently translated as "comparative religions" which, in English at least, often connotes an anthropological approach to general religious subjects without concern for historical relativity. Properly speaking, CR (Ger.: *Religionsvergleichung*) is but a part of "the history of religions" approach, the former presupposing a detailed knowledge of the history of the specific religions being compared.

The *Religionsgeschichtliche Schule* ("history of religions school" or religio-historical school) is the name given to a group of Protestant scholars in Germany who, at the turn of the century, sought to understand the religion of the Old and New Testaments within the context of their historical environment, including the other religions of that time and region. This approach, which differed radically from the German ethical idealism of the period, is associated with the names of Hermann Gunkel, Johannes Weiss, Wilhelm Bousset, Wilhelm Heitmüller, Hugo Gressmann, Albert Eichhorn, et al. It is their work which first threw light on the immense distances which separate the world of the Bible, its understandings and expectations, from that of our own, thus exacerbating the problem with which theologians struggle of making the Bible meaningful to people today.

See: **Bultmann; Form Criticism; Gunkel; Hermeneutics.**

Rhetoric. In the broadest sense, R. is the "art of speaking" and is practiced by everyone who participates in social life. The term R., therefore, may encompass all forms and aspects of human communication (philosophical, historical, critical, etc.).

See: *The Prospect of Rhetoric,* ed. Lloyd F. Bitzer and Edwin Black (Englewood Cliffs, N.J.: Prentice-Hall, Inc., 1971).

R. in the narrower sense, often called "School Rhetoric," is the art of partisan speech (as practiced by politicians, lawyers, etc.) and as a field of study traceable to the Sophists of the 5th Cent. B.C.(Cf. also the *Rhetoric* of Aristotle.) Scripture can be analyzed or described with the technical terminology of school rhetoric insofar as Scripture is apologetic in nature or persuavive in intent. See: Y. Gitay, "A Study of Amos's Art of Speech: A Rhetorical Analysis of Amos 3:1–15,"*CBQ* 42 (1980), pp. 293–309.).

Rhetorical Analysis. In recent years, the perspective and technical terms of classical rhetoric have been used in the analysis of certain Biblical texts, particularly the letters of Paul. The t.t. are derived in the main from that phase of classical speech preparation termed *inventio* (to which the second [*dispositio*] and third [*elocutio*] phases are closely related; they are not discussed separately as such in the *Handbook,* nor are the fourth [*memoria*] and fifth [*pronunciatio*]. *Inventio,* as the discovery of ideas appropriate to the intended goal of the speaker, and *dispositio,* as their selection and arrangement, are for practical purposes not separable insofar as the different parts of an address (including the letter form) present different ideas (so Lausberg; see Major Reference Works Consulted).

The parts of an address and their technical names from classical school rhetoric are:

(1) *exordium,* or *prooemium:* the brief introductory section designed to catch the hearer's attention, his goodwill and acceptance.

(2) The central section has the form: *propositio + rationes.*

(a) *propositio:* has the function of presenting the goal to be

168

achieved. It can bc expanded or even replaced by:
 (i) *partitio:* a detailing of points;
 (ii) *narratio:* a rehearsal of the course of events pertinent to the
 propositio.
 (b) *argumentatio:* has the function of carrying out the various
 (intellectual or affective) proofs. *Refutatio* is that part of the
 argumentatio given to refuting the arguments of the opponent.

(3) The (short) conclusion *(peroratio)* corresponds to the *conclusio* and
assumes that the proofs provided in the *argumentatio* are now certain. The
speaker thereby requests a judgment in his favor. The *peroratio* has two
functions:
 (a) To show the agreement between the *propositio* and the
 conclusio; and,
 (b) To repeat briefly *(recapitulatio)* the *argumentatio.*
The intended result is of course that the hearer judges in the speaker's favor.

It is suggested that Paul's letter to the Galatians is a "defense speech" cast
in the form of a letter; it essentially fits the above scheme, as follows: *Prooemium* (1:6–10), *narratio* (1:10–2:14), *propositio* (2:15–21), *argumentatio* or
probatio (3:1–4:31); the final section (5:1–6:10) is called *paraenesis* (q.v.). An
epistolary frame is given by the "prescript" (1:1–5) and the "postscript" (6:
11–18). See: Hans Dieter Betz, "In Defense of the Spirit" in Elisabeth
Schüssler Fiorenza, ed., *Aspects of Religious Propaganda in Judaism and Early
Christianity* (Notre Dame and London: University of Notre Dame Press,
1976) and his commentary, *Galatians* (Hermeneia; Philadelphia: Fortress
Press, 1979).

Rhetorical Criticism is a term adopted in 1968 by the late OT scholar
James Muilenburg to denote a methodological approach to Scripture designed
to supplement that of Form Criticism. Its task, he suggested, is to exhibit the
structural patterns employed in the fashioning of a literary unit, whether prose
or poetry, and to discern the various devices (such as **parallelism, anaphora,
epiphora,** *inclusio,* etc. [q. v.]) by which the predications of the composition
are formulated and ordered into a unified whole ("Form Criticism and Beyond," *JBL,* 88 [March 1969], pp. 1–18). Whereas Form Criticism, traditionally defined, seeks the typical and representative, RC, as Muilenburg conceived
it, seeks the unique and personal in order to trace the movement of the writer's
thought. Other scholars suggest that this does not constitute a supplement to
Form Criticism but the renewal of a proper but neglected aspect of the form-critical method, and therefore does not warrant a separate designation. See:
Jared J. Jackson and Martin Kessler, *Rhetorical Criticism: Essays in Honor of
James Muilenburg,* Pittsburgh Theological Monograph Series, No. 1 (Pittsburgh, Pa.: The Pickwick Press, 1974).

Note: The field encompassed by rhetorical studies (philosophical, histori-cal, critical, etc.) is exceedingly vast and ancient; it embraces all forms of human communication and is traceable back to the *Rhetoric* of Aristotle. See: *The Prospect of Rhetoric,* ed. Lloyd F. Bitzer and Edwin Black (Englewood Cliffs, N.J.: Prentice-Hall, Inc., 1971).
See: **Exegesis; Form Criticism; Structuralism.**

Rîb **Pattern** (Heb.: complaint; lawsuit) is a t.t. in OT studies for the com-plaint which one member of a covenant (usually Yahweh or his prophet) issues against the offending member. Also called the Prophetic Lawsuit or the Cove-nant Lawsuit. The pattern of the complaint generally includes the following elements: (a) summons to the offending party, (b) recitation of beneficent acts bestowed in former times upon the offender, (c) accusations against the offender, and (d) call to witnesses of the covenant both in heaven and on earth. (See, e. g.: Jer. 2:4–13; Isa. 1:2–9; Hos. 4:1–10; Mic. 6:1–8; Ps. 50.)

RSV is the common abbreviation for the Revised Standard Version of the Bible (NT, 1946; 1971[2]; OT, 1952; Apocrypha, 1957; expanded edition with Apocrypha, 1977), being a revision of the American Standard Version (1901), which in turn was a revision of the King James Version of 1611. The RSV sought to retain as much of the elevated style characteristic of the **KJV** as possible so that it would be suitable for public worship. The text of the RSV is closer to the original than the KJV, since ancient MSS far older than those available in 1611 have been (and are still being) discovered (see: **DSS; Textual Criticism**). A Catholic Edition of the RSV NT appeared in 1965, containing 67 slight alterations in wording; the entire Bible, including the 1957 RSV edition of the Apocrypha, appeared in 1966. The RSV "Expanded Edition" (1977) includes the OT, NT, and Apocrypha of Catholic and Protestant tradi-tion as well as 3 and 4 Maccabees and Ps. 151 of the Orthodox tradition.
The second edition of the RSV Old Testament is expected to be completed in the mid-1980's along with further revision of the NT. The greatest change is likely to be the elimination of unnecessary male-oriented language. See: **ASV; KJV; TEV; Version; Paraphrase.**

RV (Revised Version). Common abbreviation for the British revision of the King James Version of the Bible (1611), completed in 1885 (NT, 1881). It is a woodenly literal translation of the Hebrew and Greek texts purposely cast, as much as possible, in 16th cent. English following the KJV and earlier versions. The American Standard Version (1901) is a revision of the RV. See: **ASV; Douay; JB; KJV; NAB; RSV; TEV; Paraphrase; Version; esp. ASV.**

Sachexegese; Sachkritik (Ger.: subject exegesis; subject criticism). In Ger-man Biblical criticism, *Se.* may broadly refer to the analysis of the total subject matter of a text, including (1) historical data (archaeology, geography, etc.) as well as (2) theological and other leading concepts; it may however refer to (1) only, (2) being called *Begriffsexegese* (concept exegesis); or, it may refer to (2) only, (1) being called historical criticism. Some scholars argue that since Scripture clothes its theological beliefs in historical statements, no absolute distinction is possible between *Sachexegese* and *Begriffsexegese.*

In the thought of Rudolf Bultmann (1884–1976), *Sk.* refers to the interpretation of a text in light of its subject matter *(Sache)* and is based on the assumption that it would be impossible even for a Biblical author always to give adequate expression to his subject and that it is therefore necessary to distinguish between what an author says and what he means and to measure what is said by what is meant. This became one of the cardinal points of disagreement between Bultmann and Karl Barth.

Sachhälfte. See: *Bildhälfte.*

Saga. See: **Legend.**

Salvation History. See: *Heilsgeschichte.*

Samaritan Pentateuch (*siglum*: SP) is a recension of the first five books of the OT, written in Hebrew and preserved as the sacred Scriptures of the Samaritans, a religious sect in Palestine (centered in Nablus) which has claimed since Biblical times to be the faithful remnant of ancient Israel. In NT times the former region of Israel was called Samaria, its inhabitants Samaritans (see Mt. 19:1; Lk. 10:25–39; 17:11; Jn. 4:4–9; etc.). Although the best extant recension of the SP (the Abisha Scroll at Nablus) is in part of great antiquity, corroborating readings in the **LXX** and the **DSS,** its value for OT textual criticism is limited. Of its six thousand variants from the MT, many are religiously motivated: e.g., the Hebrew name for God is changed from plural (Elohim) to singular form (Gen. 20:13; 31:53; 35:7; Ex. 22:8), the reference to "the angel who has redeemed me" (Gen. 48:16) becomes "the king who has redeemed me" and so on.

See: J. D. Parvis, *The Samaritan Pentateuch and the Origin of the Samaritan Sect* (Harvard Semitic Monographs, 2; Cambridge: Harvard University Press, 1968); and R. J. Coggins, *Samaritans and Jews* (Atlanta: John Knox Press, 1975).

Sätze heiligen Rechtes (German: "sentences of holy law"). A technical term, occasionally left untranslated, proposed by Ernst Käsemann (1954) to denote what he considers to be the earliest form of Christian law, antedating the subsequent development of administrative, disciplinary, and canon law. The laws are a chiastic form of *jus talionis:* "If anyone destroys God's temple,

God will destroy him" (1 Cor. 3:17). Also 1 Cor. 14:38; 16:22; Gal. 1:9; Rev. 22:18–19; cf. Rom. 10:11, 13; Gal. 3:12; Mk. 8:38; Mt. 10:32–33. According to Käsemann, these utterances come from the early Christian prophets who, filled with the Spirit and in anticipation of the imminent *Eschaton* (the second coming of the Lord), pronounced a blessing or curse on those who broke divine law. In this way the Christian prophet, particularly in circles outside the apostles, gave leadership and order to communities prior to the formal structuring of ecclesiastical authority. (See: Ernst Käsemann, *New Testament Questions of Today* [London: SCM Press, 1969], ch. III.)

Sayings. In form-critical analyses of Scripture, the term S. is used to designate that speech which in form and content "stands midway between prose and poetry, between the story and the song" (Eissfeldt). In content it is often exalted or solemn, in form it may be free or formal (rhythmic). Categories of sayings usually include the aphorism, blessing, curse, exhortation, invective, legal demand, threat, and prophetic oracle.

Biblical Sayings are generally attributed to one of three sources: the law giver, the prophet, or the sage (revelation; inspiration/vision; observation). In the OT, collections of laws are found primarily in Ex., Lev., and Deut.; collections of prophetic sayings in Isa., Jer., etc.; and collections of wisdom sayings in Prov. In the NT, Jesus is depicted as lawgiver, prophet, and sage. The Epistle of James is not a letter but a collection of Sayings.

It is said that narrative "contribute(s) to the unity and coherence of the biblical world," whereas Sayings express "the fragmentariness of existence" (Beardslee). It must be averred, however, that wisdom sayings presuppose, even arise from, a fundamental rationality underlying human existence.

See: **Logion; Q.**

Sayings Source. See: **Q.**

SBL. The Society of Biblical Literature, founded in 1881, is the largest professional society devoted to Biblical and cognate studies in the US and Canada. It publishes the *Journal of Biblical Literature; SBL Monograph Series; Semeia; Semeia Supplements; Dissertation Series; Sources for Biblical Study; Texts and Translation Series; Septuagint and Cognate Studies and Masoretic Studies.* For information, write: Scholars Press, P.O. Box 2268, 101 Salem St., Chico, CA 95926.

Schleiermacher, Friedrich Ernst Daniel (1768–1834). Born in Breslau, Germany, and raised in a Moravian community with which he later broke, S. was a pastor in Berlin and Stolp before becoming professor of theology at Halle (1804) and later at the newly founded University of Berlin (1810), where he remained, continuing however to preach throughout his life. Although noted for his theological writings (beginning with *On Religion: Addresses in Response to Its Cultured Critics* [1799]), which have gained for him the encomium "Church Father of the 19th cent.," S's role in the development of NT criticism and hermeneutic was considerable. The first to deliver lectures on the life of Jesus (1819), he called for the study of the NT as any other literature, disputed the Pauline authorship of 1 Tim. on the basis of its language and situation, arguing that the authority of a NT writing depended on its content and not its authorship. See: **Hermeneutics.**

Scholion (pl.: scholia; Greek diminutive: "little lecture"; Latin: *scholium*). An annotation by an ancient or medieval scholar on a historical text for the purpose of instructing the reader, such as Origen's note (S.) to Ps. 118:1 (LXX) in his *Hexapla.* Codex Mosquensis (K^{ap}), dating from the 9th or 10th cent., contains scholia attributed to John Chrysostom, the great scholar-preacher. When scholia accompany the whole text and are not simply random or marginal notations, the work is called a commentary. (See: Bruce M. Metzger, *The Text of the New Testament* [London and New York: Oxford University Press, 1964].)

Schweitzer, Albert (1875–1965). Born in Kayersberg (Oberelsass, Germany); *Privatdozent* for NT (1902–12) and assistant pastor at St. Nicholas' Cathedral (1903–06) in Strassburg; began medical studies in 1905 with the intention of becoming a medical missionary, which he realized in 1913, founding a hospital in Lambarene, French Equatorial Africa (now Gabon). In this period he wrote a doctorate in philosophy (1899), became a Licentiate in theology (1900) and completed his Habilitation (requirement for teaching on the university level) in 1902. An accomplished organist, he published a study on J. S. Bach (French 1905; Ger. 1908) and on German and French organ construction (1906), the latter appearing in the same year as the first edition of his epoch-making *The Quest of the Historical Jesus.* Before his departure to Africa and in addition to lecture and recital tours, he published *Paul and His Interpreters* (Ger.: 1911; Eng.: London: A. & C. Black, 1912) and *The Psychiatric Study of Jesus* (Ger.: 1913; Eng. 1948). Interned during WW I in Europe (1917) and unable to return to Lambarene for lack of funds until 1924, S. turned to writing, this time to philosophical and autobiographical works. His last major contribution to Biblical studies, *The Mysticism of Paul the Apostle* (London: A. & C. Black), appeared in 1930.

Perhaps more than any other man S. characterized NT studies at the turn of the century. On the one hand his *Quest* embodied even as it catalogued the inadequacies of 19th cent. synoptic methodology, yet it established beyond any possibility of denial the eschatological character of Jesus' proclamation and thereby laid the basis of all dominant forms of Biblical theology in the 20th cent.

Of all the contributors to modern Biblical criticism, S. remains unsurpassed in breadth of genius, audacity of vision, and courage of moral action.

For the significance of S's *Quest,* see James M. Robinson's "Introduction" to the 1968 paperback edition, published by the Macmillan Company. See: **Quest of the Historical Jesus.**

Sellin, Ernst (1867–1945). Professor of OT in Vienna, Rostock, Kiel, and, from 1921 until his retirement in 1935, in Berlin. Sellin's most influential work is his *Introduction to the OT* (Ger., 1910; Eng., 1923; rev. by Georg Fohrer [Nashville: Abingdon Press, 1968]), in which he took a mediating position between the radical criticism of the Wellhausen school on one hand and the traditional conservative position on the other.

Semantics (fr. Gk: sēma, sēmeron: sign) is a term first employed by the French linguist Michel Breal (*Essai des semantique* [Paris: Hachette, 1897; Eng.: *Semantics: Studies in the Science of Meaning* [New York: Dover Press, 1964]) to refer to the complex rules by which linguistic expressions are created and die, how meaning changes and new expressions are chosen. Breal's interest lay in the historical (diachronic) development of the meaning of linguistic forms, an interest which in subsequent decades did not remain the central focus of S.

As a field of study today, S. is so diverse and complicated that the term itself is ambiguous and, as the Polish linguist Adam Schaff has written, "needs to undergo semantic analysis" (Ger. tr.: *Einführung in die Semantik* [Berlin: 1966], Preface). In general usage the term may refer to (1) the study of the relationship between the meaning and content of words and phrases; (2) **semasiology** (q.v.); (3) that aspect of language analysis which studies the relationship of linguistic units to the objects and processes described by them; and (4) the empirical investigation of the meaning (content) of linguistic signs and sign combinations, in brief, "the study of meaning" (see: Th. Lewandowski, *Linguistisches Wörterbuch* 3[Heidelberg: Quelle & Meyer, 1975], ad hoc).

Semasiology (fr. Gk.: sēma, sēmeion: sign) usually refers either to (1) the study of meaning, and is equivalent to **semantics** (q.v.), or (2) that branch of linguistics which investigates the lexical meanings of words in terms of their synchronic and diachronic aspects. According to Th. Schippan (*Einführung in die Semasiology* [Leipzig: Bibliographisches Institut, 1972]), S. is the heart of lexicology; it is the study of words and their origins, particularly the lexical division of a language and of the variations occurring within it. S. investigates the structure of the "lexic" ("vocabulary"; cf. lexicon), the meaning of its elements and lexical units and their semantic relationships; it describes the changes in a vocabulary, the causes and conditions lying behind them; and, it investigates the connection between the development of a society and vocabulary adaptation and creation. The foundations of S. go back to the Latin studies of C. K. Reisig in Germany.

(For this definition see: Th. Lewandowski, *Linguistisches Wörterbuch* 3 [Heidelberg: Quelle & Meyer, 2nd rev. ed., 1976].)

Semiology, Semiotics (fr. Greek: sēma, sēmeion: sign, signal) are t.t., now used interchangeably, to denote studies toward a general theory of signs or sign systems. At present, S. is perhaps more a field of studies waiting to be unified into a single discipline than a single discipline unifying diverse phenomena by way of a comprehensive semiotic model (U. Eco). The field of semiotics includes studies in a vast range of communicative processes (semiosis); such studies assume that underlying each process is a *system of significations* (or "Code") which makes communication possible. Individual semiotic studies may concentrate on the production (encoding), performance, or reception (decoding) of signs, since each is an inherent part of every event of communication. Areas encompassed by contemporary research are: Zoosemiotics, tactile communication, codes of taste, paralinguistics (voice sets, qualities, etc.), kinesics (gesturing), musical codes, formalized languages (e.g., algebra), written languages, natural languages, plot structure, visual communication, text theory, cultural codes, mass communication, rhetoric, etc. (In any single event of human communication a number of discrete systems [codes] is likely to be involved.)

In recent years Biblical criticism has experienced the growing impact of semiotic studies. These include the general theoretical studies of Ferdinand de Saussure (*Course in General Linguistics* [New York: McGraw-Hill, 1959; French orig.; 1916]), C. S. Peirce (*Collected Papers* [Cambridge: Harvard University Press, 1931–1958]), and Charles Morris (*Writings on the General Theory of Signs* [Approaches to Semiotics, 16, The Hague/Paris: Mouton, 1971]), and, of particular interest, the more specialized investigations within the field of narrative or plot structure, e.g., Vladimir Propp (*Morphology of the Folktale* [The Hague: Mouton, 1958; 2nd ed. Austin, TX and London: University of Texas Press, 1968; Russian orig.: 1928]), A. J. Geimas (*Sémantique structurale* [Paris: Larousse, 1966]), and Roland Barthes (*Mythologies* [Paris: Seuil, 1957]).

For a listing of approximately 1900 books and articles relating semiotic theory to religious studies, see: Alfred M. Johnson, Jr., *A Bibliography of Semiological and Structural Studies of Religion* (Pittsburgh: Clifford E. Barbour Library, Pittsburgh Theological Seminary, 1979).

See: **Structure, Structuralism.**

Semitism (also Semiticism). Broadly speaking, a S. is a word or idiom derived from a Semitic language; in Biblical study it more specifically designates a feature of LXX or NT Greek which shows the influence of Semitic (Hebrew or Aramaic) style and terminology. Except for Daniel, the LXX contains only Hebraisms; the Hebraisms of the NT may point either to a quotation from the LXX or to an imitation of LXX style (Lk.-Acts)—just as the style of the KJV is imitated today. Proven Aramaisms in the NT, however, are likely to go back either to Jesus or to early Palestinian Christianity; terms such as *"Abba"* ("Father," Mk. 14:36), *"Maranatha"* ("Our Lord, come," 1 Cor. 16:22), and *"Talitha cumi"* ("Little girl, arise," Mk. 5:41) are examples. In general, Semitic style is characterized by a frequency of parataxis (the sequential ordering of subjects and main verbs rather than using subordinate clauses—e. g., Mk. 10:32), parallelism (e. g., Lk. 12:48), and *chiasmus* (Mt. 9:17; 1 Cor. 5:2–6, etc.), which, however, are also found, though to a far less degree, in Greek. The Semitic style of the *Magnificat* (Lk. 1:46–55), the *Benedictus* (1:68–79), and the *Nunc Dimittis* (2:29–32), plus other considerations, have led scholars to postulate their pre-Christian origin within the movement associated with John the Baptist. See: Heuman, Fred S., *The Uses of Hebraisms in Recent Bible Translations* (New York: Philosophical Library, 1977). See: **Latinism; Septuagintism.**

Sensus Litteralis (Latin: literal sense) names the first of the fourfold sense of Scripture given to a text in medieval hermeneutics, along with allegorical, moral (tropological) and anagogical (see: **Allegory; Tropology; Anagogy**).

Sentences of Holy Law. See: *Sätze heiligen Rechtes.*

Septuagint (Latin: seventy; *siglum:* LXX; sometimes called the Old Greek or Proto-LXX translation) is the name of the earliest Greek translation of the Hebrew Torah; it later came to include the whole OT and the Apocrypha. According to tradition it was prepared at the order of Ptolemy II (*ca.* 285–247 B.C.) in Alexandria, Egypt, by 70 (or 72) Hebrew elders, whence its name and symbol. It became the favored translation of the OT in the early Church and for this reason fell into disfavor among Jews. In OT text-critical discussions, the symbol LXX often denotes the Lucianic recension of the LXX (Lucian d. A.D. 312), hence terms such as "Old Greek" or "Proto-LXX" refer to the earliest forms of the text. Further, "Proto-Lucian" (2nd–1st cent. B.C.) denotes a form of the Old Greek text revised in the direction of the Palestinian Hebrew text. Another early recension of the Old Greek is called the Proto-Theodotion or *Kaige* recension (1st cent. A.D. or earlier). By Jerome's day (*ca.* A.D. 400) there were three editions of the LXX called the *Trifaria Varietas:* the Hexaplaric text of Origen, another by Hesychius of Egypt, and Lucian's. See: **Aquila; Theodotion; Symmachus.**

Septuagintism ("belonging to the Septuagint"). Words or phrases that are peculiar to or especially characteristic of the Greek OT (the **Septuagint;** q. v.) and are used by NT writers in imitation (conscious or otherwise) of its style and expression are called Septuagintisms. Luke in particular appears to have cast his history of the early Church (the book of Acts) in the style of the LXX. The expressions "lifted up his voice," "let this be known," and "give ear" all in Acts 2:14 are examples of Ss. The subsequent speech by Peter (Acts 2:15–39) and another in 3:12–26 are generally recognized as Lukan imitations of Septuagint Greek. A S. may be, but is not necessarily, also a Semitism. For example, Matthew's use of *parthenos* (virgin) in his quotation of Isa. 7:14 (Mt. 1:23) follows the LXX and may be termed a S., since the Hebrew reading contains *'almāh* meaning "a young woman." The use of *parthenos* is peculiar to the LXX and has nothing to do with Hebrew (Semitic) terminology or expression. This is one of the reasons 1st–2nd cent. Judaism rejected the LXX. See: **Semitism; Latinism.**

Setting in Life. See: *Sitz-im-Leben.*

Shema (Hebrew: hear) is the common name given to the three prayers offered daily by the pious Jews of the 1st cent. A.D., taken from Dt. 6:4–9; 11:13–21; and Num. 15:37–41; the term *(S.)* itself is from the longest section of the second prayer beginning, "Hear, O Israel: The Lord our God, the Lord is One." In their brief form the prayers are (1) *Yoser,* "Blessed art thou, O Lord, Creator of the luminaries"; (2) *Ahabah,* "Blessed art thou, who hast chosen thy people in love" (the *S.* follows here ending, "I am the Lord your God, who brought you out of the land of Egypt, to be your God; I am the Lord your God"); (3) *Geullah,* "Blessed art thou, O Lord, who redeemest Israel." In NT faith, cf. Rom. 3:30; Gal. 3:20; Jas. 2:19; esp. 1 Cor. 8:6; Phil. 2:6–11.

Shemoneh Esreh (Hebrew: Eighteen) or "The Eighteen Benedictions" formed the center of the service of worship in the Jewish synagogues of 1st cent. Palestine. The prayer, beginning "O Lord, open thou my lips and my mouth shall show forth thy praise," contains eighteen (since ca. A.D. 100, nineteen) benedictions concerning (1) the Patriarchs, (2) making the dead live, (3) sanctification of the name, (4) understanding, (5) repentance, (6) forgiveness, (7) redemption, (8) healing, (9) the blessing of the year, (10) the gathering of the dispersed, (11) restoration of the Judges, (12) against heresy, (13) the blessing of proselytes, (14) Jerusalem, (15) hearing prayer, (16) worship, (17) thanksgiving, and (18) peace.

177

Sich realisierende Eschatologie. A German phrase commonly given the awkward translation: "eschatology in the process of being realized." See: **Eschatology; Realized Eschatology; Wrede.**

Signs Source. This t.t. derives from the source-critical analysis of the Gospel of John, specifically that section of the Gospel containing the seven miraculous "signs" of Jesus' divine power (chs. 2–11), which in whole or part is thought to have existed in written form prior to the compilation and redaction of the Gospel. This theory, first proposed by A. Fauré (1922), is generally accepted though debated in its details (content, setting-in-life, etc.). The word "sign" is a literal translation of the Greek *sēmeion* which the author uses in place of the common word for miracle (see Jn. 2:11, 18, 23; 3:2; 4:54; 6:2, 14, 26, 30, etc.). For a discussion, see: Robert T. Fortna, *The Gospel of Signs: A Reconstruction of the Narrative Source Underlying the Fourth Gospel* (Cambridge: Cambridge University Press, 1970). See: **Literary Criticism.**

Simile. See: **Metaphor.**

Sitz-im-Leben (Ger.: setting in life, or life situation) has become a t.t. in Form Criticism to refer to that sociological setting within the life of Israel or the early Church in which particular rhetorical forms (legends, sayings, liturgical formulae, psalms, prophecies, parables, etc.) first took shape. (See: Martin J. Buss, "The Idea of Sitz-im-Leben—History and Critique," ZAW 90 [1978] 157–70.)

As first employed by Hermann Gunkel (1906) it referred to the social setting of literary form in Israel *(Sitz-im-Volksleben Israels)*. Martin Dibelius *(From Tradition to Gospel* [London: Ivor Nicholson and Watson, Ltd.; repr. James Clarke, 1971; New York: Charles Scribner's Sons, 1935; Ger.: 1919]) applied the concept to the NT, particularly to the Gospel materials because, unlike the NT epistles, they had existed in oral form prior to being written down in the Gospels. Here the term functioned in the sense of "the setting in the life of the Church" *(Sitz-im-Leben der Kirche).* According to Dibelius, it was the Church's need for sermonic and didactic material which was the "life situation" that had either created or formatively shaped and determined the content of the traditions.

C. H. Dodd *(The Parables of the Kingdom* [London: Nisbet & Co., 1935]) and Joachim Jeremias *(The Parables of Jesus* [New York: Charles Scribner's Sons, 1955; London: SCM Press, 1972; Ger.: 1947; 1971⁸]) sought to go behind the sociological setting of the Church to the "setting in the life of Jesus" *(Sitz-im-Leben Jesu),* which they defined in part as the impending crisis of Divine Judgment and Jesus' controversies with the Pharisees.

In NT Redaction Criticism, however, the term, or rather a modification of it, refers not to a sociological but to a literary setting, viz., "the setting in the Gospel" (*Sitz-im-Evangelium;* i. e., in Mt., Mk., Lk., or Jn.) which the various traditions (parables, miracle stories, sayings, etc.) have been given by the writers. Here it is recognized that linguistic forms have been adapted to the kerygmatic, catechetical, and apologetic purposes of the Gospel writers and that their meaning and function for the writer can in part be ascertained by the literary setting he gives them.

See: **Form Criticism;** *Kultgeschichtliche Schule;* **Mowinckel; Tradition Criticism.**

Sociological Interpretation stresses that knowledge of the social milieu in which the texts of Scripture arose is necessary for any adequate understanding of the texts themselves.

Following N. K. Gottwald one can say that SI seeks to understand typical patterns of human relations in their structure and function, both at a given time in history (synchronics) and in their trajectories of change over a specified time span (diachronics). The hypothetically "typical" in collective human behavior is ascertained by comparative study of societies and expressed theoretically in "laws," "regularities," or "tendencies" that attempt to abstract structures and processes of a translocal and transtemporal character. As a method the SI of Scripture includes all the methods of inquiry proper to the social sciences (such as anthropology, sociology, political science, and economics), as well as those typical of the humanities (history, comparative religions, literary criticism, form criticism, rhetorical criticism, redaction criticism, tradition history, etc.).

The assumptions generally characteristic of SI are (1) that humanistic and sociological methods are equally valuable and complementary methods for reconstructing the ancient past; (2) that religion is best understood as one part of a wider network of social relations in which it has intelligible functions to perform; (3) that changes in religious behavior and thought are best viewed as aspects of change in the wider network of social and economic relations; and (4) that religion is intelligible to the degree that it exhibits lawful behavior and symbolic forms which can be predicted and retrodicted within limits set by the total matrix of changing social and economic relations (cf. Norman K. Gottwald, *The Tribes of Yahweh: A Sociology of the Religion of Liberated Israel, 1250–1050* B.C.E. [Maryknoll, N.Y.: Orbis Books, 1979], Preface, xxiii; also "Sociological Method in the Study of Ancient Israel," in Martin J. Buss, ed., *Encounter with the Text: Form and History in the Hebrew Bible* [Missoula: Scholars Press, 1979]).

Since its inception at the turn of the century, the application of sociological theory to ancient Israel and to Christian beginnings has been sparse and sporadic. Among the earliest practitioners in OT studies were W. Robertson

Smith (*Lectures on the Religion of the Semites. The Fundamental Institutions* [London: A. & C. Black, 1901]), Max Weber (*Ancient Judaism* [Glencoe, Ill.: Free Press, 1952; Ger.: 1923]), and Johannes Pedersen (*Israel, Its Life and Culture,* I–IV [London: Oxford University Press, 1926–40]); in the NT those usually cited are Shailer Mathews (*The Social Teaching of Jesus* [New York: The Macmillan Co., 1906]), Shirley Jackson Case (*The Social Origins of Christianity* [Chicago: Chicago University Press, 1923]), and Adolf Deissmann (*St. Paul: A Study in Social and Religious History* [London: Hodder and Stoughton, 1912]).

In recent years, studies combining sociological theory and methodology to Biblical texts have demonstrated four different (though often overlapping) approaches and/or concerns: (1) a description of *social facts* related to the material culture: institutions, occupations, economics, food, etc., e.g., R. de Vaux, *Ancient Israel: Its Life and Institutions* (New York: McGraw-Hill, 1961); Martin Hengel, *Judaism and Hellenism* (Philadelphia: Fortress Press, 1974); Joachim Jeremias, *Jerusalem in the Time of Jesus* (London: SCM Press, 1969); and, Ronald F. Hock, *The Social Context of Paul's Ministry* (Philadelphia: Fortress Press, 1979); (2) the development of the *social history* of a movement integrating hard data with social and political history by means of a theoretical framework, e.g., G. E. Mendenhall, *Law and Covenant in Israel and the Ancient Near East* (Pittsburgh, PA: The Biblical Colloquium, 1955); Abraham Malherbe, *Social Aspects of Early Christianity* (Baton Rouge, LA: Louisiana State University Press, 1977); and Robert M. Grant, *Early Christianity and Society* (New York: Harper and Row, 1977); (3) an account of the *social organization* involved in a movement's origins and developments, e.g., N. K. Gottwald's work cited above; Gerd Theissen, *Sociology of Early Palestinian Christianity* (Philadelphia: Fortress Press, 1978); and Leander Keck, *The New Testament Experience of Faith* (St. Louis: Bethany Press, 1976); (4) the reconstruction of the *social world* of a religious movement, attempting to suggest what it is like to live in a world structured by the symbols, rituals, and language used by the movement, e.g., Peter Berger, *The Sacred Canopy: Elements of a Sociological Theory of Religion* (Garden City, N.Y.: Doubleday and Co., 1967). For this synopsis, see James A. Wilde, "The Social World of Mark's Gospel: A Word about Method" in *SBL Seminar Papers,* Vol. 2, ed. by Paul J. Achtemeier (Missoula: Scholars Press, 1978), pp. 47–70; also, Walter Brueggemann, "Trajectories in OT Literature and the Sociology of Ancient Israel," *JBL* 98 (1979), pp. 161–85.

See: *Trägerkreis,* **Reception Theory.**

Source Criticism. See: **Literary Criticism.**

SP. Common abbreviation for the **Samaritan Pentateuch**.

Spät-Judentum (German: "late Judaism"). See: **Late Judaism.**

Sprachereignis (Ger.: "language event"). See: **Language-event.**

Stich, *stichos* (Greek: row, line, verse; fr. *steichein,* to go, walk). See: **Colon.**

Strack-Billerbeck is the common call name of the *Kommentar zum Neuen Testament aus Talmud und Midrash,* vols. I–IV/2; edited by (Hermann L. Strack and) Paul Billerbeck (Munich: C. H. Beck Verlag 1926–28), which is an indispensable tool for the comparative study of early Christianity and 1st–4th cent. Judaism. See: **Exegesis.**

Strauss, David Friedrich (1808–1874). Born in Ludwigsburg (Württemberg), Germany, a student of F. C. Baur in Blaubeuren (1821) and Tübingen (1825), and later influenced by F. E. D. Schleiermacher in Berlin (1831–32), S. became "infamously famous" (Karl Barth) for his *Life of Jesus Critically Examined* (Ger.: 1835–36 [reprint 1969]; Eng.: 1846), which declared the Gospels to be myths without historical foundation. The resulting controversy ended his academic career (with pension) in 1839 before it had really begun. S's subsequent position moderated but this did not alter critical opinion toward him, and he died embittered. His last works included *The Old Faith and the New* (Ger.: 1872; Eng.: 1873) and *Der Christus des Glaubens und der Jesus der Geschichte* [*The Christ of Faith and the Jesus of History*] (Ger.: 1864; reprint 1971; Eng. reprint: Philadelphia: Fortress Press, 1973).

Streeter, Burnett Hillman (1874–1937), a Fellow at Queen's College, Oxford, is noted in Textual Criticism particularly for his theory concerning the text Family used by Origen in Palestine, called the Caesarean text; and, in Source Criticism for his Four Document (or Source) Hypothesis, with which he proposed to replace the older Two Source Hypothesis, through the establishment of two additional ancient documents known as "M" and "L" encompassing material peculiar to Mt. and Lk. respectively. See: **Four Document Hypothesis.**

Streitgespräch (Ger.: "controversy dialogue"). In OT form-critical studies, *S.* is a descriptive term used in reference to the book of Job; in NT studies it is a t.t. employed by Rudolf Bultmann as a subcategory of **Apophthegms** (q. v.); it includes e. g., Mk. 2:1–12, 15–17; 3:1–5; 7:1–23; 10:2–12, 17–30; 12:13–17, etc.

Strophe (Greek: lit., turning). In the wider sense, a S. is one of two or more series of lines possessing metrical regularity which form the divisions of a lyric poem. In Greek choral and lyric poetry, the term pertained to a metrical structure which was repeated in a following series of lines called the antistrophe. In the study of OT poetry, the applicability of the term is much disputed, since Hebrew poetry is characterized by parallelism of thought, not by rhyme or metrical regularity. When the term S. is used in OT criticism, therefore, it is loosely applied and may mean simply a verse paragraph of indeterminate length uncontrolled by any formal artistic scheme (G. B. Gray, *Forms of Hebrew Poetry* [New York: Ktav Publishing House, 1970], p. 192), or, more closely defined, as a series of parallel figures (bicola or tricola) with a discernible beginning and ending, possessing identifiable unity in thought, structure, and style. Sometimes the Ss are opened with particular formulae ("Behold," "Praise," "How Long?" "O Lord") or closed with a refrain (Pss. 39; 42; 43; 46; 49; 56; 57; 59; 62; 67; 78; 80; 99; 107; 114; 136; 144; 145; cf. Amos 1; 2; 4; Isa. 4; 5; 9; and 10), with alteration in length of line or meter. Strophic division is more frequently marked by the sense of the poem itself, since the structuring of thought patterns into parallel forms is the basic characteristic of Hebrew poetry. Occasionally, a poem is structured by acrostic (Pss. 9–10; 25; 34; 37; 111; 112; 119; 145; Lam. 1–4; and Nahum 1). See: **Colon.**

Structuralism, like existentialism in earlier decades of this century, is a way of thinking about reality present in a range of intellectual disciplines so diverse as to preclude any single definition even in terms of its usage within any one of them. At best perhaps, one can say that S.—whether in linguistics, sociology, ethnology, mathematics, psychology, the physical sciences, philosophy, literary criticism, etc.—has as its primary intention "the construction of a theory of [its] object from which the fundamental characteristics of this object can be deduced" (Raymond Boudon, *The Uses of Structuralism,* trans. Michalina Vaughan [London: Heinemann, 1971]). In Biblical criticism, this "theory" or set of principles is at present primarily derived from other disciplines, from the structuralist anthropology of Claude Lévi-Strauss and from the structuralist literary critic Roland Barthes, et al., but especially from general linguistics where S. began in the seminal thought of Ferdinand De Saussure. It is not first of all the structure of texts (the "object" of Biblical criticism) that is preconceived in theory, but the *structure of language* to which individual texts as particular linguistic expressions must conform in order to be intelligible. Structural linguistics deals primarily with the sentence and smaller units. Biblical and literary critics are interested in larger units. It is suggested that the structure of language predetermines the structure of its genres and that genres are in turn predeterminative of any given instance of their expression. Hence the task of the structuralist is to establish the rules by which language functions and to deduce principles therefrom for analyzing the structure of texts. "Structure" here refers to that theoretical model or system of interrelated elements (texts or text-parts) from which the content and function of the elements themselves are derived. This differs from "structure" as the internal organization of a text, its linguistic patterns, sequence, etc. as commonly used in recent form-critical studies. Rather, "structure" here is a trans-textual rather than simply an intra-textual "reality." So conceived (and some structuralists would disagree with the above), the whole (the structure) is more than or other than the sum of the parts; further, the whole determines the parts, a path structuralists contend is irreversible (cf. *the hermeneutic circle* under **Hermeneutics**).

Major concepts and terms in structural linguistics and the sub-disciplines related to them include:

1. Language *(langue)*, as the social side of speech, is distinct from speaking *(parole)*, as any individual act of language use. According to Saussure, this distinction separates the social from the individual, the essential from the accessory or accidental. Only *langue* therefore constitutes the proper study of linguistics.

2. Every language is a coherently ordered and explicable system of signs and of rules (the subject of semeiology) which function (non-interchangably) on three levels: a. sounds *(phonemes,* the subject of phonology), b. units of meaning *(morphemes,* the subject of morphology) consisting of word stems *(lexemes)* and (or including) functional indicators such as prefixes and suffixes, and c. the sentence *(syntagm),* formed through the combination and opposition of constituent elements of meaning (the subject of grammar [syntax] and semantics). Some here add d. the literary unit or *texteme* composed of macro-syntactical elements marked off by introductory and closing signifiers, etc.

3. Every linguistic act, whether word or sentence, is made up of (a) a verbal sign, the sound-image or signifier, and (b) a concept, or that which is signified (Saussure). The relationship between the signifier and the signified is arbitrary, as the multitude of languages proves.

4. The structure of a linguistic system is basically one of combinations, contrasts, and oppositions, since the elements of language achieve meaning only in relationship. Sounds which do not conform to the phonetic rules of a linguistic system cease to function as components of verbal signs (see 1 Cor. 14), just as verbal signs which do not conform to the rules of syntax when combined fail to function as units of meaning. The sequence of relationships here, for both sender and receiver, whether oral or written, is linear or *syntagmatic.* At the same time, every word and every sentence arouses in those who know the language associations with other related unspoken signs within the total linguistic system; such relationships are of a *paradigmatic* type. The relationship of verbal signs within a language at any given time is *synchronic* (lit., "at the same time"); they are mutually and simultaneously interdependent.

The relation of signs to their antecedents within the same or cognate language is *diachronic* (lit., "through time"). S. deals with synchrony not diachrony, with language at a given time, not the evolution of language through time.

S. thus differs in focus from that of historical-critical methodologies (Classical Literary Criticism, Form Criticism, Redaction Criticism, et al.) in that the category of history is essentially absent. Considering the historical nature of Biblical theology, the role of S. in Biblical criticism is naturally circumscribed, but, as it relates to Biblical exegesis, the approach is still in its infancy and much remains to be answered.

For examples of S. applied to Scripture and for an extensive bibliography (53 pages) see, Roland Barthes et al., *Structural Analysis and Biblical Exegesis: Interpretational Essays,* trans. Alfred M. Johnson, Jr., Pittsburgh Theological Monograph Series, Number 3, (Pittsburgh: Pickwick Press, 1974). For additional bibliography, see: **Semiology; Structure.**

See: **Biblical Criticism; Exegesis; Form Criticism; Hermeneutics; Morpheme; Parable; Phoneme.**

Structure. The term S. has a wide variety of applications, some of which stand in theoretical contradiction to each other; it therefore lends itself to no single definition. Even works expressly devoted to analyzing the S. of texts rarely directly offer any definition of the term itself (J. Pouillon).

In non-structuralist studies, S. often refers to poetic, literary, or rhetorical style, such as metric pattern, parallelism, anaphora, diatribe, etc. S. here pertains to the surface structures of a text rather than to so-called "deep structures." The basic unit of research is the sentence or colon.

In structuralist studies, whose basic units are supra-sentential, the term S. is no less varied in usage. Broadly speaking, it refers to the inner organization of the lexical-semantic or thematic content through which the text receives its intelligibility; it is the arrangement of the constituent elements (whether ideas or characters) and the network of relationships existing between them. The inner organization or network of relationships, however, is perceived to exist below the surface of the text as deep structures not as surface ones. Just as (the constituent elements of) a sentence must conform to underlying grammatical rules if the sentence is to be coherent so, it is argued, must (the constituent elements of) narratives and myths (called narrative syntagma and mythemes) conform to underlying "laws" or "constraints" in order to be intelligible. And just as grammatical rules generate, that is, are the origins of sentence intelligibility, so the "laws" or "deep structures" of narratives and myths can be thought of as "generative grammars" of the same. Therefore it is less accurate to say that a narrative or myth *has* a structure than that it conforms to a structure, the formulation or diagrammatization of which is accomplished theoretically only by the study of a large number of texts.

184

What the relationship is of surface structures to deep structures, what constitutes a deep structure and how it is to be modeled or diagrammed, are all moot points. For example, U. Eco writes that a structure "is a model built and *posited* in order to standardize diverse phenomena from a unified point of view" (*A Theory of Semiotics* [Bloomington/London: Indiana University Press, 1976], p. 46, n. 4). In this sense, the "structure" of a text is less an objective reality than an operational hypothesis. A concurring but qualifying caveat is offered by Jean Pouillon: "A model is not a structure. It is a simplification of reality, which is tested in order to make it undergo variations which will permit the structure to be more easily read. And the diagram, thanks to which the model appears, refers to the analysis and to its method, not to a particular reality whose representation it would be" ("Structuralism: A Definitional Essay," in *Structuralism and Biblical Hermeneutics,* ed. and trans. by Alfred M. Johnson, Jr. [Pittsburgh: The Pickwick Press, 1979], pp. 42–43).

In point of fact, few structural models for narratives and myths exist, and none which has remained undisputed or unqualified. Although it is not possible here to explain structure or structural models in detail, the following will illustrate what is involved. Claude Lévi-Strauss, a structural anthropologist, suggests that the structure or myths can be expressed by the formula: $F_x(a) : F_y(b) :: F_x(b) : F_{a-1}(y)$, in which opposing subjects (or states) a and b with functions (F) x and y are resolved by a transformation of states and an inversion of functions.(Claude Lévi-Strauss, *Structual Anthropology* [New York/London: Basic Books, Inc., 1963], p. 228.)

A. J. Greimas and proponents of his theories, working on the structural analysis of narratives, have attempted to deduce from large numbers of texts *actantial* and *functional* "constants" or "elements of structure" operative in all narratives. The functions of actants in narratives are said to be seven in number: (1) Arrival vs. Departure or Departure vs. Return, (2) Conjunction vs. Disjunction, (3) Mandating vs. Acceptance or vs. Refusal, (4) Confrontation, (5) Domination vs. Submission, (6) Communication vs. Reception, (7) Attribution vs. Deprivation. Actants or "spheres of action" (not to be confused with the various characters of the narrative) which are deemed constant structural elements in every narrative are expressed in the following actantial model:

SENDER————————————▶OBJECT————————————▶RECEIVER
HELPER————————————▶SUBJECT———————————▶OPPONENT

For detailed explanations of these "structures," see: Jean Calloud, *Structural Analysis of Narrative* (Missoula, MT.: Scholars Press, 1976), and Daniel and Aline Patte, *Structural Exegesis: From Theory to Practice* (Philadelphia: Fortress Press, 1978).

A highly simplified but useful application of structuralist insights on the catechetical level is André Fossion's "Structural Readings of Scripture in

185

Catechesis" in *Lumen Vitae* 33 (1978), pp. 446–70. See also in Johnson (cited above): "Appendix: Structural Readings: How to do them," pp. 183–208.
See: **Semiotics; Structuralism.**

Sub-Pauline. See: **Deutero-Pauline.**

Sui ipsius interpres (Latin: "itself its own interpreter") is the classic principle of Scriptural interpretation arising from the Reformation, first enunciated by Martin Luther in opposition to the Roman Catholic practice of interpreting Scripture according to the Councils and the Church Fathers; the phrase comes from *sacra scriptura sui ipsius interpres* ("Holy Scripture itself is its own interpreter"). According to this principle Luther judged the epistle of James' doctrine of justification by works by Paul's teaching of justification by faith and found the former lacking. The idea that one part of Scripture can judge another is referred to as "the canon [rule of faith] within the canon" (i. e., the Bible).
See: **Canon; Hermeneutics.**

Surface Structure. See **Structure.**

Symmachus (abbrev.: Symm. or Σ.). According to Eusebius, S. was an Ebionite Christian who translated the OT freely into Greek during the second half of the 2nd cent. His translation, known by his name, made use of the LXX, Aquila, and Theodotion. Although of minor importance for OT textual criticism, it did influence Jerome's Latin translation, the Vulgate. It is extant primarily only in fragments of Origen's *Hexapla*. See also: **Aquila;** *Hexapla;* **Septuagint; Theodotion.**

Symploce (Greek: a weaving together) is the technical term for the rhetorical device of combining **anaphora** and **epiphora** (q. v.) in the same structure, as e. g., Ps. 67.

Synchronic. See: **Diachronic.**

Synecdoche (Greek: to receive together) in rhetoric is a figure of speech by which (a) a part stands in the place of the whole ("the circumcised" for "the followers of the Law," i. e., Jews; Gal. 2:7–9); or (b) the whole for a part (Jn. 3:16, either: world = humankind; or, as in [a] above, world = creation; cf. also Rom. 8:22); or (c) the species for the genus (cross = self-sacrifices; Mt. 10:38; 16:24 par.); or (d) the genus for the species (creature = humankind; Rom. 1:25). See: **Metonymy.**

Synonymous Parallelism. See: **Parallelism.**

Synopsis. In NT Criticism, a S. is a book which presents Mt., Mk., and Lk. (sometimes Jn.) in parallel columns, arranged to show where the Gospels agree and disagree; also called a Gospel Parallel. The best known in Greek are Albert Huck's *Synopse der drei ersten Evangelien* (9th ed., edited by Hans Lietzmann [Tübingen: J. C. B. Mohr (Paul Siebeck), 1950]), and Kurt Aland's *Synopsis Quattuor Evangeliorum* (Stuttgart: Württembergische Bibelanstalt, 1969[6]); and in English (following Huck's format): *Gospel Parallels,* ed. Burton H. Throckmorton, Jr. (New York: Thomas Nelson and Sons, 1957[2], 1967[3]); Kurt Aland, *Synopsis of the Four Gospels: Greek-English Edition of the Synopsis Quattuor Evangeliorum with the Text of the Revised Standard Version* (New York: United Bible Societies, 1972), which omits material in the earlier Greek edition, such as extra-canonical parallels, Greek and Latin patristic quotations, and the Gospel of Thomas; and H. F. D. Sparks, *The Johannine Synopsis of the Gospels* (New York: Harper and Row, 1975). The useful *A Diagram of Synoptic Relationships* by Allan Barr (Edinburgh: T. & T. Clark, 1938, 1957[3]) is still in print. *The Horizontal Line Synopsis of the Gospels* in English by Reuben J. Swanson (Dillsboro, N.C.: Western North Carolina Press, 1975) provides a new format and will be followed by a Greek edition with textual variants in footnotes at a subsequent date.

Akin to a synopsis of the Gospels is the recent *Pauline Parallels* by Fred O. Francis and J. Paul Sampley (Philadelphia: Fortress Press, 1975); each of the ten chief letters attributed to Paul is divided into thematic units with related passages placed in parallel lines.

Synoptic Parallel. In NT Criticism a SP refers to a passage in Mt., Mk., or Lk. which is parallel in content with one or both of the remaining synoptic Gospels; in OT criticism the term is sometimes used in discussions of parallels between 1 Sam.-2 Kings and 1–2 Chron. A SP is usually referred to by the abbreviation "par.(s)."

Synoptic Problem (The) derives from the observation that the first three books of the NT (Mt., Mk., and Lk.) contain a strikingly high degree of verbal agreement between them and, further, that the order of the material in each is in large measure the same. It is for this reason that the three books are called the "synoptic Gospels" or simply the "synoptics" (meaning, "with the [same] eye"). The SP, therefore, is to explain how this similarity came to be. What is the literary relationship of these Gospels? Who copied from whom? Luke explicitly states that others preceded him (1:1–4). To whom does he refer? The early Church Fathers (Papias, Clement of Alexandria, Augustine) do not agree in their explanation of the relationship of the Gospels.

The problem is best seen with the aid of a Greek or English **synopsis** (q. v.), which places the texts of the Gospels in parallel lines. In lieu of a synopsis, compare the following passages in any standard translation: Mt. 26:20–29 and Mk. 14:17–25; Mt. 26:36–46 and Mk. 14:32–42; Mk. 5:1–20 and

Lk. 8:26–39; Mk. 9:37–40 and Lk. 9:48–50; Lk. 3:7–9 and Mt. 3:7–10; Lk. 4:1–13 and Mt. 4:1–11; or Mt. 12:1–8 and Mk. 2:23–28 and Lk. 6:1–5.

Theoretically, there are eighteen different solutions to the problem of literary dependence. (See: William R. Farmer, *The Synoptic Problem* [New York: The Macmillan Company, 1964], ch. 6.) Most of these are ruled out by the literary data itself. But variations on the viable alternatives, including the postulation of primitive sources (see: *Urevangelium;* **Logion; Q; "M"; "L"**), intermediary documents (see: *Urmarkus;* **Proto-Luke**), or divergent recensions of the existing Gospels, extend the number of alternatives almost indefinitely.

In spite of this, widely accepted solutions have been few in number: (1) the Augustinian Hypothesis (*ca.* 400) accepted the canonical order (Mt., Mk., Lk., Jn.), stating that each Gospel depended on its predecessor; (2) the Griesbach Hypothesis (1783) excluded Jn. from consideration and made Mk. an abridger of Mt. and Lk.; (3) the Two Source Hypothesis (formally stated by H. J. Holtzmann, 1863) proposed a primitive collection of the sayings of Jesus (subsequently called *"Quelle"* or *"Q"*) and an earlier form of Mk. *(Urmarkus),* both of which were used by Mt. and Lk. independent of each other; and, (4) the Four Source Hypothesis proposed by B. H. Streeter in 1924, which is but a modification of the Two Source theory.

In recent years, W. R. Farmer (op. cit.) and others have argued in defense of the Griesbach Hypothesis with a degree of success. The majority of scholars, however, accept some variation of the Two Source Hypothesis upon which almost all modern Gospel criticism, esp. Redaction Criticism, rests.

Syntagm/Syntagmatics/Paradigmatic.

A Syntagm is a t.t. in linguistics first used by Ferdinand de Saussure to refer to a word-chain or combination of words such as "the good life," "towards us," "to go away," etc.), which, when constructed according to strict rules, forms that level of meaning within a language which falls between the word and the sentence; grammatically speaking, such word sequences or S. are equivalent to single words.

Syntagmatics is the analysis of linguistic units as they exist within a given speech continuum; it deals therefore with the relationships existing between units of an utterance in contrast to the *(paradigmatic)* relationship which exists between mutually exclusive units from which the speaker, in the speech continuum, selected his words; e.g. "the good life" makes sense, in part, by virtue of its paradigmatic contrast to "the bad/low/high/etc./life." See: Lewandowski, ad hoc.

Syntax

Syntax (fr. Gk.: syntaxis: arrangement, organization, etc.) most commonly refers to (1) the study of the rules (or simply the rules themselves) by which sentences are constructed in a given language; more technically, it may refer to (2) that subdivision of **semiotics** which deals with the arrangement and relationship of linguistic signs to each other (in distinction from two other subdivisions: semantics and pragmatics).

Synthetic Parallelism. See: Parallelism.

Tale. The term T. has several connotations, most of which are unrelated to Biblical criticism; in its literary sense, however, it refers to any story or narrative usually briefly told for its inherent interest. The term enters Biblical criticism as a technical translation of Martin Dibelius' form-critical category *"Novelle"* (*From Tradition to Gospel* [London: Ivor Nicholson and Watson, Ltd., 1934; repr. James Clarke, 1971; New York: Charles Scribner's Sons, 1935], ch. IV), which he distinguished from paradigms on the one hand and legends on the other. Dibelius identified nine pericopes in Mark as "Tales": Mk. 1:40–45 (the leper); 4:35–41 (the storm); 5:1–20 (the demons and the swine); 5:21–43 (Jairus' daughter and the woman with an issue of blood); 6:35–44 (the feeding of the 5000); 6:45–52 (the walking on the sea); 7:32–37 (the deaf mute); 8:22–26 (the blind man); and 9:14–29 (the epileptic). In addition are five stories in John developed from Ts: Jn. 2:1ff. (the marriage at Cana); 4:46ff. (the Centurion's son); 5:1ff. (the lame man); 9:1ff. (the man born blind); and 11:1ff. (Lazarus); also similar is Lk. 7:11ff. (the raising of the widow's son). In more recent criticism, this category has been subsumed under the larger genre of miracle story or aretalogy. See: **Aretalogy; Dibelius; Form Criticism.**

Talmud (fr. Hebrew: *lamad*, "study," *limmah*, "instruction"). The word T. is the comprehensive term for the Mishna and its accompanying commentary, called the Gemara (here meaning "teaching"). The Gemara contains a wide variety of material bearing directly or remotely on the subjects of the Mishna (proverbs, tales, customs, folklore, etc.) as well as strict exposition on the text. The structure of the T. is therefore that of the Mishna, having six orders divided into sixty-three tractates, which is the form it had obtained by the 3rd cent. The Gemara, being the work of the rabbis known as Amoraim (expounders), developed primarily in two centers, Babylon and Palestine (Tiberias), from the 3rd to the 5th cent.

The two editions of T., though similar in form, differ greatly in content. The Babylonian T., being 5894 pages of standard pagination, is four times the length of the Palestinian, since the latter was in large part lost in antiquity. For this reason, the Babylonian T. has in past centuries been the authoritative document. According to some authorities, the halachic portions of the Palestinian T. are more irenic and temperate, the haggadic portions purer and more rational than the corresponding material in the Babylonian T. Of the sixty-three tractates in the Babylonian T., only thirty-six contain Gemara (commentary).

See: **Mishna.**

Tanak (also Tanach) is a Hebrew abbreviation for the OT derived from the initial letters of the names of its three divisions: Torah (Pentateuch), *Nebiim* (Early and Later Prophets), and *Ketubim* (Writings or Hagiographa). See: **Hagiographa; Pentateuch; Prophets.**

Tannaim, Tannaitic Literature (fr. Aramaic *teni:* to teach orally, learn).

The term *tanna* (pl.: -im) generally "designates a teacher either mentioned in the Mishnah or of Mishnaic times" (i.e., 20–200 C.E.; *Enc. Jud.*), whose teachings were compiled to form the TL. The T. are credited with preserving Jewish tradition threatened by extinction after the Fall of Jerusalem (70 C.E.), the defeat of the Bar Kokba revolt (135 C.E.) and the rise of Christianity. TL falls under two main headings: (a) Mishnah—succinct halakic formulations arranged under various legal categories or other mnemonic devices and (b) halakic Midrashim—arranged as extended exegetical commentaries to the books of the Pentateuch, such as the Tosefta, Mekilta, Mekilta of R. Simon, Sifra on Leviticus, Sifre on Deuteronomy, Sifre Zutta, Sifre on Numbers, and Midrash Tannaim. Also belonging to the TL is the Seder Olam Rabbah. Leading T. of the 1st century included Hillel (20 B.C.E.-20 C.E.), Shammai (30 B.C.E.), Gamaliel I (20–50 C.E.), Simeon ben Gamaliel (d. 70 C.E.), and Johanan ben Zakkai (d. ca. 80 C.E.). Concerning the earliest period of the T., see: Jacob Neusner, *The Rabbinic Traditions About the Pharisees Before 70;* Vol. I–III (Leiden: E. J. Brill, 1971).

Targum (Aramaic: translation, interpretation). In broad uses, the word T. means "translation" or "interpretation"; as most frequently used however it refers specifically to Aramaic versions of the OT. In rabbinic literature the word may refer simply to the Aramaic portions, even single words, of the Bible, as found in Ezra, Nehemiah, and Daniel. The T. arose out of the synagogal practice of accompanying the reading of the Hebrew text with an Aramaic translation (T.) for the benefit of Aramaic-speaking Jews. The translation, however, was provided with interpretive additions, making the T. an expanded paraphrase of the original. No single T., therefore, existed; rather, numerous T. traditions arose on the various books of the OT—except those listed above. The most authoritative (esp. for orthodox Jews) is T. Onkelos, a version of the Palestinian T. developed by Babylonian Jews. A reportedly Palestinian T. of the Pentateuch containing a tradition going back possibly to the 1st cent. A.D. was discovered by A. Diez Macho in the Vatican Library in 1956, called Neofiti I. Pseudo-Jonathan is the name of another Babylonian version of the Palestinian T., also of the Pentateuch alone. See: **Daughter Translation; Version.**

Tatian (*ca.* A.D. 120–173). A Syrian convert to Christianity and pupil of Justin Martyr in Rome (*ca.* 160), T. is best known for his *Diatessaron*, a harmony of the life of Christ based on the four Gospels, and for *Oratio ad Graecos*, a bitter polemic against Greek culture. T. broke with Orthodox Christianity as interpreted in the West, and returned to Syria to found an ascetic order known as Encratites. His views were in the main repudiated by the Western Church.

Teaching of the Twelve Apostles. See: **Didache.**

Tell Mardikh. See: *Ebla.*

Tendenz Criticism (Ger.: *Tendenzkritik*) refers to the analysis of the intention of an author or, more pointedly, to the particular bias with which the author treats his subject matter. The term is especially identified with the work of F. C. Baur (1792–1860) who contended that the *Tendenz* of the author of the book of Acts was to minimize the differences between Peter and Paul in order to depict the early Church as unified and harmonious.

Terminus ad quem is a Latin term which means "a fixed date or point to which"; similarly, its counterpart, *terminus a quo* means "a fixed date or point from which" and together they set the terminal limits for the dating of an event or a document. E. g., A.D. 27 and A.D. 33 mark the *t. a quo* and the *t. ad quem* respectively of the crucifixion of Jesus.

Terminus a quo. See: *Terminus ad quem.*

Terminus technicus (abbrev.: t.t.). Latin for "technical term."

Tertium comparationis (Latin: point of comparison). See: *Bildhälfte.*

Tetragrammaton (Greek: "having four letters") is the name of the four Hebrew consonants YHWH, usually written Yahweh or Jahweh, and translated "Lord." Following the Exile (539 B.C.) it became the most sacred name for God among the Jews and was not pronounced, the Hebrew term for Lord (*Adonai*) being pronounced in its stead. In English translations it is now the standard convention always to translate the T. with capital letters, so KJV, RSV, NEB, NASV, NAB, etc. The Jerusalem Bible employs the proper noun, Yahweh. The word *Jehovah* is an artificial term dating from the 16th cent. and is a combination of the four consonants of the T. with the vowels of the Hebrew

191

word *Adonai;* it is found in early editions of the KJV, in the ASV, et al. Where the convention above is followed, the Hebrew divine name *Elohim* is translated "God."

Tetrateuch (Greek: four books) is a t.t. derived from Greek for the first four books of the OT: Genesis, Exodus, Leviticus, and Numbers. See: **Pentateuch.**

TEV. Common abbreviation for the Today's English Version (NT, 1966; OT 1976), published by the American Bible Society. The NT, better known as *Good News for Modern Man,* was translated by Robert G. Bratcher; the OT by a number of OT scholars under Bratcher's chairmanship. The translation places emphasis on clarity of meaning rather than on literary form. It employs a standard of English common to all who speak the language, whether of a high or low level of education. Since it avoids technical, traditional language (e. g., synagogue, scribe, etc.), it is not as useful a study Bible as the RSV, JB, or NEB. It is however a faithful, highly readable version. See: **ASV; KJV;** *LB(P);* **Paraphrase; RSV; Version.**

Text Fragment refers to those texts in Scripture, particularly in the OT, which are incomplete or "fragmentary" as they now read and which derive from earlier, complete but now otherwise lost texts or traditions. An example is found in the story of Noah's ark; here two flood stories are combined at the expense of one of the stories (or "texts"), fragments of which may be found in Gen. 7:8–9, 13–15, 19–21; 8:1–5—although the precise identity of the "fragments" is disputed. Cf. also Gen. 6:1–4 and in the NT, 2 Cor. 6:14–7:1.

Textual Criticism. The function and purpose of TC is of a dual nature: (1) To reconstruct the original wording of the Biblical text; and (2) to establish the history of the transmission of the text through the centuries. The first of these two goals is in fact hypothetical and unattainable. In every instance the original copy (called the autograph) of the books of the Bible is lost, hence every reconstruction is a matter of conjecture. TC's task, therefore, is to compare existing MSS, no two of which are alike, in order to develop a **"critical text"** (q. v.) which lists variant readings in footnotes, called a **"critical apparatus."** Modern translations of the Bible are, in the main, based on such critical texts (TEV, JB, NEB). (Note: The readings of the TEV are explained by Bruce M. Metzger, *A Textual Commentary on the Greek New Testament* [New York and London: United Bible Societies, 1971].) In this way, TC not only provides an idea of how the original text may have read, it also provides knowledge of how in fact it did read, and in some respects how it was interpreted, at various centers of faith at various times in Christian history. For example, at some time after A.D. 300, and first in MSS of the Western Church, there was added to John's Gospel the pericope of the woman caught in adultery (Jn. 7:53–8:11). This fact, attested by TC, provides data for understanding the Church of the 4th cent., the status of the canon, etc., irrespective of the authenticity of the passage itself. This is a dramatic illustration from the history of textual transmission, but scores of other examples could be adduced. The student unfamiliar with Hebrew, Aramaic, and Greek, the languages in which the Bible was originally written, can nevertheless gain some idea of the results of TC by comparing modern standard English translations with the KJV. The latter, written in 1611 prior to the discovery of all the major vellum and papyrus MSS (q. v.) of the Bible, was prepared from MSS less ancient than and notably inferior to those available today. The Dead Sea Scrolls of the OT, found 1947–54, are an example.

In antiquity and until the invention of the printing press, MSS were copied by hand; none, therefore, is free of error, each inevitably carrying within it the errors of the MS from which the new copy was made. *Variations* between MSS arose from a variety of causes: (a) physical damage, by accident and decay, leaving holes (lacunae) in the text; (b) accidental omission by slip of the copyist's eye (see: **Dittography; Haplography; Homoioteleuton, homoioarchton**); (c) aural mistakes (as in English dictation one might confuse "their" with "they're," so ancient scribes misheard the reader of the text); (d) exegetical misjudgment (placing the wrong vowels on the Hebrew consonants, or misdividing Greek letters into words, since the original Hebrew OT texts appear with consonants only [see: **Masoretic Text**], and the original Greek NT texts possessed neither word division nor punctuation); and, (e) deliberate alteration of the text for purposes of clarification, correction, and apologetic (see: **Gloss; Conflation; Assimilation**).

The *sources of OT* TC are vastly fewer in number than for NT: (a) the Greek OT, known in its various ancient editions (some of which are preserved only fragmentarily, as in quotations of the Church Fathers and in marginal notations of the LXX): **Aquila;** *Kaige;* **Lucianic; Old Greek (LXX); Symmachus;** and **Theodotion** (q. v.); (b) the **Dead Sea Scrolls** (q. v.), which antedate by nearly 1000 years all previously known MSS of the Hebrew OT; (c) the Masoretic Text (MT) of the Hebrew OT, dating from the 11th cent. A.D.; (d) ancient versions of the LXX (called **"Daughter Translations"**): Old Latin, Coptic, Ethiopic, Syro-Hexaplar, et al.; (e) ancient versions of the Hebrew OT: **Targums,** the **Peshitta,** and the Latin **Vulgate;** and, (f) the Samaritan Pentateuch. (Note: The dearth of Hebrew examplars of the OT is due in no small measure to the destruction of Jewish antiquities by anti-Semites, Christian and otherwise.)

The *sources of NT* TC present a different picture, with MSS numbering over 5000. MSS are categorized according to a system initiated by J. J. Wettstein (1751) and since expanded to include: (1) **papyrus MSS,** the oldest extant NT MSS and the most recently discovered being the Chester Beatty and

THE DEVELOPMENT OF OLD TESTAMENT TEXTS

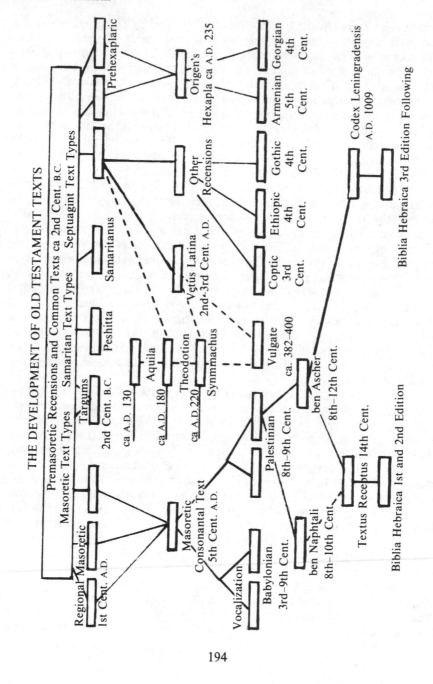

Premasoretic Recensions and Common Texts ca 2nd Cent. B.C.

Masoretic Text Types   Samaritan Text Types   Septuagint Text Types

Prehexaplaric

Origen's Hexapla ca A.D. 235

Armenian 5th Cent.   Georgian 4th Cent.

Other Recensions

Gothic 4th Cent.

Ethiopic 4th Cent.

Coptic 3rd Cent.

Vetus Latina 2nd-3rd Cent. A.D.

Samaritanus

Peshitta

Targums 2nd Cent. B.C.

Aquila ca A.D. 130

Theodotion ca A.D. 180

Synmmachus ca A.D. 220

Vulgate ca. 382-400

Regional Masoretic 1st Cent. A.D.

Masoretic Consonantal Text 5th Cent. A.D.

Vocalization

Babylonian 3rd-9th Cent.

Palestinian 8th-9th Cent.

ben Naphtali 8th-10th Cent.

ben Ascher 8th-12th Cent.

Codex Leningradensis A.D. 1009

Biblia Hebraica 3rd Edition Following

Textus Receptus 14th Cent.

Biblia Hebraica 1st and 2nd Edition

194

Bodmer papyri in the 1930s; (2) **uncials,** or MSS written in capital letters, such as Codex Sinaiticus; (3) **minuscules,** or MSS written in cursive letters, dating from the 9th cent.; (4) ancient **versions,** such as Syriac, Coptic, Ethiopic, Old Latin, etc.; (5) quotations from the **Church Fathers;** and, (6) ancient **lectionaries** (quotations from Scripture used in public worship and private devotion). Of little but historical interest are **ostraca** and talismans inscribed with Scripture as memory exercises and charms.

The principles of TC are little more than rules of thumb, or "codified common sense" as someone has suggested, or "common sense and use of reason" (A. E. Housman). These include: (1) External criteria. Since every MS of a given text is theoretically related to all other MSS of that text, it is possible to treat MSS genealogically, as sub-families within one large family. These sub-families are called text-types, or in some instances simply "families" (see: **Family**). Text-types are divided, more or less accurately, into the geographical area of their origin, such as **Alexandrian** (Egypt), **Western, Byzantine.** The nomenclature and the categories are themselves debated by TC. Text-types vary in value. A MS from an inferior family, though ancient, may be of less value than a more recent MS of a superior type. It is the evaluation of given MSS and of the theories of text-types that occupies much of TC today. (2) Internal Criteria. The following are the traditional formulations: (a) The more difficult reading is often preferred *(lectio difficilior potior).* (b) Which reading would be more likely to have given rise to the other? (c) The shorter reading is generally preferred. (d) The reading characteristic of the author is generally preferable. That these "rules" are considered by some scholars as circumlocutions for the truism *melior lectio potior* ("the better reading is to be preferred") indicates that TC is not yet an objective science and shares in some of the subjectivism ascribed to so-called "Higher Criticism" (see: **Lower Criticism**).

The history of TC cannot be sketched here. It is the oldest of the critical approaches to Scripture, dating back at least to Origen (*ca.* A.D. 185–254). As a critical methodology, however, TC began in the 17th and 18th cent., with the work of John S. Mill (1645–1707) and others in England, J. A. Bengel (1687–1752), J. J. Wettstein (1693–1754), J. S. Semler (1725–1791), and J. J. Griesbach (1745–1812) on the Continent. (See: F.M. Cross and S. Talmon, eds., *Qumran and the History of the Biblical Text* [Cambridge, London: Harvard University Press, 1975]; Ralph W. Klein, *Textual Criticism of the Old Testament: The Septuagint after Qumran,* Guides to Biblical Scholarship: Old Testament Series, ed. Gene M. Tucker [Philadelphia: Fortress Press, 1974]; Jack Finegan, *Encountering New Testament Manuscripts* [Grand Rapids: William B. Eerdmans Publishing Company, 1974] Ernst Würthwein, *The Text of the Old Testament,* rev. ed. [Grand Rapids: William B. Eerdmans, 1980].)

In addition to terms and names above, see: **Biblical Criticism; Codex Alexandrinus** et al.; **Erasmus; Nestle Text; Palimpsest; Recension; Old Latin**

MSS; *Textus Receptus;* **Vellum; Vulgate; Tischendorf; Westcott** (and Hort).
See also: Bruce Metzger, *The Text of the New Testament: Its Transmission, Corruption and Restoration* (New York and London: Oxford University Press, 1968²) and his *The Early Versions of the New Testament: The Origin, Transmission, and Limitations* (Oxford: Clarendon Press, 1977).

A significant new cache of ancient Greek MSS, uncials and minuscules, plus other MSS in Arabic, Armenian, Coptic, Ethiopic, Georgian, Karshuni, Latin, Slavic, Syria Estrangela, and Syriac was discovered at St. Catherine's Monastery on Mt. Sinai in May, 1975. They are expected to shed much light on the history of the Greek text of the Bible, on Byzantine art and Greek calligraphy, particularly for the "period of great silence"—7th–9th centuries. Both canonical and extra-canonical writings *(Testament of the Twelve Patriarchs)* were found, including Homer's *Iliad* and certain "lost" books of Christian tradition.

See: *Biblical Archaeologist* 43 (Jan.–Feb., 1980), pp. 26–34.

Textus Receptus. Latin for "received text," the name given in Britain to the 1550 edition of the Greek NT published by Robert Stephanus in Paris which essentially reproduced Erasmus' text of 1535. On the Continent, the accepted or "received (Greek) text" was the 1633 edition of Elzevir (or Elsevir), a Dutch printing house. Until the 19th cent., the *TR* was the authoritative text of the NT. See: **ASV; Critical Text; KJV; RSV; Textual Criticism.**

In OT textual criticism, the term TR denotes the Second Rabbinic Bible of Jacob ben Chaim (also Chayyim), which was published in Venice in 1524–25 by Daniel Bomberg (hence it is also called Bombergiana). In addition to the Hebrew text the TR includes the Aramaic translation and commentaries by the most influential of the Rabbis (Rashi, Ibn Ezra, etc.). The TR was used as the basis for the first two editions of Kittel's *Biblia Hebraica,* then replaced in the third edition by Codex Leningradensis.

See: **"L"; Masorectic Text.**

Theios Aner in Greek means "Divine Man" and was particularly applied to spiritual leaders with purportedly miraculous powers. See: **Aretalogy.**

Theodotion (abbrev.: Theod.). The traditional name of a Greek version of the OT which may be a revision of the LXX in the direction of the Hebrew text or a more literal translation of the Hebrew. It has been argued that Theod. was based on a still earlier revision called Proto-Theodotion, but this theory has been questioned by some scholars. The Theodotionic recension was widely used by the church fathers of the 3rd and 4th cent. A.D.; it came to supplant the LXX text of much of Job and Jeremiah. It formed the sixth column in Origen's *Hexapla* and was used by him to fill lacunae in the LXX text at his disposal. Little is known of Theodotion himself; it is thought that he lived during the second half of the 2nd cent. and was a proselyte Jew. So-called "Theodotion" of Daniel, citations of which appear in the NT, replaced the LXX of Daniel in all LXX MSS except two (mss 88 and 967 in Rahlf's list). "Theodotion-Daniel," to be dated in the 1st cent. B.C., is not in the same textual tradition as Theodotion. See: **Aquila; Symmachus; Textual Criticism.**

Theodotion Daniel. See: *Kaige* **Recension.**

Theological Interpretation may refcr either to (a) the purely descriptive task of explaining what the Biblical texts say about God, his nature and/or relation to creation as understood within the context of their original historical setting, or to (b) the essentially prescriptive task of interpreting for contemporary faith what the texts say on these subjects.

The theological interpretation of Biblical texts may in general be categorized according to four major types, although the distinctions between them, both in theory and in practice, are not precise. They are:

(1) Those TIs which concentrate on describing what the text meant to its original hearers/readers. Here Biblical religion rather than Biblical theology is central, e.g.,

> (a) R. Pfeiffer, *Religion in the Old Testament* (New York: Harper Bros., 1961).
> (b) Wilhelm Bousset, *Kyrios Christos: A History of the Belief in Christ from the Beginnings of Christianity to Irenaeus,* tr. John Steely (Nashville: Abingdon Press, 1970; Ger.: 1913).

(2) Those TIs which concentrate on what the text means to contemporary hearers/readers, e.g.:

> (a) Frederick Herzog, *Liberation Theology: Liberation in the Light of the Fourth Gospel* (New York: Seabury Press, 1972).
> (b) Jon Sobrino, *Christology at the Crossroads,* tr. John Drury (Maryknoll, N.Y.: Orbis Books, 1978; Spanish: 1976).

(3) Those TIs which either equate "what the text meant" with "what it means" or ignore the possibility of any difference, e.g.:

> (a) G. E. Wright, *God Who Acts: Biblical Theology as Recital* (London: SCM Press, 1952).
> (b) Joachim Jeremias, *New Testament Theology: The Preaching of Jesus,* tr. John Bowden (New York: Charles Scribner's Sons/London: SCM Press, 1971; Ger.: 1971).

(4) Those TIs which deny the possibility of any simple equation of "what it meant" with "what it means" but who nevertheless seek some meaningful and unifying perspective by which the historical distance (hermeneutical diff-

erence) can be overcome. In some instances, "what the text means" becomes, "what it *truly* meant." The numerous examples vary widely from (a) essentially Biblical concepts, themes, motifs, or ideas to (b) fundamentally philosophical/theological (systematic) concepts, etc., by which the texts are unified and interpreted, e.g.,

    a. (1) Covenant: W. Eichrodt, *Theology of the Old Testament,* 2 vols. (Philadelphia: Fortress Press, 1961–1967; Ger.; 3 vols.: 1933–1939).

    (2) Deuteronomic Concept of History: G. von Rad, *Old Testament Theology,* 2 vols. (New York: Harper and Row, 1962–64; Ger.: 1957–1960).

    (3) Canon as Context: B. S. Childs, *Introduction to the Old Testament as Scripture* (Philadelphia: Fortress Press, 1979).

    b. (1) Existentialist Philosophy: R. Bultmann, *The Theology of the New Testament,* 2 vols. (New York: Charles Scribner's Sons, 1951–55; Ger.: 1948–53).

    (2) Process Philosophy: R. Pregeant, *Christology Beyond Dogma: Matthew's Christ in Process Hermeneutic* (Philadelphia: Fortress Press, 1978).

    (3) Linguistics: E. Güttgemanns, "Linguistic Literary Critical Foundation of a New Testament Theology" in *Semeia* 6 (1976), 181–215.

    (4) Literary Criticism: L. L. Thompson, *Introducing Biblical Literature: A More Fantastic Country* (Englewood Cliffs, N.J.: Prentice-Hall, 1978).

For a survey and examination of problems see: Gerhard Hasel, *Old Testament Theology: Basic Issues in the Current Debate* (Grand Rapids: William B. Eerdmans, 1972; rev. 1975); ibid., *New Testament Theology: Basic Issues in the Current Debate* (Grand Rapids, Eerdmans: 1978), and Henrikus Boers, *What Is New Testament Theology?* (Philadelphia: Fortress Press, 1979).

See: **Biblical Theology (Movement); Hermeneutics.**

Theologumenon (Gk.: __a: pl.; pres. pass. ptc., neuter, of theologein: to speak of God.) In Roman Catholic tradition a T. is defined as "a proposition expressing a theological statement which cannot be directly regarded as official teaching of the Church, as dogma binding in faith, but which is the outcome and expression of an endeavour to understand the faith by establishing connections between binding doctrines of faith . . ." (K. Rahner, *Sacramentum Mundi* 6, ad hoc). In recent Biblical criticism (Protestant and Catholic), T. has been more loosely defined as "the historicizing of what was originally a theological statement" (R. Brown). So defined, the genealogy of Jesus and perhaps his virginal conception may be understood as theologumena, that is, as the "historization" of the theological assertions that Jesus was "Son of David" and "Son of God" respectively. What constitutes a T., what is historical and what is presented as history are debated.

Theophany (Greek: a manifestation of God). See: **Epiphany.**

Tischendorf, Constantin (1815–1874). Professor of NT at Leipzig, Germany, beginning as a *Privatdozent* in 1839. An ardent traveler throughout Europe and the Near East, T. discovered a number of important and ancient uncial manuscripts of the Bible, most notably Codex Sinaiticus, Codex Vaticanus, and Codex Claromontanus, and succeeded in deciphering the difficult palimpsest Codex Ephraemi. He published editions of the Greek NT and the Greek OT; his last critical text of the NT, known as the *Editio Octava Critica Maior* (1869/72), is still a standard tool of NT Textual Criticism.

Topos, Toposforschung, Topik. Topos (pl.: Topoi; Greek: place) is a t.t. in ancient Greek rhetoric whose ancient meaning is discussed under the Latin equivalent: *locus.* The term T. was introduced into modern literary criticism with a change in meaning and spelling (*Topik:* topics) by Ernst R. Curtius (*European Literature and the Latin Middle Ages* [Princeton: Princeton University Press, 1953; Ger.: 1948) and the school of *Toposforschung* (topos research) after him. The term refers to a general concept which through cultural and literary tradition has become the common possession of at least a certain strata of society and is used by an author in a finite and concrete way in the treatment of the subject. A T. is therefore often, but one-sidedly, understood as merely "something handed down in literature and taken over as a stereotype, i.e., defined as a traditional formula, inherited motif or thought schemata" (see Edgar Mertner, "Topos und Commonplace" in *Strena Angelica,* Festschrift für Otto Richter; G. Dietrich and F. W. Schulze, eds. [Halle: M. Niemeyer, 1956]). So defined, works such as the Kittel-Friedrich, *Theological Dictionary of the New Testament,* or the Botterweck-Ringgren, *Theological Dictionary of the Old Testament,* can be termed examples of *T.-forschung* in that they attempt to illumine history or literature on the basis of the smallest elements of the tradition (viz., single words).

Recent *topos* research, however, recognizes the ancient and primary role of *topoi* in the discovery *(inventio)* of arguments for use in a given rhetorical situation. Such analysis begins by postulating the general *topoi* (*loci communes* or "commonplaces") through which the argument of a given text received its structure. The *topos* has been likened to a vessel sometimes filled with water, sometimes with wine, i.e., a form possessing different functions at different times depending on what is deemed appropriate to the rhetorical situation. The reader, who because of ignorance of the *topos* considers a specific formulation of an author to be a completely original creation of the moment, overestimates its meaning and errs just as the reader who, filled with his knowledge of the *topos,* considers the passage nothing but a semantically empty filler (Cf. Lausberg, p. 39). For example: In I Cor. 1:20–21; 26–30; 2:6–7, Paul contrasts the wisdom of the world with the wisdom of God. This theme is not to be understood as originating with the apostle Paul but as a *topos* of Hellenistic Jewish (-Christian) missionaries in competition with the miracle workers and magicians of the Gentile world (so K. Berger). (Paul, of course, finds its most telling example in the crucifixion of Jesus of Nazareth.) See: Dan. 2:27–28; Jos. Ant. 2.286; 10.203; Hippolytus, *Dan.* 2:3,27; Justin, *Apol.* 60:11; Syr. Apoc. of Dan (Pseudo-Daniel) 1:16. Similarly, a central paraenetic *topos* is that of not being ashamed under adversity, e.g., Rom. 1:16; 2 Tim. 1:8,12,16; 2:15; Ps. Ign. Eph. 2:2.

See: **Rhetorical Analysis.**

Torah has several connotations: strictly and commonly speaking, T., defined as "law," refers to the Pentateuch, the first five books of the OT; more broadly, it may refer to the whole OT, and more widely still to the whole of Jewish religious writing, both ancient and modern, in which case it is defined as "teaching" or "guidance."

Tractate (Latin: to treat). A treatise or essay on a specific subject.

Tradition Criticism, also Tradition History or Traditio-historical Criticism, are all acceptable translations for the German t.t. *Traditionsgeschichte* and are increasingly used as translations of the word *Überlieferungsgeschichte* (lit., "the history of transmission") even though in Germany the latter has been used in contradistinction to *Traditionsgeschichte.* For *Ü.* some scholars prefer the longer but more accurate "history of the transmission of tradition," but this is deemed unnecessarily redundant. In English the word tradition denotes both the process of transmission (Latin: *traditio*) and that which is transmitted *(traditum),* as does the word *Überlieferung.*

Broadly stated, T-HC is the study of the history of oral traditions during the period of their transmission. In this sense it is usually distinguished from Form Criticism, Textual Criticism, Literary Criticism, and Redaction Criticism. But since the scope and methods of these disciplines are not rigid, particularly LC and FC, it is not surprising that T-HC is variously represented as the same as FC (von Rad) or as an extension of it (Klaus Koch), as reliant upon the observations of LC (Noth) or as basically antithetical to them (Engnell), as distinct from the other methodologies (Wolfgang Richter) or as a special amalgam of them all (Magne Saebø).

What constitutes the focus of T-HC is defined in an equally varied manner. In the main, however, it is the history of oral traditions that is in view. Sometimes this excludes compositional stages, but more often it includes the reconstruction of the whole history of a literary unit from its hypothetical origin and development in its oral stage to its composition and final redaction in literary form. So-called "streams of tradition" also come under investigation, that is, the socio-religious milieu of the traditionists (e. g., prophetic and priestly circles) which gave shape and significance to certain bodies of tradition such as the festival rites accompanying the annual renewal of the divine covenant. Considerable conjecture has also been given to the geographical site of origin for these various traditions, such as Shechem, Jerusalem, Bethel, etc. Other tradition historians focus not on specific units of Scripture or on particular oral forms but on certain ideas, themes, or motifs, and their development.

Traditionsgeschichte, as employed by Swedish OT scholar Ivan Engnell (1906–1964), applied almost completely to the final stage of the tradition. Denying the possibility of discerning the original wording of the tradition or the stages of its transmission, he analyzed instead the end product with reference to compositional techniques, patterns, motifs, and purposes as well as the smaller units of the tradition in relationship to their context within the text. At the same time, he called for the use of all other relevant data: literary, ideological, psychological, sociological, archaeological, and cultural. However, Engnell's emphasis on the final stage of the tradition has met with criticism and has led to the suggestion that his use of this term was inappropriate, Motif-criticism being suggested in its place.

Interest in the oral stages of the Biblical traditions prior to their literary formulation dates back to the 18th cent. and before; it remained essentially dormant throughout the 19th cent. finally to be revived by Hermann Gunkel, Hugo Gressmann, et al. at the turn of the cent. (See: **Form Criticism.**) T-HC, however is especially identified with Gerhard von Rad (1901–1971) and Martin Noth (1902–1968) in Germany, Sigmund Mowinckel (1884–1965) and Ivan Engnell in Scandinavia. For a historical overview of T-HC methodologies and their assessment, see Douglas A. Knight, *Rediscovering the Traditions of Israel* (Missoula, Mont.: Society of Biblical Literature, 1973).

In NT studies, T-HC is concerned with the development of tradition in the pre-Pauline period, *ca.* A.D. 30–50. It has dealt especially with the oldest liturgical fragments, hymns, juridical formulas (see: *Sätze heiligen Rechtes*), etc., within the context of baptism, the eucharist, catechesis, proclamation, etc.

Traditionist(s), Tradent, Trägerkreis. A person, or group of persons (Ger.: *Kreis:* circle; cf., *Schule:* school), who preserve and transmit (Ger.: *Träger;* lit.: one who bears) traditional material, whether written or oral. (Also used is the Latin *Tradent:* "a person who delivers or hands over any property to another," OED.) Recent interest in the social history of Judaism and early

Christianity, quickened by studies in the sociology of knowledge, Liberation Theology, and both Old and New Testament *Traditionsgeschichte* (q.v.) has focused attention on the socio-theological perspectives of the Ts. The questions being asked are: Who is responsible for preserving and transmitting the traditions (canonical or extra-canonical)? What socio-theological perspectives are present in the traditions? How do these views fit into the socio-theological matrix of ancient society?

For bibliography, see: **Sociological Interpretation.**

Traditionsgeschichte (Ger.: the history of the tradition; tradition history). See: **Tradition Criticism.**

Translation. See: **Version.**

Transliteration is the act or process by which the words, letters, or characters of one language are written in the letters or characters of another.

Biblical languages, and the languages of the Bible's environment, are often transliterated into Roman script. Unfortunately, there is no single system in common use for transliterating Hebrew. Normally, such systems as are employed attempt to transliterate Hebrew so that both letters (mainly consonants) and vowels will be perfectly or nearly perfectly represented. These systems require the adaptation of diacritical marks to the Roman alphabet.

Listed below are four systems in current use in Great Britain, Germany, and America (2):

Hebrew Consonants	ROWLEY	*RGG*³	*JBL*:1971	1976	*IB*
א	'	'	'	'	'
ב	b	b	b		b
כ	b̲		(b)*		bh
ג	g	g	g		g
ג	g̲		(g)		gh
ד	d	d	d		d

ROWLEY H. H. Rowley, *The Old Testament and Modern Study* (Oxford: Clarendon Press, 1951, 1952²), p. xiii.

*RGG*³ *Die Religion in Geschichte und Gegenwart,* 3. Aufl.; Heraus. Kurt Galling (Tübingen: J. C. B. Mohr [Paul Siebeck], 1957–1965), I, xxx.

JBL Journal of Biblical Literature, 90 (December 1971), p. 513.; and *JBL* 95 (June 1976), pg. 334; only changes are indicated.

IB The Interpreter's Bible, ed. George Arthur Buttrick (Nashville: Abingdon Press, 1951), VII, xxii.

*The spirant form of b, g, d, k, p, and t is normally not indicated; when absolutely needed, the underlined letter (here in parenthesis) is used.

Hebrew	ROWLEY	RGG³	JBL:1971	1976	IB
ד	ḏ		(d)		dh
ה	h	h	h		h
ו	w	w	w		w
ז	z	z	z		z
ח	ḥ	ḥ	ḥ		ḥ
ט	ṭ	ṭ	ṭ		ṭ
י	y	j	y		y
כ	k	k	k		k
ך כ	ḵ		(ḵ)		kh
ל	l	l	l		l
ם מ	m	m	m		m
ן נ	n	n	n		n
ס	s	s	s		ş
ע	ʿ	ʿ	ʿ	ʿ	ʿ
פ	p	p	p		p
ף פ	p̱		(p̱)		ph
ץ צ	ṣ	ṣ	ṣ		ç
ק	ḳ	q	q		q
ר	r	r	r		r
שׂ	ś	ś	ś		s
שׁ	š	š	š		sh
ת	t	t	t		t
ת	ṯ		(ṯ)		th
ָ	o or ā**	å or a	o or ā		o or ā
ַ	a	ă	a		a
ֶ	e	ae	ę	e	e
ֵ	ē	e	ē		ē
ִ	i	i	i or ī***	i****	i or î
ֹ	ō	o	ō		ō
ֻ	u	u	u or ū***		u
(ו)ָ	â(w)	â(w)	ā(y)w		â(w)
יֶ		âe	ę(y)	ê	
יֵ	ê	ê	ê		ê
יִ	î	î	î	i	î
ֹו	ô	ô	ô		ô

**qāmeṣ ḥāṭûp or qāmeṣ
*** defectively written long vowel
****defectively written short ḥireq

ן	û	û	û		û
‍ָ‍	o	ă	o	ŏ	o
‍ַ‍	a	a	a	ă	a
‍ֱ‍	e	ae	e̦	ĕ	e
‍ְ‍	e	e	e	ĕ	e
‍ַ‍	a	a	a	a	a
הָ		ā	āh		
הֳ		āē	eh		
הֵ		ē	e̦h	ēh	
הֺ		ō	ōh		

Greek is normally transliterated as follows:

A	α	a		Ξ	ξ	x
B	β	b		O	o	o
Γ	γ	g		Π	π	p
Δ	δ	d		P	ρ	r
E	ε	e		Σ	σ(ς)	s
Z	ζ	z		T	τ	t
H	η	ē		Y	υ	y or u**
Θ	θ	th		Φ	φ	ph
I	ι*	i		X	χ	ch
K	κ	k		Ψ	ψ	ps
Λ	λ	l		Ω	ω	ō
M	μ	m			ͺ***	h
N	ν	n				

Treaty Form. The form-critical study of ancient Near Eastern treaties, particularly from the archives of the Hittite empire, reveals a sixfold structure, parallels of which scholars have sought in the OT. The classic form, not always present in every part or in order, contains six members: (1) preamble introduc-

---

*iota subscript is often omitted or represented by a cedilia under the vowel concerned: ᾀ = ą̄ , -= ͺe, ῳ = ǭ
**used in dipthongs (e.g., au, eu, ui)
***rough breathing mark

ing the speaker (cf. Deut. 1:1); (2) historical prologue describing previous relations (cf. Deut. 1:3–4); (3) stipulations detailing the obligations of the vassal state (cf.1 Deut. 24:7); (4) document clause providing for the safekeeping and regular public reading of the agreement (cf. Deut. 27:8); (5) the gods who are witnesses to the treaty (cf. Deut. 32:1; Isa. 1:2, Ezek. 17:12–21); (6) curse and blessing formula (cf. Deut. 28). See, e. g., Dennis J. McCarthy, *Treaty and Covenant*, rev. ed. (Rome: Pontifical Biblical Institute, 1978). See: **Law.**

Tricolon (pl.: tricola). See: **Colon.**

Triple Tradition refers to material common to Mt., Mk., and Lk.; the term is used to avoid implying the nature of the source or the direction of dependency, if any, between the three Gospels. See: **Double Tradition; Q; Synopsis; Synoptic Problem; Two Source Hypothesis.**

Trito-Isaiah. See: **Deutero-Isaiah.**

Trope (Greek: a turn). A figure of speech; the use of a word in a sense other than its normal meaning. The four basic kinds of tropes are **metaphor, metonymy, synecdoche,** and **irony** (q. v.).

Tropology. An archaic mode of Scriptural interpretation which dealt with the moral sense of Scripture purportedly existing behind its literal sense and in addition to its allegorical and anagogic meaning (see: **Allegory; Anagogy**) Employed by Justin Martyr (*ca.* 160), Jerome (*ca.* 400), et al., through the Middle Ages. See: **Hermeneutics.**

"Tu es Petrus" pericope (Latin: "You are Peter"; pericope: Greek: passage). The Latin name for Mt. 16:18–19, which is the Scriptural basis for the Roman Catholic doctrine of the Church. See: **Pericope.**

Tugendkatalog (German: catalog of virtues). See: *Lasterkatalog.*

Two Source Hypothesis (The) proposes a solution to the **Synoptic Problem** (q. v.) by postulating independent use by Mt. and Lk. of two distinct sources in the writing of their Gospels: (1) Q(*uelle*), a no longer extant collection of sayings (except as recoverable from Mt. and Lk.) and (2) Mark's Gospel. This solution replaced the **Griesbach Hypothesis** (q. v.).See: **Four Document Hypothesis; Holtzmann; Lachmann; Q; Streeter; Synoptic Problem;** *Urevangelium.*

Typology (fr. Greek *typos:* pattern, archetype). A method of Biblical exegesis or interpretation in which persons, events, or, things of the OT are interpreted as being foreshadowings or prototypes, of persons, events, or things in the NT; for example, in 1 Cor. 10:1–6, Paul interprets the Exodus as a type of baptism and as an event by which a subsequent generation (his) was to be instructed (vs. 11); in Rom. 5:14, Adam is declared a "type" of the one who was to come, viz., Jesus; in Heb. 7, the author patterns the priestly office of Jesus after the OT priest Melchizedek, etc. T. differs from allegory in that the latter sees the hidden, spiritual meaning of a narrative whereas the former sees the revelatory connection between two historically distinct but religiously significant persons or events. See: **Allegory; Hermeneutics.**

Überlieferungsgeschichte (Ger.: history of transmission). See: **Tradition Criticism.**

Uncial is a technical term for 3rd to 10th cent. codices of the Bible written in majuscule or capital letters on parchment or vellum. Technically, papyrus MSS are also uncials (written in capital letters) but are designated instead by the material on which they are written (*siglum:* P). The uncial style of writing was ordinarily reserved for formal and literary documents; the autographs of Paul's letters were likely written in cursive. The most important Us of the NT and certain extra-canonical writings (in whole or part) are: B (Vaticanus); or S (Sinaiticus); D (Bezae); L (regius); θ (Koridethi); A (Alexandrinus); C (Ephraemi); and W (Washingtonianus or Freer).

Ugarit, Ugaritic Texts. See: *Ras Shamra* **Texts.**

Urevangelium (Ger.: original or primal gospel) is the name given by G. E. Lessing in 1778 to a Hebrew or Aramaic document which he believed lay behind and thus explained the relationship of the first three Gospels, a shorter version of which was used by Mk.; a theory supplanted by the **Two Source** and **Four Document Hypotheses** (q. v.). See: *Urmarkus.*

Urgemeinde, Urkirche (German: *ur:* primitive, primal, original, ancient, early. *Gemeinde:* congregation, community. *Kirche:* church). See: **Early Church, The.**

Urmarkus (German: primitive, original or primal Mk.) is the name given by H. J. Holtzmann in 1863 to a hypothetical source document behind, and abbreviated (Holtzmann), or expanded (Hermann von Soden [1905], Paul Wendland [1908], Hugo Gressmann [1925–31], et al.) by Mk. The existence of doublets (e. g., the feeding of the five thousand and its sequel in 6:30–7:37 and the feeding of the four thousand and its sequel in 8:1–26), the collections of logia (4:21–25; 8:34–9:1; 9:42–50; and 13:1–37), and the apparent absence of 6:45–8:26 in Lk. (called the "Great Omission") have led to the common conviction that Mk. used sources in the writing of his Gospel. Whether these sources formed an *U.* prior to its redaction by Mk., or were added to an *U.* at various stages by a redactor(s) is debated. What could constitute an *U.* is also not clear; e. g., Rudolf Bultmann has written "it is . . . probable that the text of Mark which the two other evangelists used lay before them in an older form than that in which we have it today. This *Urmarcus* (as it is usually called) was altered and enlarged at certain points; but it can scarcely be distinguished from the present text of Mark in any important way" (*Form Criticism,* ed. F. C. Grant [New York: Harper and Row, 1962], pp. 13–14). See: **Synoptic Problem; Two Source Hypothesis.**

Urrolle (Ger.: *Ur:* earliest, original. *Rolle:* scroll) is occasionally employed as a t.t. (German) for the *earliest* form of a document presumably written on a *scroll,* that is, as originally composed prior to any additions or redactions —as are found for example in the book of Jeremiah in the OT.

Variant Reading. In Textual Criticism, VR refers to a variation in the wording of a passage of Scripture (whether parts of words, words, or sentences) as found in the comparison of two or more MSS of the text in hand. All the variant readings in all the MSS of the NT, added together, would number over 500,000, mostly minor variations in spelling and word order. The difference between Mk. 1:2 in the KJV and the RSV is due in part to MS variation.

Vaticinium ex eventu (pl.: *vaticinia*) is a Latin phrase meaning "a prophecy from an outcome." In NT criticism it is used to designate a passage in the Gospels which foretells an event that was in fact first known to and experienced by the early Church and then placed back as prophecy on the lips of Jesus. For example: Mk. 10:38–39; 14:28; and Lk. 19:42–44 are probably *v. ex e.*

Vaux, Roland Guérin de (1903–71), born in Paris, studied at the Sorbonne and at the Seminary of St. Sulpice, entering the Dominican Order of the Roman Catholic Church in 1929. In 1933 he went to the École Biblique et Archéologique de St. Etienne in Jerusalem, where he served in various capacities including Professor of Biblical History (1935–70), of Biblical Archaeology and Israelite Institutions (1935–70), and as Director (1945–65). As Chairman of the Board of the Palestine Archaeological Museum, he was intimately involved in the purchase and publication (as editor-in-chief) of the Dead Sea Scrolls (see: DJD) and was Director of the excavation of Khirbet Qumran (1953–58). His major works include *Ancient Israel: Its Life and Institutions,* trans. John McHugh (New York: McGraw-Hill, 1961); *Archaeology and the Dead Sea Scrolls* (The Schweich Lectures of the British Academy for 1959; Oxford: Oxford University Press, 1973); and, *The Early History of Israel,* trans. David Smith (Philadelphia: Westminster Press, 1978); he also translated Genesis, 1 & 2 Samuel, and 1 & 2 Kings for the *Bible de Jérusalem.* He received nine honorary degrees from universities in Europe, Great Britain, and the United States.

Vellum (Latin: *pellis vitulina*) in the proper sense refers to calfskin processed for writing; the skins of all other animals when used for writing are technically known as parchment. In current usage, however, this distinction is no longer observed and the term V. can denote the skin of any animal prepared as writing material. While dating from about the 2nd cent. B.C., V. came into dominance *ca.* 4th cent. A.D. 2 Tim. 4:13 refers to such parchments with the Latin loan word *membrana;* the author (Paul?) may be speaking of OT Scriptures. See: **Papyrus; Textual Criticism; Uncial.**

Verbal Inspiration (also known as "mechanical insp." or the "dictation theory of insp.," implying that every word [*litera*] is of God or is filled with his Spirit; hence, also "literal inspiration").

In reaction to the rise of historical criticism in the 18th and 19th cents. which, by discovering errors in Biblical fact and reason, threatened Scripture as the authoritative Word of God, there developed a theory of Biblical inspiration in which every word was defended as direct from God. V-I usually but not always implied absolute inerrancy, e. g., "God employed men in writing. But these men were so controlled by Him, that He is the Author of the writing; and so [completely] the Author, that any charge of inaccuracy against the record, or Scripture, as originally given, must be preferred against Him" (Kennedy, *The Doctrine of Inspiration,* 1878, p. 6; quoted by Marcus Dods, "Inspiration" in *A Dictionary of Christ and the Gospels,* ed. James Hastings [New York: Charles Scribner's Sons, 1906], I, 833). Other views of V-I, based on passages such as Mt. 10:20; Ex. 4:11–12; Jer. 1:9; Ezek. 3:27, conceded the possibility of defects but not apart from God's permission or as being inconsistent with his purpose. See John Robson, *The Bible: Its Revelation, Inspiration, and Evidence* (London: Hodder and Stoughton, 1883).

See: **Hermeneutics.**

Version. In Textual Criticism the term V. denotes an early translation of the NT from Greek into another language; these early versions of the NT are in Latin, Coptic, Syriac, Armenian, Arabic, Ethiopic, Persian, Gothic, Georgian, and Slavonic. In the field of Bible translation, however, the word V. (e. g., KJV, RSV, TEV) denotes an edition of the Bible which incorporates something of the language and style of a previous translation or V. in the same language; a "translation" on the other hand, in contradistinction to a "V.," proceeds directly from the Hebrew, Aramaic, or Greek text without the conscious influence of an earlier V.: *The Complete Bible,* translated by J. M. Powis Smith, Edgar J. Goodspeed, et al. (Chicago: University of Chicago Press, 1935), is an example of a translation. In OT criticism, the term "daughter translation" is sometimes used of translations of the LXX into Latin, Coptic, Ethiopic, etc., because they are not translations of the original Hebrew (and Aramaic) Scriptures, but a translation of a prior (Greek) translation. See: **Paraphrase.**

Volksspruch (Ger.: popular, or folk, saying). In OT Form Criticism a distinction is sometimes made between proverbial sayings of the common people and those arising first with the sages, the former called *Volksspruch,* the latter *Kunstspruch* (an artistic saying or aphorism). So defined the book of Proverbs in the OT is classified as *Ks.* Examples of the folk saying are 1 Sam. 10:11; 19:24: "Is Saul also among the prophets?" and Jer. 31:29; Ezek. 18:2: "The fathers have eaten sour grapes, and the children's teeth are set on edge"; cf. Jer. 23:28; 1 Sam. 24:13; 1 Kgs. 20:11. The origin of proverbs is a matter of conjecture and hence the distinction is disputed.

Vorlage (Ger.: copy, model, text; lit., "that which lies before") is a t.t. borrowed from German scholarship to denote a particular copy of a document used as a source; e. g., to refer to "Luke's Markan *Vorlage"* is to draw attention to the fact that Luke's copy of Mark may have differed in important ways from the recension of Mark as it comes to us in the major MSS or from the copy used by Mt.

Vulgate (Latin: common, popular) is the name given to that version of the Latin Bible recognized by the medieval Church and later by the Council of Trent (1546) to be the *vetus et vulgata editio* (the "old and popular edition").

The Council decreed that it was to be the official Bible of the Roman Church. Most of the books of this version stem from Jerome (*ca.* 340–420), who undertook the translation of the Bible at the behest of Pope Damasus (382) in order to end the proliferation of inferior (Old Latin) versions. Jerome's translations, completed in 405, circulated separately until bound in a single volume in the mid-6th cent. These bound editions, however, later known as the Vulgate, included translations not attributable to Jerome. Although all the OT is from Jerome, of the Apocrypha only Tobit and Judith, and of the NT only the Gospels can be ascribed to Jerome with certainty. The remainder are older Latin versions. The textual history of the Vulgate is however a matter of debate. See: **Jerome; Old Latin MSS.**

Weiss, Bernhard (1827–1918). Born in Königsberg, Germany, W. taught NT studies at Königsberg (1852–63), Kiel (1863–1876), and Berlin (1877–1908). He published a number of commentaries (in the H. A. W. Meyer series) and theological works. English translations include *Biblical Theology of the NT* (Edinburgh: T. & T. Clark, 1882–1883) and *The Life of Christ* (Clark, 1883).

Weiss, Johannes (1863–1914). Born in Kiel, the son of Bernhard Weiss and the son-in-law of the famed theologian, Albrecht Ritschl, he taught in the field of NT at Göttingen (1888–1895), Marburg (1895–1908), and Heidelberg (1908–1914). An advocate of the methodology of comparative religions *(Religionsgeschichtliche Schule),* his major contribution to subsequent NT exegesis and theology was the discovery of the eschatological nature of Jesus' proclamation of the kingdom of God (*Jesus' Proclamation of the Kingdom of God;* Ger.: 1892; Eng.: London: SCM Press, 1971; Philadelphia: Fortress Press, 1971), a dominant factor in Biblical criticism and theology ever since.

Wellhausen, Julius (1844–1918). Born the son of a Lutheran pastor in Hameln, Germany, W. studied under the famed OT scholar Heinrich Ewald in Göttingen, and became Prof. of OT on the theological faculty in Greifswald in 1872, a position from which he resigned because of ecclesiastical opposition to his radically historical approach to OT studies, most notably to his theories concerning the formation of the Pentateuch. Subsequently, he became prof. of Semitic languages in Halle (1882), Marburg (1885), and Göttingen (1892). Accomplished in NT and Islamic studies as well as the OT, W's great influence on Biblical criticism nevertheless derived largely from his classic work, *Prolegomena to the History of Ancient Israel* (1878, 1883[2]; reprint: Gloucester, Mass.: Peter Smith, 1973). See: **Graf-Wellhausen Hypothesis; Literary Criticism.**

We-sections is a term of convenience referring to those passages in the book of Acts in which the autobiographical first person plural ("we") appears instead of the biographical third person (Acts 16:10–17; 20:5–15; 21:1–18; 27:1–28:16; Codex Bezae adds 11:28). Generally thought to be from Luke's own "travel diary," but is possibly a convention of Hellenistic narrative style.

Westcott, Brooke Foss (1825–1901). Educated in Birmingham and at Trinity College, Cambridge, England; taught at Harrow (1852–69); Regius Professor of Theology at Cambridge (1870–90); Bishop of Durham (1890–1901). An author of numerous studies on NT theology and history, W. is most widely noted for his critical edition of the Greek NT (1881), prepared with F. J. A. Hort. See: **Critical Text; Textual Criticism.**

Western Text, The. In NT Textual Criticism, WT is one of the geographical place names given to MSS of the NT bearing similar textual characteristics. WTs are in the main the bilingual Graeco-Latin MSS, Old Latin MSS, and quotations from the Latin Fathers, all associated with Italy, Gaul, and Africa. The term is only partly accurate (since some Old Syriac and Coptic MSS show the same textual characteristics) and is replaced by some scholars with the designation "Delta," after its central witness, Codex Bezae Cantabrigiensis (D or D^{ea}). According to E. J. Epp, the WT is one of only two distinct early text-types and can be traced from P^5 and P^{29} through P^{48}, P^{38}, P^{37} and 0171 to D and thereafter to more recent centuries, to F and G (9th cent.) and to MSS 614 and 383 (13th cent.). (See Epp, *JBL*, 93 [1974], pp. 386–414.) It is suggested that by the 5th cent., the WT and the Neutral (Alexandrian) text had been melded together to form the Byzantine Text, the dominant text-type of subsequent centuries.

Wie es eigentlich geschehen ist is a German phrase meaning "as it actually happened," and is sometimes quoted as a catchphrase to characterize the assumption prevalent among 19th (and 20th) cent. rationalistic historiographers that past history could be reconstructed *"wie. . . ."* See: **Historical Critical Method; Psychological Reconstruction; Quest of the Historical Jesus.**

Wisdom Literature, broadly defined, is the name given to those ancient writings that deal primarily with man's acquisition of knowledge about and mastery of life; its explanations appeal to reason, experience, and human initiative, rather than to revelation and to divine initiative; in Jewish tradition, WL, narrowly defined, is made up of Job, Proverbs, Ecclesiastes (also called *Qoheleth* or *Koheleth*), Ecclesiasticus (also called the Wisdom of Jesus ben Sira or Sirach), and the Wisdom of Solomon; to these is sometimes added the didactic poem in Baruch 3:9–4:4. The last three appear only in the Greek canon of the OT.

James L. Crenshaw suggests that, on the basis of the above texts, WL can be divided into four kinds: (1) juridical, (2) nature, (3) practical, and (4) theological. He further distinguishes between "(1) family/clan wisdom, the goal of which is the mastery of life, the stance hortatory and the style proverbial; (2) court wisdom, with the goal of education for a select group, the stance secular, and method didactic; and (3) scribal wisdom, with the aim of providing education for everyone, a stance that is dogmatico-religious, and a dialogico-admonitory method." Crenshaw also notes eight categories in which WL appears: (a) proverbs (see the book of Proverbs), (b) riddle (Judg. 14:10–18), (c) fable (Judg. 9:8–15; Num. 22:21–35; Gen. 37:5–11, etc.) and allegory (Prov. 5:15–23; Eccles. 12:1–6), (d) hymn (e. g., Prov. 1:20–33; 8; Job 28; Sirach 24:1–22; Wisd. of Solomon 6:12–20; 7:22–8:21; Pss. 1; 32; 34; 37; 49; 112; 128) and prayer (e. g., Sirach 22:27–23:6; 36:1–17; 51:1–12; Wisd. of Solomon 9:1–18), (e) dialogue (the book of Job), (f) confession or autobiographical narrative (e. g., Prov. 4:3–9; 24:30–34; Eccles. 1:12–2:26; 8:9–9:1; Sirach 33: 16–18; 51:23–30; Wisd. of Solomon 7–9), (g) lists or *onomastica* (q. v.; e. g., Job 38; Sirach 43), and (h) didactic poetry (e. g., Pss. 37; 49; 73; 139) and didactic narrative (e. g., Prov. 7:6–23; Sirach 44–50; Wisd. of Solomon 10–19). (See: *Old Testament Form Criticism,* ed. John H. Hayes [San Antonio: Trinity University Press, 1974], p. 227ff.).

In contemporary scholarship the nature and limits of Wisdom are widely debated; some scholars include practically all non-revelatory speech in this category, such as the narratives of primeval history (Gen. 1–11), the Joseph saga (Gen. 37–50), etc. A mediating position is found in Gerhard von Rad's *Wisdom in Israel* (Ger.: 1970; Eng.: London: SCM Press, 1972). (See: James L. Crenshaw, ed., *Studies in Ancient Israelite Wisdom* [New York: KTAV, 1976).]

Woe-Oracle. See: **Oracle.**

Wortgeschehen (Ger.: word event) is a t.t. in the hermeneutical theory of Gerhard Ebeling. See: **Language-event.**

Wrede, William (1859–1906). Pastor (1887–89), later *Privatdozent* (lecturer) in NT studies at Göttingen, Germany; Assoc. Prof. (1893) and Prof. (1895–1900) at Breslau. Noted primarily for his book, *Das Messiasgeheimnis in den Evangelien* (Göttingen: Vandenhoeck and Ruprecht, 1901; see: **Messianic Secret**), which revealed the theological structure of Mark's Gospel, ending the current view that it contained an essentially objective and historically accurate account of Jesus' ministry on which a "Life of Jesus" could be based. See: **Redaction Criticism.**

Writings, The. See: **Hagiographa.**

Yahwist. See: **J (Yahwist).**

Zadokite Document (or Fragments), The. See: **Dead Sea Scrolls.**

Zweiquellentheorie (Ger.: two source theory). See: **Two Source Hypothesis.**

ABBREVIATIONS IN TEXTUAL CRITICISM
plus common Latin words and phrases

A:	Codex Alexandrinus (q. v.)
a.: ante:	before
ab origine:	from the origin
ab ovo:	from the beginning
ad:	at, to
add., addit:	add(s)
addendum:	something to be added
ad infinitum:	to infinity
ad loc.:	at the passage discussed
a fortiori:	with stronger reason
Agnus Dei:	Lamb of God
al.:	other(s)
aliq.:	other form
al. omn.:	all others
al. pc.:	a few others
al. pl.:	very many others
alt.:	the other (alternate)
ante:	before
ap., apud:	with, according to
a posteriori:	to argue from effect to cause
app.:	apparatus
append.:	appendix
a priori:	to argue from cause to effect
argumentum e silentio:	an argument from silence
aut:	or
B:	Codex Vaticanus (q. v.)
bis:	twice
C:	Codex Ephraemi Rescriptus (q. v.)
c., cum:	with
ca.:	about
cet., cett.:	another, others
cf.:	compare
cj.:	conjecture

215

cod., codd.:	codex, codices
col.:	column(s)
comm.:	commentary
comma:	phrase
cont.:	continued
cor., corr.:	corrector, corrected
cum grano salis:	with a grain of salt
D:	Codex Bezae Cantabrigiensis (q.v.); Codex Claromontanus D^P
def.:	is lacking; *also:* definition
de facto:	in reality
del.:	effaced
de novo:	anew
de profundis:	out of the depths
desideratum:	a thing desired
deus ex machina:	a god out of a machine
E:	Codex Basiliensis; E^a: Codex Laudianus
e:	the Gospels
e, ex:	from
ead.:	likewise
ed., edd.:	editor(s)
editio princeps:	first edition
e. g.:	for example
ergo:	therefore
err.:	error
et, etiam:	also
et al.:	and others
evl.:	Gospel
exc.:	except
F:	Codex Boreelianus
fere:	almost
fin.:	the end
fluct.:	varies
fol., foll.:	leaf, leaves
fort., fortasse:	perhaps, probably
frg. (frgg.):	fragment(s)
G:	Codex Boernerianus
hab.:	has
hapaxl.:	hapaxlegomenon (q.v.)
hiat.:	is lacking
hoc:	this
ibid., id., idem:	the same
i. e.:	that is, in other words
infra:	below
in limine:	at the threshold
in ovo:	in the inception
int., interp.:	interpretation

inter alia:	among others
in toto:	entirely
in vacuo:	in empty space
ipsissima mens:	the very mind
ipsissima verba:	the very words (q.v.)
ipsissima vox:	the very voice
ipso facto:	obvious from the facts
item:	thus
κτλ:	and so forth
l:	lectionary
leg.:	it reads
loc.:	place
LXX:	Septuagint
magnum opus:	a great work
mal:	badly
matres lectionis:	consonants used to represent vowel sounds
metri causa:	for the sake of meter
mg.:	margin
MS (MSS):	manuscript(s)
M.S.:	second hand
MT or Mas.:	Masoretic Text
mu., mult.:	many
non:	not
nonnul.:	some
novum:	a new thing
numerus:	number
obeliscus:	obelisk
occidentalis:	Western
om.:	omit
omn.:	all
opt.:	the best
P.:	papyrus
p.:	post (after) or page
par(s).:	parallel(s) or paragraph(s)
pari passu:	side by side
partim:	in part, some
passim:	everywhere
patr.:	the Church Fathers
pauc., pc.:	few
permulti:	very many
petitio principii:	to beg the question
pl., pler.:	very many
plur.:	plurality
plus:	more
pon.:	put, place
post:	after

217

pr.:	first occurrence
praem.:	precede(s)
punct.:	punctuation
q. v.:	which see (that is, see the preceding item)
recto:	right hand page
redivivus:	returned to life
regula fidei:	rules of faith
rel., rell.:	remaining
S:	Codex Sinaiticus (q. v.)
saec.:	century
schol.:	scholion
scil.:	that is to say, to wit
sec.:	second occurrence
sec., secundum:	according to
sed:	but
sem.:	only one
seq.:	the next
sic:	thus, note
siglum (a):	sign(s)
sim.:	similar
sine:	without
sine qua non:	without which not (an indispensible condition)
sive . . . sive:	either . . . or
solum:	alone
sq., sqq.:	the next verse(s)
sui generis:	of its own kind
supp., suppl.:	supply
supra:	above
s. v.: sub voce, sub verbo:	under the entry
tant., tantum:	this alone
tert.:	third
tertium non datur:	a third does not exist
tertium quid:	a third something
tot.:	all
t.t.: terminus technicus:	technical term
unice:	alone, solely
usque:	as far as
ut:	as
V. or vide:	see
v. or vs. (vv. or vss.):	verse(s)
vacat:	absent
varr.:	variant reading
vers.:	version
verso:	left hand page
vid.:	apparently

vide:	see
v. l.:	variant reading
vol.	volume
VT:	Old Testament
W:	Codex Washingtonianus or Freer (q.v.)

ABBREVIATIONS OF WORKS
commonly cited in Biblical studies

Periodicals, Reference Works, and Serials

'A *or* Aq.	Aquila (q. v.)
AA	*Alttestamentliche Abhandlungen*
AAA	*Annals of Archaeology and Anthropology*
AASOR	*Annual of the American School of Oriental Research*
AB	The Anchor Bible
ABR	*Australian Biblical Review*
Acts Pil.	Acts of Pilate
ACW	*Ancient Christian Writers*
Add. Esth.	Additions to Esther
Adv haer	Irenaeus, *Adversus Haereses*
AevTh	*Abhandlungen zur evangelischen Theologie*
AFO	*Archiv für Orientforschung*
AGSU/AGAJU	*Arbeiten zur Geschichte des (Spätjudentums) antiken Judentums und des Urchristentums*
AJA	*American Journal of Archaeology*
AJSL	*American Journal of Semitic Languages and Literature*
AnBib	*Analecta Biblica*
ANEP	*The Ancient Near East in Pictures* (ed. Pritchard, 1955)
ANET	*Ancient Near Eastern Texts* (ed. Pritchard, 1955²) (q. v.)
ANF	*The Ante-Nicene Fathers*
AnOr	*Analecta Orientalia*
ANQ	*Andover-Newton Quarterly*
Ant	Josephus, *Antiquities*
AO	*Alte Orient*
Apoc.	Apocrypha
Apoc. Bar. (2–3)	Apocalypse of Baruch (Syriac, Greek)
Apoc. Mos.	Apocalypse of Moses
Apoc. Pet.	Apocalypse of Peter
APOT	*Apocrypha and Pseudepigrapha of the Old Testament* (ed. R. H. Charles)
ASNU	*Acta seminarii neotestamentici upsaliensis*

Assump. Moses	Assumption of Moses
ASTI	*Annual of the Swedish Theological Institute*
ASV	American Standard Version
ATD	*Das Alte Testament Deutsch*
ATR	*Anglican Theological Review*
AV	Authorized Version (King James Version)
BA	*Biblical Archaeologist*
BAG	W. Bauer, W.F. Arndt, and F.W. Gingrich, *Greek-English Lexicon of the New Testament*
Bar.	Baruch
Barn.	Epistle of Barnabas
BASOR	*Bulletin of the American Schools of Oriental Research*
BBB	*Bonner biblische Beiträge*
BDB	Brown-Driver-Briggs, *Hebrew and English Lexicon of the Old Testment*
BDF	Blass-Debrunner-Funk, *A Greek Grammar of the New Testament and Other Early Christian Literature*
Bel.	Bel and the Dragon
BevTL	*Beiträge zur evangelischen Theologie*
BGBE	*Beiträge zur Geschichte der Biblischen Exegese*
BGBH	*Beiträge zur Geschichte der Biblischen Hermeneutik*
BH(S) or (K)	*Biblia Hebraica* (Stuttgartensia) or (Kittel)
BHT	*Beiträge zur historischen Theologie*
Bib	*Biblica*
Bib. Ant.	Ps. Philo, *Biblical Antiquities*
Bib Stud.	*Biblische Studien*
Bib Today	*Bible Today*
BiK	*Bibel und Kirche*
BiL	*Bibel und Leben*
BiT	*The Bible Translator*
BJRL	*Bulletin of the John Rylands Library*
BK	*Biblischer Kommentar*
BNTC	Black's New Testament Commentaries
BO	*Bibliotheca Orientalis*
BR	*Biblical Research*
BS	*Biblische Studien*
BWANT	*Beiträge zur Wissenschaft vom Alten und Neuen Testament*
BZ	*Biblische Zeitschrift*
BZAW	*Beihefte zur Zeitschrift für die alttestamentliche Wissenschaft*
BZNW	*Beihefte zur Zeitschrift für die neutestamentliche Wissenschaft*
CAH	*Cambridge Ancient History*
Cant.	Canticles

CAT	*Commentaire de L'Ancien Testament*
CBQ (ms)	*Catholic Biblical Quarterly* (monograph series)
CDC (or CD)	Zadokite Document (Cairo Genizah Document), Damascus Document
CGTC	*Cambridge Greek Testament Commentary*
Chr.	Chronicles (1&2)
ClassBul	*Classical Bulletin*
Clem.	Clement (1&2)
CNT	*Commentaire du Nouveau Testament*
Col.	Colossians
Comm.	*Commonweal*
Cor.	Corinthians
CrossCurr	*Cross Currents*
D	Deuteronomic Source
Dan.	Daniel
Deut. *or* Dt.	Deuteronomy
Dial.	*Dialog*
Did.	Didache (q. v.)
Diogn.	Epistle to Diognetus
DJD	*Discoveries in the Judean Desert* (q. v.)
DSS	Dead Sea Scrolls (q. v.)
E	Elohist Source (q. v.)
EB	*Enchiridion Biblicum*
EBi	*Encyclopaedia Biblica*
EBib	*Etudes bibliques*
Eccl. *or* Eccles.	Ecclesiastes
Ecclus.	Ecclesiasticus
EH	*Exegetisches Handbuch zum Alten Testament*
EKL	*Evangelisches Kirchenlexikon*
Elen	*Elenchus*
Enc	*Encounter*
EncJud	*Encyclopaedia Judaica*
Enoch (1–2–3)	Enoch (Ethiopic, Slavonic, Hebrew)
Ep. Arist.	Epistle of Aristeas
Eph.	Ephesians
Ep. Jer.	Epistle of Jeremiah
Esd.	Esdras (1&2)
Esth.	Esther
ET	*Expository Times*
Euseb.	Eusebius
EvK	*Evangelische Kommentare*
EvTh	*Evangelische Theologie*
Ex. *or* Exod.	Exodus
ExpT	*Expository Times*
Ezek.	Ezekiel

223

4 Ezr.	Apocalypse of Ezra (= 2 Esdras chs. 3–14)
FRLANT	*Forschungen zur Religion und Literatur des Alten und Neuen Testaments*
FzB	*Forschungen zur Bibel*
Gal.	Galatians
Gen.	Genesis
GKC	*Gesenius' Hebrew Grammar,* ed. E. Kautzsch, tr. A. E. Cowley
Gos. Eb.	Gospel of the Ebionites
Gos. Eg.	Gospel of the Egyptians
Gos. Heb.	Gospel According to the Hebrews
Gos. Naass.	Gospel of the Naassenes
Gos. Pet.	Gospel of Peter
Gos. Thom.	Gospel of Thomas
GTT	*Gereformeerd theologisch Tijdschrift*
Hab.	Habakkuk
Hag.	Haggai
HAT	*Handbuch zum Alten Testament*
HDB	Hastings' *Dictionary of the Bible*
HDCG	Hastings' *Dictionary of Christ and the Gospel*
Heb.	Hebrew *or* The Letter to the Hebrews
Herm. (Man., Sim., Vis.)	The Shepherd of Hermas (Mandates; Similitudes; Visions)
Hev	Naḥal Ḥever caves or texts
HK	*Handkommentar zum Alten Testament*
HNT	*Handbuch zum Neuen Testament*
HNTC	*Harper's New Testament Commentary*
Hos.	Hosea
HTR	*Harvard Theological Review*
HTS	*Harvard Theological Studies*
HUCA	*Hebrew Union College Annual*
IB	*The Interpreter's Bible*
ICC	*International Critical Commentary*
IDB (Sup)	*The Interpreter's Dictionary of the Bible (Supplementary Volume)*
IEJ	*Israel Exploration Journal*
Ign.	Ignatius
Ign. Eph.	Ignatius' Letter to the Ephesians
Ign. Magn.	Ignatius' Letter to the Magnesians
Ign. Phld.	Ignatius' Letter to the Philadelphians
Ign. Pol.	Ignatius' Letter to Polycarp
Ign. Rom.	Ignatius' Letter to the Romans
Ign. Smyrn.	Ignatius' Letter to the Smyrnaeans
Ign. Trall.	Ignatius' Letter to the Trallians
Int.	*Interpretation*
Iren.	Irenaeus
Isa.	Isaiah

ITQ	*Irish Theological Quarterly*
J	Yahwist Source (see J: [Yahwist])
JAAR	*Journal of the American Academy of Religion*
JAOS	*Journal of the American Oriental Society*
Jas.	James
JB	Jerusalem Bible
JBC	*Jerome Biblical Commentary*
JBL	*Journal of Biblical Literature*
Jdt.	Judith
JEA	*Journal of Egyptian Archaeology*
Jer.	Jeremiah
JES	*Journal of Ecumenical Studies*
Jn. (1–2–3 Jn.)	John (1–2–3 Epistles of John)
JNES	*Journal of Near Eastern Studies*
Jos.	Josephus
Josh.	Joshua
JPS	Jewish Publication Society
JQR	*Jewish Quarterly Review*
JR	*Journal of Religion*
JSJ	*Journal for the Study of Judaism*
JSOR	*Journal of the Society of Oriental Research* (1917–1932)
JSS	*Journal of Semitic Studies*
JT	*Journal of Theology*
J.T.	Jerusalem Talmud
JTS	*Journal of Theological Studies*
Jub.	Jubilees
Jud.	*Judaica*
Judg.	Judges
Just.	Justin Martyr
KAT	*Kommentar zum Alten Testament*
KB	Koehler-Baumgartner Hebrew Lexicon
KBANT	Kommentare und Beiträge zum Alten und Neuen Testament
Kgs.	Kings (1 & 2)
KJV	King James Version
L	Lukan Source
Lam.	Lamentations
LangStyle	*Language and Style*
LB(P)	*Living Bible, Paraphrased*
LCL	Loeb Classical Library
Lev.	Leviticus
Ling.	*Linguistics*
Lk.	Luke
LThK	*Lexikon für Theologie und Kirche*
LXX	Septuagint (seventy) (q. v.)
M	Matthaean Source

M.	Mishna (q. v.)
Macc.	Maccabees (1–2–3–4)
Mal.	Malachi
Mart. Isa.	Martyrdom of Isaiah
Mart. Pol.	Martyrdom of Polycarp
Mas	Masada texts
Meyer *(KeK)*	*Kritisch-exegetischer Kommentar über dem Neuen Testament*
Mic.	Micah
Mird	Khirbet Mird texts
Mk.	Mark
MNTC	Moffatt New Testament Commentary
Mt. *or* Matt.	Matthew
MTZ	*Münchener theologische Zeitschrift*
Mur	Wadi Murrabba'ât caves or texts
NAB	New American Bible
Nah.	Nahum
NASV	New American Standard Version
NCE	*New Catholic Encyclopedia*
NEB	New English Bible
Neh.	Nehemiah
NF	Neue Folge ("New Series")
NICNT	New International Commentary on the New Testament
NIDNTT	*The New International Dictionary of New Testament Theology*
NJV	New Jewish Version
NovT (Sup)	*Novum Testamentum (Supplements)*
NT	New Testament
NTA	*New Testament Abstracts*
NTAbh	*Neutestamentliche Abhandlungen*
NTD	Das Neue Testament Deutsch
NTS	*New Testament Studies*
NTT	*Nieuw theologisch Tijdschrift*
NTTS	*New Testament Tools and Studies*
Num.	Numbers
OAB	*Oxford Annotated Bible*
Obad.	Obadiah
ODCC	*Oxford Dictionary of the Christian Church*
Odes Sol.	Odes of Solomon
OED	Oxford English Dictionary
OLZ	*Orientalistische Literaturzeitung*
Or	*Orientalia*
OrLitt	*Orbis Litterarum*
OT	Old Testament
OTS	*Old Testament Studies*
P	Priestly Source (q. v.)

p.	Pesher (commentary)
PCB	*Peake's Commentary on the Bible*
PEQ	*Palestine Exploration Quarterly*
Pet.	Peter (1&2)
PG	J. P. Migne, Patrologia graeca
Phil.	Philippians
Philem.	Philemon
PL	J. P. Migne, Patrologia Latina
Polyc.	Polycarp
Polyc. Phil.	Polycarp to the Philippians
Pr. Azar.	The Prayer of Azariah
Pr. Man.	The Prayer of Manasseh
Prot. Jas.	Protoevangelium of James
Prov.	Proverbs
Ps. (Pss.)	Psalm(s) (q. v.)
Pseudep.	Pseudepigrapha
Pss. Sol.	Psalms of Solomon
PW *(RKA)*	Pauly-Wissowa, *Realenzyklopädie der klassischen Alter-tumswissenschaft*
Q	Quelle (Source) (q. v.) or Qumran
1QH	Thanksgiving Hymns (See: Dead Sea Scrolls for this, the following and other DSS abbreviations.)
1QIs[a]	Isaiah Scroll (pub. by ASOR)
1QIs[b]	Isaiah Scroll (pub. by Hebrew University, Jerusalem)
1QM	War Scroll
1QpHab	Habakkuk Commentary
1QS	Manual of Discipline
1QSa	Rule of the Congregation
3Q15	Copper Scroll from Qumran Cave 3
RAC	*Reallexikon für Antike und Christentum*
RB	*Revue Biblique*
RE	*Review and Expositor*
Rev.	Revelation
RGG[1-3]	*Die Religion in Geschichte und Gegenwart* (1st–3rd ed.)
RHR	*Revue de l'histoire des religions*
RinL	*Religion in Life*
RQ	*Revue de Qumran*
RR	*Ricerche religiose*
RS	*Revue sémitique*
RScRel	*Revue des sciences religieuses*
RSV	Revised Standard Version
Sam.	Samuel (1&2)
SANT	*Studien zum Alten und Neuen Testament*
SBS	*Stuttgarter Bibelstudien*
SBT	*Studies in Biblical Theology*
SE	*Studia Evangelica*

Sem.	*Semiotica*
Semeia	*Semeia*
Sib. Or.	Sibylline Oracles
Sir.	Sirach or Jesus Ben Sirach, The Wisdom of
SNTSMS	Society for New Testament Study Monograph Series
SONTSMS	Society for Old Testament Study Monograph Series
SPB	*Studia Post-Biblica*
StNT	*Studien zum Neuen Testament*
Str-B	Strack-Billerbeck, *Kommentar zum Neuen Testament aus Talmud und Midrash*
STZ	*Schweizerische theologische Zeitschrift*
SUNT	*Studien zur Umwelt des Neuen Testament*
Sus.	*Susanna*
SVT	*Supplements to Vetus Testamentum*
Symm.	Symmachus (q. v.)
SZ	*Stimmen der Zeit*
T. 12 Patr.	Testament of the Twelve Patriarchs
Targ.	Targum
T. Asher, T. Levi, etc.	Testament of Asher, Levi, etc.
TB	Babylonian Talmud
TDNT	*Theological Dictionary of the New Testament*
TDOT	*Theological Dictionary of the Old Testament*
TEV	Today's English Version *(Good News for Modern Man)*
ThB	*Theologische Bücherei*
ThD	*Theology Digest*
Theo.	*Theology*
Theod.	Theodotion (q. v.)
Thess.	Thessalonians
ThLZ	*Theologische Literaturzeitung*
ThQ	*Theologische Quartalschrift*
ThR	*Theologische Rundschau*
ThRev	*Theologische Revue*
ThS	*Theological Studies*
ThSt	*Theologische Studien*
ThZ	*Theologische Zeitschrift*
Tim.	Timothy
Tit.	Titus
Tob.	Tobit
TSK	*Theologische Studien und Kritiken*
TT	*Theologisch Tijdschrift*
TU	*Texte und Untersuchungen zur Geschichte der altchristlichen Literatur*
TWNT	*Theologisches Wörterbuch zum Neuen Testament*
UF	*Ugarit-Forschungen*
USQR	*Union Seminary Quarterly Review*
VC or *VigChr*	*Vigiliae Christianae*

Vcaro	*Verbum caro*	
VD	*Verbum Domini*	
Verk F	*Verkündigung und Forschung*	
VS	*Verbum salutis*	
VT	*Vetus Testamentum*	
Vulg. *or* Vg	Vulgate	
WDB	*Westminster Dictionary of the Bible*	
WHAB	*Westminster Historical Atlas to the Bible*	
Wisd. Sol. (or Wis)	Wisdom of Solomon	
WMANT	*Wissenschaftliche Monographien zum Alten und Neuen Testament*	
ZAW	*Zeitschrift für die alttestamentliche Wissenschaft*	
ZDPV	*Zeitschrift des deutschen Palästina-Vereins*	
Zech.	Zechariah	
Zeph.	Zephaniah	
ZKG	*Zeitschrift für Kirchengeschichte*	
ZNW	*Zeitschrift für die neutestamentliche Wissenschaft*	
ZS	*Zeitschrift für Semitistik*	
ZST	*Zeitschrift für systematische Theologie*	
ZThK	*Zeitschrift für Theologie und Kirche*	

Orders and Tractates in the Mishna and Related Literature

ABBREV. (JBL)	NAME	COMMON ALTERNATE SPELLING
ᵓAbot	ᵓAbot	ᵓAboth
ᶜArak.	ᶜArakin	ᶜArakin
ᶜAbod. Zar.	ᶜAboda Zara	ᶜAbodah Zarah
B. Bat.	Baba Batra	Baba Bathra
Bek.	Bekorot	Bekoroth
Ber.	Berakot	Berakoth
Beṣa	Beṣa	Bezah
Bik.	Bikkurim	Bikkurim
B. Meṣ.	Baba Meṣiᶜa	Baba Meẓiᶜa
B. Qam.	Baba Qamma	Baba Kamma
Dem.	Demai	Demai
ᶜErub.	ᶜErubin	ᶜErubin
ᶜEd.	ᶜEduyyot	ᶜEduyyoth
Giṭ.	Giṭṭin	Giṭṭin
Ḥag.	Ḥagiga	Ḥagigah
Ḥal.	Ḥalla	Ḥallah
Hor.	Horayot	Horayoth
Ḥul.	Ḥullin	Ḥullin
Kelim	Kelim	Kelim
Ker.	Keriotot	Kerithoth

Ketub.	Ketubot	Kethuboth
Kil.	KilɔAyim	KilɔAyim
Maᶜas.	Maᶜaserot	Maᶜaseroth
Mak.	Makkot	Makkoth
Makš.	Makširin (=Mašqin)	Makshirin
Meg.	Megilla	Megillah
Meᶜ il	Meᶜ ila	Meᶜ ilah
Menaḥ.	Menaḥot	Menaḥoth
Mid.	Middot	Middoth
Miqw.	Miqwaɔot	Mikwaɔoth
Moᶜed	Moᶜed	Moᶜed
Moᶜed Qaṭ.	Moᶜed Qaṭan	Moᶜed Kaṭan
Maᶜas. Š.	Maᶜaser Šeni	Maᶜaser Sheni
Našim	Našim	Nashim
Nazir	Nazir	Nazir
Ned.	Nedarim	Nedarim
Neg.	Nega im	Nega im
Nez.	Neziqin	Nezikin
Nid.	Niddah	Niddah
Ohol.	Oholot	Oholoth
ᶜOr.	ᶜOrla	ᶜOrlah
Para	Para	Parah
Peɔa	Peɔa	Peɔah
Pesaḥ.	Pesaḥim	Pesaḥim
Qinnim	Qinnim	Kinnim
Qidd.	Qiddušin	Kiddushin
Qod.	Qodasin	Kodashin
Roš. Haš.	Roš Haššana	Rosh Hashanah
Sah.	Sanhedrin	Sanhedrin
Šabb.	Šabbat	Shabbath
Šeb.	Šebi ᶜit	Shebiᶜ ith
Šebu.	Šebuᶜot	Shebuᶜoth
Šeqal.	Šeqalim	Shekalim
Soṭa	Soṭa	Soṭa
Sukk.	Sukka	Sukkah
Taᶜan.	Taᶜanit	Taᶜanith
Tamid	Tamid	Tamid
Tem.	Temura	Temurah
Ter.	Terumot	Terumoth
Ṭohar.	Ṭoharot	Ṭoharoth
Ṭ. Yom	Ṭebul Yom	Ṭebul Yom
ᶜUq.	ᶜUqṣin	ᶜUkẓin
Yad.	Yadayim	Yadayim
Yebam.	Yebamot	Yebamoth
Yoma	Yoma (=Kippurim)	Yoma

Zabim	Zabim	Zabim
Zebaḥ.	Zebaḥim	Zebaḥim
Zer.	Zera^c im	Zera^c im

Note: Since these names are also used for tractates in the Tosepta (Tosefta), Babylonian Talmud, and the Jerusalem Talmud, they are often preceded by abbreviations designating these works, such as Mish., M., or m. for Mishna; Tos., T., or t. for Tosepta; Bab. Talm., Bab., B.T., or b. for Babylonian Talmud; and, Jer. Talm., Jer., or y. for Jerusalem Talmud.

Major Reference Works Consulted
in addition to those listed in the text

Berger, Klaus. *Exegese des Neuen Testaments.* Heidelberg: Quelle & Meyer, 1977.

Encyclopaedia Judaica, vols. 1–16. Jerusalem: Keter Publishing House, 1972.

Fokkema, D.W., and Elrud Künne-Ibsch. *Theories of Literature in the Twentieth Century: Structuralism, Marxism, Aesthetics of Reception, Semiotics.* London: C. Hurst & Co., 1977.

Garvin, Paul (ed.). *A Prague School Reader on Esthetics, Literary Structure, and Style.* Washington: Georgetown University Press, 1969.

Lausberg, H. *Handbuch der literarischen Rhetorik.* Munich: Huebner Verlag, 1923².

Lewandowski, Theodor. *Linguistisches Wörterbuch.* Heidelberg: Quelle & Meyer, Vol. 1, 1973; Vols. 2 & 3, 1975.

Lexikon für Theologie und Kirche. 2. Aufl. Heraus. Josef Höfer und Karl Rahner. Bände I-XI. Freiburg: Herder Verlag, 1957–1967. Abbrev. *LThK*

The Oxford Dictionary of the Christian Church. 2nd ed. Ed. F. L. Cross and E. A. Livingstone. London: Oxford University Press, 1974. Abbrev. *ODCC*

Reallexikon für Antike und Christentum. Bände I-VIII. Heraus. Theodor Klauser. Stuttgart: Hiersemann Verlag, 1950–1972. Abbrev. *RAC*

Die Religion in Geschichte und Gegenwart. 2. Aufl. Heraus. Hermann Gunkel und Leopold Zscharnack. Bände I-V. Tübingen: J. C. B. Mohr (Paul Siebeck), 1927–1931. Abbrev. *RGG²*

Ibid. 3. Aufl. Heraus. Kurt Galling. Bände I-VI. Tübingen: J. C. B. Mohr (Paul Siebeck), 1957–1965. Abbrev. *RGG³*

Appendix

A Simplified Guide for Writing an Exegetical Paper on the Synoptic Gospels Employing Historical-Critical Methods

I. Preparation
   A. Consult the *Handbook* for a definition of exegesis and a list of exegetical tools. (See: **Exegesis; Exegetical Method, Exegetical Tools.**)
   B. Become acquainted with the various types of exegetical tools such as (for English exegesis) concordances, Biblical and theological dictionaries, commentaries, monographs and periodicals. Learn how to use cardfiles and bibliographic aids. (See: **Bibliography.**)
   C. Selecting a passage for exegesis. Read the *Gospel Parallels* (Burton H. Throckmorton, Jr., ed. [Nashville: Thomas Nelson, 1973³]) until a single passage arouses special interest, either by the power of the ideas or events it records or the questions it evokes. Passages in the double tradition (Mt. and Lk.) or the triple tradition (Mt., Mk. and Lk.) are often the most challenging because they offer the possibility of sketching the history of a tradition.

   Select an entire pericope rather than a segment of a pericope. In almost every instance each section of the *Gospel Parallels* (marked with a paragraph sign and number) constitutes a single pericope.

II. Study
   A. Level One
      1. The Limits of the Passage. Although the layout of the *Gospel Parallels* has set the limits (beginning and end) of your passage, note how this is done. Is it clear to you that the demarcation is accurate? How does the passage open and close? Is it clearly a self-contained unit? Jot down your observations.
      2. The Context. How is the pericope related to the Gospel material before and after? Is the pericope essentially dependent or indepen-

dent of this material? What are the reasons for your conclusion? Jot down your tentative analysis of the context.

3. Literary Structure. What is the structure of the pericope? This can best be ascertained by outlining the major ideas or events in the text very briefly. The outline should be so constructed as to show the inner movement of the text as well as the relationship of ideas, persons and/or events within it. In what ways does the structure of the pericope inform your understanding of it? Elements of style may also be clues to structure; see below. (Note: Traditionally, the historical-critical method has dealt only with the surface structures of a text. Structuralist exegesis, a method in and of itself, deals with deep structures and is not proposed here. Students interested in these methods should begin with the articles on **"Structure"** and **"Structuralism"** and pursue the bibliography listed there.)

4. Literary Style. What rhetorical elements are present in the pericope (such as paronomasia, parallelism, hyperbole, simile, metaphor, etc.)? Do they suggest spontaneity or deliberation in composition? Are they typical of oral or written speech? Does the poetic function of these elements outweigh their cognitive function? In what ways does the presence of these elements affect the meaning of the text?

5. Terminological Clarification. List the theological and historical terms in the text which need clarification. Check Biblical dictionaries and atlases for historical and geographical terms. Jot down findings. The precise meaning of theological terms is more difficult to discover and more important. Theological dictionaries such as Kittel's *Theological Dictionary of the New Testament* (based on the Greek) or Alan Richardson's *Wordbook* are helpful here, but must be used with caution.

   Use a concordance to discover other places in the Gospel(s) or the Bible as a whole where the specific terms and phrases in question are also used. Does the passage at hand employ the terms in their traditional meaning, or are the nuances given to the meaning of the terms not found elsewhere?

6. Comparison of Translations. The text of the *Gospel Parallels* is that of the RSV. With this translation compare at least three other major translations. A good cross-section would be the **KJV, LB(P)** and **JB, NEB, NIV** or **TEV.** Slight variations (different words having the same meaning [e.g., house/dwelling]) can be ignored. When significant variations occur, explain the differences and state the preferred reading. Check commentaries devoted to the translation in question. (See: **Commentary.**) Become conversant with the difference between a dynamic and a formal translation.

7. In preparation for Level 2 of your study, be sure that you have the necessary critical tools readily at hand: concordances written for the translation(s) you are dealing with; modern critical commentaries (do not use devotional commentaries); Biblical and theological dictionaries (be careful to use recent and accepted critical works); monographs relevant to your passage, and periodical articles. (See esp.: *New Testament Abstracts* for building a Bibliography.)

B. Level Two

1. Form Critical Analysis.

   a. Analyze the text according to its form(s), that is, outline the verses or verse segments according to their formal characteristics (redactional narrative, introductory formula, logion, parable, makarism, floating logion, etc.).

   b. On the basis of the above analysis, is the text a self-contained unit or a composite? In other words, is the use of sources (oral or written) evident? (Many of the sections making up Matthew's "Sermon on the Mount," just as the traditions in "Q" generally, are self-contained words of Jesus in a narrative setting (chria/pronouncement story) and are composite.

      i. If the text is composite, the identifiable units within the text may go back to different periods in the traditioning process: the life of Jesus, the preaching of the early church, the hand of the Gospel writer. Jot down your initial guess concerning the origins of the compositional elements.

      ii. If the text is a self-contained tradition, the exegete must determine the setting in which the text originally arose. It, too, may go back to Jesus, to the life of the early church, or to the hand of the Gospel writer. Jot down your initial answer.

2. Literary Form (Type) and "Setting in Life." (See: *Sitz-im-Leben*.)

   a. Setting in Life. What recognizable literary forms or types are present in the passage under study? What is the usual social setting for this linguistic form? (For example: doctrinal or paraenetic teaching, baptism, preaching, eschatological warning, worship, etc.). What is the *typical* content and function of of the literary form in question? What are its typical elements? Does the text at hand show any divergence from the usual form? What explanation can be given for these divergencies? Write out tentative answers to these questions.

   b. Setting in the Life of Jesus/the Early Church. Can the literary forms identified (the unit as a whole or subunits within it) be placed historically either within the historical situation of Jesus or the early Church? What would such a setting be? (Would it be at the beginning, middle, or end of Jesus' ministry? In Galilee or Jerusalem? etc.) Who is being addressed? What was the meaning and possible significance of what is being said in its historical context? In brief: Who, what, where, when, to whom, why, how? Sketch out your answer. How can your historical reconstruction be defended?

   c. The Setting in the Gospel **(Redaction Criticism).** In what ways is the text in question related to the material preceding and following it in the Gospel? To the Gospel as a whole? Is it apparent that the content of the text has been affected by its context? (An analysis of parallel passages in one of the other Gospels, if any exist, may help you decide.) What is the function of the text within the larger composition? What is the historical or theological significance of the redactional treatment of the traditional material?

  3. Summary.

On the basis of your study, jot down your understanding of the intention of the text. Your answer may have more than one level as you consider the meaning/intention of the text (or a segment thereof) to Jesus, to the early Church, or to the Gospel writer. The least hypothetical level is perhaps the last of these.

III. Writing Up Findings.

Exegetical study and an exegetical paper are not the same, any more than a research paper is identical with all the research that went into it. The following is but one way of writing up the findings arrived at in your study.

  A. Text. If the text is of moderate length, write it out in full as the first page of the paper.

  B. General Discussion. Present your analysis of the Text's:

    1. Limits.

    2. Context.

    3. Structure.

  C. Verse by Verse Analysis. Proceeding verse by verse, discuss the content of the unit. Note in this section translational variations, textual problems (see critical apparatus in the *Gospel Parallels*), special terms (theological or historical) needing clarification, redactional elements, etc.

  D. The "Settings" of the Text. What can be said concerning the history of the unit as it has been traditioned from Jesus' own situation (if that be the case) to that of the early Church, to the mind of the Gospel writer?

  E. Theological Interpretation.

1. What have theologians said concerning the text? The Reformers are often helpful (Martin Luther, John Calvin) as well as contemporary theologians (Protestant and Catholic).
2. In your own dialogue with the text, what discoveries have you made? How do you read/hear the text? Can you say why you hear it that way?

F. Footnotes. These may appear either at the bottom of the page or at the end of the paper. It may be helpful to follow Kate Turabian's *Manual for Writers of Term Papers,* (Chicago, 4th edition).

G. Bibliography. List all books studied, whether quoted or not. Follow Turabian.